8.30.21
$39.95

SWORD OF EMPIRE

SWORD

OF EMPIRE

The Spanish Conquest of the Americas
from Columbus to Cortés, 1492–1529

DONALD E. CHIPMAN

State House Press
at Schreiner University
Kerrville, TX
325-660-1752
www.mcwhiney.org

Cataloging-in-Publication Data
Names: Chipman, Donald E., author.
Title: Sword of empire: the Spanish conquest of the Americas from Columbus to Cortés, 1492-1529 / Donald E. Chipman.
Description: First edition. | Kerrville, TX: State House Press, 2021. | Includes bibliographical references and index.

Identifiers: ISBN 9781933337883 (soft cover); ISBN 9781933337906 (e-book)
Subjects: LCSH: Columbus, Christopher. | Cortés, Hernán, 1495-1547. | America – Discovery and Exploration – Spanish. | Latin America – History – To 1600.
Classification: E123 (print) | DCC 970.01

First edition 2021

Cover and page design and production by Allen Griffith of Eye 4 Design.

Distributed by Texas A&M University Press Consortium
800-826-8911
www.tamupress.com

For My Son, Jason Chipman

CONTENTS

ACKNOWLEDGEMENTS

The year 2019 marked the five-hundredth anniversary of Spaniards landing in Mexico, soon named New Spain by them. In February and March, I posted on Facebook a sort of "you are there" narrative paragraph that followed Hernando Cortés day by day for a month prior to his arrival at Veracruz harbor on Holy Thursday, as observed in 1519. It attracted perhaps a score of readers. Among them was historian Donald S. Frazier in Kerrville, Texas. Frazier emailed me with the suggestion that I write a book-length manuscript on Spanish contact with the major Caribbean islands and Mexico. He included an invitation to send the completed work to the Grady McWhiney Research Foundation for possible publication by State House Press.

Thus, I wish first to thank Don Frazier for the genesis of this book. Second, I wish to express appreciation to my son Jason Chipman for urging me to sit down and write, while asking almost daily how the writing was going and putting up with my complaints about having to learn Microsoft Word at age ninety. I used WordPerfect almost exclusively in writing or co-authoring prior books. I would like to dedicate this book to Jason, who was also my tech specialist on many occasions.

Friends and historians Harriett Denise Joseph, F. Todd Smith, Carol A. Lipscomb, and Randolph B. "Mike" Campbell read the entire manuscript and offered valuable suggestions as well as correcting typos and infelicities that marred my prose. Mary Jo O'Rear in Corpus Christie likewise lent encouragement and support. Professor Graham Cox made two "house calls" to correct problems I perhaps created with an unintentional keystroke that caused Microsoft Word to change margins and layout in my manuscript. Assistance also came from Melody Specht Kelly, ace book-finding sleuth and Associate Dean of Libraries Emeritus at the University of North Texas. Jim Doyle, a nephew in Little Rock, was helpful in solving problems, which he assures me Microsoft Word creates on its own and even overnight while I sleep to ensure employment for computer tech specialists like him.

I also wish to thank Montse Vilahur Gies, a young woman and chiropractor in Barcelona whom I have known since her parents lived in Denton, Texas, and her late father took one of my classes at the University of North Texas. As a favor, Montse photographed the Columbus Statue in Barcelona's Plaza de Colón that appears as an illustration in the book and granted permission to publish it.

Alexander Mendoza, friend and associate professor of history at the University North Texas, deserves special mention and thanks for his assistance. Alex was adept at taking my pencil drawings and turning them into professional quality maps and genealogy charts. All such materials appearing in the book are Alex's excellent adaptations or independent cartography.

The final edit of this manuscript profited from the invaluable assistance of Mike Campbell. He worked with me from our homes in Denton by reading identical texts linked by iPhone on speaker. This was necessary because both of us are sheltered due to the COVID-19 pandemic of 2020-21. For more than fifty years, it has been great having Mike as best friend, evidenced once again by his help on this book.

INTRODUCTION

This book is primarily intended for students and general readers. It traces the contributions of Christopher Columbus and Hernando Cortés in establishing foundations for the Spanish Empire in the Caribbean Sea and Mexico. My knowledge of Columbus is based on reading secondary sources. During quincentenary observances of his epic first voyage in 1492 that was celebrated throughout much of 1992, I spoke on the mariner in Austin, Denton, and Houston, as well as at Eastern Michigan State University and Fresno State University.

By contrast, my knowledge of Hernando Cortés runs deeper. Professor France V. Scholes was my mentor in graduate school at the University of New Mexico. When I received my Ph.D. in 1962, Dr. Scholes, forced to retire that year under UNM age limitations for its professoriate, had received a grant from the Bollingen Foundation, funded by Paul and Mary Mellon. By accepting the grant, Scholes agreed to write a magisterial three-volume biography of Cortés, and it is a tragedy of some proportions that my mentor's interests shifted, causing him to void the contract. Sometime later, Professor Scholes left Albuquerque and accepted a lateral appointment at Tulane University in New Orleans where he continued to teach graduate students much to their benefit, as he had done for me.

Professor Scholes and I remained in close contact for twenty years, and in more than ninety handwritten letters that I have in my possession, he occasionally shared insights into the multi-layered complexities of a man who began life in

1484 with the baptismal name of Fernando Cortés. (As I explain elsewhere in the book, it is best to use Hernando in referring to Cortés's first name.)

After the death of Professor Scholes in 1979, I was pleased that Sir Hugh Thomas published *Conquest: Montezuma, Cortés, and the Fall of Old Mexico* in 1993. I have read and reread portions of this wonderfully well-researched book for more than a quarter of a century. With the aid of only one research assistant, Teresa Alzugaray, a specialist in Spanish paleography, Thomas read materials in the Archivo General de Indias, the Archivo de Protocolos de Seville, the Archivo General de Simancas and other depositories in writing his book, which is rich in detail and analysis. The reader will perhaps note that Thomas's book appears in the bibliography of all chapters following those devoted to Columbus, but I also have used such original materials as the eye-witness account of the conquest of Mexico written decades later by Bernal Díaz del Castillo, translations of the extensive letters Cortés sent to the Crown, and some archival materials such as wills and other legal instruments.

Columbus and Cortés differed in many ways. The former may not have been a great mariner in that he relied more on dead reckoning than celestial navigation. Nonetheless, dead reckoning should not be dismissed out of hand, because it was a rare talent that permitted Columbus to know the sea almost as well as many of us might know an expanse of land in our home county. The Admiral's chief critic who sailed with him on the 1492 voyage was Martín Alonso Pinzón, and he thought the more famous mariner took too many chances. But Samuel Eliot Morison, Pulitzer Prize-winning biographer of Columbus, believed the man's daring was essential, since so little was known about the Americas at the time of his explorations. Morison did agree with other historians who have labeled Columbus an inept colonial administrator. Just how much his mismanagement can be attributed to difficulties he encountered as a foreigner born on the Italian peninsula at Genoa in 1451 cannot be measured with certainty.

It is certain, however, that the post-Columbian world is the modern world. Columbus's contributions along with those of mariners who sailed south to the America of the Southern Hemisphere and eastward toward Asia where they discovered lands for Europeans that have never since lost contact with each other. Columbus's four voyages helped place "the world on the path toward global interdependence, with enormous consequences—both good and ill." In his lifetime in Spain, Columbus was often the victim of disparaging comments due to his Genoese origins. For example, Morison lends credence to an account that while at Court in Spain requesting support for one of the later voyages, a critic repeatedly belittled Columbus's accomplishments by asserting he had never done anything out of the ordinary. Tiring of the man, one day Columbus arrived with a chicken egg, sat down at a table beside his detractor, and asked him if he could stand the egg on it on its smaller and more pointed end. After repeated failures, the man pronounced it an impossibility. The egg was probably hardboiled, and Columbus after tapping it gently to form a base stood it upright. Whereupon the Admiral apparently commented that it took genius to accomplish the impossible.

Hernando Cortés, born a generation and half after Columbus, was also a genius when it came to his leadership in the conquest of Mexico. There is, nonetheless, a prevailing misconception that the Conqueror led conquistadors who were soldiers in the Spanish army. That professional military unit was formidable but campaigned on the European continent, and often on the Italian peninsula in battles fought with the French during the lifetime of Cortés. By contrast, conquistadors in the Americas were free-lance entrepreneurs operating under the umbrella of absolute monarchy. Men in the ranks who followed Cortés had to buy their own weapons, armor, mail, and helmet with the hope of striking it rich in the Indies. They respected the eventual Conqueror of the Aztecs because like Andrew Jackson centuries later in the United States he never asked those under his command to do anything he would not do twice. Even so, not all of Cortés's men-at-arms liked him, and a few entered plots to assassinate the captain general—at their peril. Through inspirational speeches, Machiavellian cunning, and at times harsh discipline, Cortés became a great captain in the conquest of Mexico—supported significantly by lesser ranked sub captains such as Pedro de Alvarado, Cristóbal de Olid, and Gonzalo de Sandoval.

In present times, the often favorably held view of Indian nations and their cultures, as opposed to those of European countries, has led some to the extreme position that Columbus was worse than Hitler, attributing to him all Indian deaths that occurred since 1492. In Mexico there are to the best of my knowledge no streets, plazas, or schools named after Cortés. But Columbus and Cortés brought

Western Civilization to the Americas by laying the foundations of the Spanish Empire in North America.

An important subtheme in this book is the crucial role performed by the Spaniards' Indian allies in the conquest of Mexico. Many of them had suffered under the Aztec Empire with its demands for mandatory tribute paid in young men's lives as offerings to its gods as well as in Indian women who were often violated and invariably enslaved. It would have been virtually impossible for Cortés and his fellow conquistadors to have had the supplies and weaponry necessary on their march to the Aztec capital without Totonacs who served as burden bearers and auxiliaries. En route Cortés fought three battles with the Tlaxcalans, two of which can best be described as indecisive engagements. Nonetheless, Tlaxcalan elders decided their future and that of their people would be best served under Spanish control, instead of remaining at war with Moctezuma and his legions. That decision was essential to Spanish success in defeating the Aztecs and occupying their great city of Tenochtitlan after a bitter eighty-day siege.

We shall never know how the Aztec Empire might have evolved without European conquest and occupation, but beyond doubt it would have lasted well beyond 1519–1521 had it not been for Cortés's ability to employ Indians allies to his advantage. There is scant evidence the Aztec Empire had reached its largest extent possible or was in danger of decline. The Mexica, as the Aztecs preferred to call themselves, collected tribute from subject people that stretched from Totonacs in the present-day Mexican state of Veracruz in the north to Oaxaca in the south and beyond to the northern limits of Central America—in all, sixteen provinces. That changed in 1521, and by 1529 when this study ends, Spaniards had become the new overlords, receivers of tribute, and agents of power in Mexico.

Donald E. Chipman
Denton, Texas, 2021

SWORD OF EMPIRE

CHAPTER 1

The Admiral at Sea: Voyages One and Two

Just minutes after midnight on October 12, 1492, Rodrigo de Triana stood watch on *Pinta*. The ship had joined *Santa María* and *Niña* out of Las Palmas in the Canary Islands and was on day thirty-three at sea. Christopher Columbus, known to the Spanish as Cristóbal Colón, was worried. Crews on the three ships muttered mutiny, thinking how could they possibly return home safely after so many days at sea? Mindful of their concerns, Columbus had kept two logs—an accurate one showing approximate distance traveled and one that deliberately underestimated distance, which he shared with ship captains and officers to allay their fears. Whether by instinct or careful observation, Columbus had altered course, a southward adjustment some four days prior. He had observed the flight of land-dwelling petrels that seemed to veer a bit to the left of the latitude traveled since leaving port in the Canaries. Had Columbus not changed course, he would likely have made landfall on the east coast of Florida, and that would have changed everything. False sightings of land had happened more than once—usually a low-lying cloud on the horizon, or perhaps tricks played on the eyesight of increasingly desperate men who conjured mirages. This time, the lookout saw what appeared as an elongated dark mound on the horizon, but there was also faint light emitting from it—probably from a continuously fed campfire on a beach. Triana shouted the magical words that all aboard the three vessels had so desperately longed to hear: *"Tierra! Tierra!"* The deck of *Pinta* soon filled with excited sailors, and word spread to men within earshot on the other ships. The island sighted would be named San Salvador (Holy Savior).

So how did Columbus, who was born on the Italian peninsula in 1451, come to command such a history-making Spanish sea expedition to the Americas in 1492? As the 500th anniversary of his discovery approached in 1992, scholars began searching Spanish archives and libraries in the probably vain hope of finding new information on him. Among them was the late historian Eugene Lyon, perhaps the best researcher in the United States, an archival bloodhound. He had previously found in the great Archive of the Indies in Seville the manifest of the *Nuestra Señora de Atoche*, an incredibly rich treasure ship that sank off the Florida Keys in 1622. Later, in a Madrid archive, Lyon discovered a bundle of unmarked papers that contained information not previously known about Columbus. For example, Lyon found the name of his parents in Genoa, and he learned that they were wool weavers and merchants. Son Christopher, however, had no interest in the family business. Instead, he had a passion for all things related to sea exploration—maps, charts, instruments of celestial navigation, and different kinds of sailing vessels. The country with the foremost knowledge of exploration beyond the European continent was Portugal. Columbus decided to go there, and go he did in 1476, but his arrival was less than auspicious. Shipwrecked off the Portuguese coast, Columbus swam ashore.

During his ten years in the more western Iberian kingdom, Columbus made several oceanic voyages along the northwest coast of Africa as well as to islands that had been settled by the Portuguese. These may have included the Azores, Cape Verdes, and Madeiras. Nonetheless, Portugal's major thrust of exploration was southward along the great Atlantic coast of Africa, and foreigner Columbus was not welcome on those sailings. There is good evidence Columbus may have been a crewmember on a vessel that reached waters off Iceland. What is certain is Columbus's marriage in Portugal and the birth of his eldest son Diego around 1480.

By the middle years of the 1480s, it had become clear to Columbus that Portugal would eventually reach India by rounding Cape Agulhas at the southern tip of Africa. That happened with the preliminary voyage of Bartolomew Dias in 1488, and the later sailing of Vasco da Gama to India in 1497. Regarding his own prospects, Columbus had shown prescience by relocating to Spain around 1485, along with five-year-old son Diego. They took passage from Lisbon to Palos de la Frontera, a port in far southwest Spain near Huelva. Also close by was the Franciscan friary La Rábida where Columbus and his son were occasional residents for the next six and a half years.

Columbus arrived in Spain with his plan for the great "enterprise of the Indies"—the proposal to demonstrate the feasibility of sea voyages from Spain to Asia by sailing west, which would thereby increase the availability of spices to Western European buyers and decrease their cost. To make his idea more appealing, he grossly misrepresented the circumference of the world. His calculations were not logical but then neither was he. The numbers he produced had to make his enterprise more feasible to attract a sponsor in Spain—so he purposely miscalculated the circumference of planet Earth by about 25 percent. In doing so, Columbus placed the distance from the Canary Islands to Japan at 2,400 nautical miles. That distance would have placed him at the Virgin Islands —considerably short of Japan. In fact, it was approximately 5,600 miles short on a straight line, and no map in existence showed the intervening continents of North and South America.

Columbus's timing in relocating to Spain from Portugal was premature by nearly seven years. The almost eight centuries of periodic war by Christians against Muslim-occupied Spain known as the Reconquest (circa 720 to 1492) was in its final phase. Its conclusion took precedence over all other considerations for the Catholic Monarchs, Isabella of Castile and Ferdinand of Aragon. Columbus had made repeated entreaties to them at court in the later 1480s. Queen Isabella had always expressed interest but ultimately demurred. The Reconquest *had* to come first. To that end, the Catholic Monarchs set up a new command center at Santa Fe, a military encampment just ten miles from Granada where the last core of Muslim resistance held out until January 2, 1492. Thereafter, Columbus's enterprise of the Indies would receive a more favorable royal hearing, but even so it was nearly rejected.

Columbus had grown weary of not finding a sponsor for his western approach to Asia. But during his lengthy stay in Spain, he had learned Spanish, the only language in which he wrote. Early in 1486 the would-be mariner traveled to

Córdoba seeking an audience with the Catholic Monarchs but just missed them as they had departed for Madrid. While languishing in Córdoba, Columbus entered a relationship with a young woman named Beatriz Enríquez de Harana. She would bear his second son Ferdinand out of wedlock in late summer of 1488. Having failed to find gainful employment in Spain and often dependent on the kindness of the Franciscan friars at La Rábida, Columbus had two sons to support. He decided to try one last time to win favor with the King and Queen after Granada fell in early January 1492. Should he fail to do so, Columbus was determined to leave Spain and seek support of King Charles VIII of France.

Fortunately, the monarchs were then more willing to listen, but negotiations in newly won Granada between Columbus and the King and Queen were complex, and initially they did not go well. Ferdinand, always more interested in diplomacy than other affairs of state, disliked Columbus personally and his proposed voyage even more. Isabella, however, liked him. They were close in age and of similar disposition. She remembered seeing Columbus's shabby apparel on earlier occasions when he had been at court, and she wanted him to appear well dressed on this occasion. Remarkably, she sent the prospective mariner 20,000 maravedís with orders to buy decent clothing and a mule. All seemed to augur well when Columbus appeared in Granada, and then the axe fell. Royal counselors regarded his plans to reach Japan by sailing west as a cockamamie scheme. He was sent away on orders of both the King and Queen. But matters then changed dramatically in the span of a few hours. Columbus would soon catch a favorable wind that would blow him all the way to San Salvador.

Luis de Santangel, keeper of the privy purse of King Ferdinand, had befriended Columbus while he was at court. The same day the dismissed mariner left Granada, Santangel sought an audience with Queen Isabella. He stressed to her majesty that she had always demonstrated resolute spirit in matters of import, so why not take a chance on Columbus that would cost little but carried the potential of glory and riches redounding to her realm. Don Luis then made persuasive points—Isabella was deeply devout, and Columbus's enterprise might prove of great service to God and the exaltation of the Catholic faith. Furthermore, if money were a consideration, Santangel said he himself would finance the proposed expedition. The Queen was much impressed. She sent a messenger on horseback to overtake Columbus, who was riding his mule just ten miles from Granada and only four miles beyond Santa Fe. Royal commands demanded obedience, and Isabella's orders were clear. As her subject, Columbus had to return to court, and negotiations would get underway on a contract that would authorize and finance his great enterprise of the Indies. Those complex discussions would last three months.

In initial exchanges between Columbus, the Catholic Monarchs, and their advisors, the mariner had enough peasant cunning to not ask for everything at once. The Queen was his ally, and she remained skeptical of her so-called learned advisors who counseled the sovereigns against being overly generous to Columbus. In her sixteen years of reign, Isabella realized that these men often did not know what they were talking about. But she persisted in believing there was little risk for possible vast gain as argued by Luis de Santangel. Still, Ferdinand and Isabella had to agree on everything, and the King no doubt reminded his wife that don Luis was his official and not hers. And there was the expense of the first voyage into the unknown, estimated at two million maravedís. The Queen had proposed to raise the money by selling her jewels, but that became unnecessary. Santangel and a partner were joint treasurers of the Santa Hermandad, an efficient police force with its own endowment. From its treasury came a loan for 1,400,000 maravedís; Columbus himself invested 250,000 maravedís of borrowed money; and the balance may have been paid from Santangel's own monies. With financing out of the way, a contract known as the Capitulations of Santa Fe was signed on April 17, 1492, by the King and Queen.

The Capitulations contained five major provisions. They would loom large for years to come in Spain's administration and settlement of the four major islands in the Caribbean Sea. (1) Their Highnesses appointed don Cristóbal Colón as Admiral over all islands and mainlands discovered by his labor and industry. Colón and his heirs were to enjoy the title of Admiral in perpetuity. (2) Cristóbal Colón would receive the title of Viceroy and Governor General over all islands and mainlands discovered by him. An additional provision allowed Colón to nominate three candidates for each office established therein, and the

Sovereigns could pick one. (3) Colón could keep one tenth of all precious metals, gems, and spices obtained within the limits of his domains, and all were free of taxes. (4) Cases arising over merchandise or products within Colón's domains were to be adjudicated by him or his deputy. (5) Colón was offered the option of paying an eighth of the expenses of any ship sailing to his possessions and of receiving a likewise eighth of all profits therefrom—an option Columbus chose to accept.

By almost any measure, the Capitulations of Santa Fe were exceedingly generous. Historians have suggested that the broad concessions made to Columbus were an inverse measure of the Catholic Monarchs' confidence that he would be successful in sailing west to Japan. In short, the Sovereigns could promise the moon if they believed their commitment would never fall due. Little did they know in 1492 that it would take the finest legal minds in Spain to abrogate the binding contract to Columbus and later to his heir Diego, or that those efforts would extend decades into the next century. In the meantime, the mariner enjoyed heady times. Imagine what it must have been like for a man who loved everything about the sea to bear the title of Admiral.

It is remarkable that in only the few hours during which Columbus had ridden just fourteen miles on mule back, his fate changed. He was spared from being an obscure supplicant and again a foreigner seeking favors at the French court of Charles VIII. Instead, his name centuries later would adorn many cities and towns in the United States and its federal district in Washington, DC. Although the spelling has vowel changes, Colombia in South America is also indebted to Columbus for its name.

As the newly titled Admiral, traveling again by mule back, headed to Palos and La Rábida to organize his enterprise, it is appropriate to comment on what the year 1492 held in store for Spain. Foremost, on January 2 the nearly the eight-hundred-year Reconquest ended with the surrender of the Moors. There is also little doubt Ferdinand and Isabella regarded that as their greatest achievement. Their mortal remains lie in lead coffins below a magnificent sarcophagus in Granada's Cathedral. The contract with Columbus in April of course brought profound changes to the Americas, and importantly to Spain itself. For example, consider what happened to the Spanish language in 1492. Even paleographers, scholars skilled in reading longhand, have great difficulty reading fifteenth-century Spanish documents written prior to 1492. Commissioned by Queen Isabella, a panel of linguists and philologists headed by Antonio de Nebrija began efforts to standardize the Spanish language. Their great achievement is titled: *Arte de la Lengua Castellana* (Art of the Spanish Language.) When presented to the Queen, Nebrija prophetically remarked: "Language, your majesty, is the instrument of Empire." Consequently, if one knows Spanish, he or she can with proper instruction read hand-written records such as lawsuits, royal decrees, and wills dated post-1491. Perhaps only in an absolutist monarchy can a head of state decree such sweeping reforms of a language but readers of posterity can be grateful for them. Lastly, in an event that had tragic consequences for thousands of Spanish Jews, on March 31, while discussions with Columbus were still ongoing, Ferdinand and Isabella issued a decree from the Alhambra in Granada that compelled those practicing Judaism to either convert to Catholicism or leave Spain in ninety days. That deadline fell on July 31, 1492, just a few days before Columbus sailed for the Indies.

Focus shifts here to organizing the departure of *Niña*, *Pinta*, and *Santa María* from the port of Palos. [**Figure 1**] Armed with credentials, full of energy, eager to depart, and with money to spend, Columbus arrived at the port on May 22. He did not choose Cádiz, as it had been designated as the point of departure for exiled Jews. Indeed, some 8,000 families had sailed from there in the summer of 1492. But aside from congestion and lack of ships at Cádiz, Palos nevertheless would almost certainly have been the chosen port of departure for Columbus's enterprise. The mariner carried a decree signed by the King and Queen addressed to Paleño officials and inhabitants. Because of their unspecified "misdeeds committed to the disservice of the King and Queen," they had to provide two equipped caravels at their expense and hand them over to the Admiral as restitution. The malefactors were also required to provide four months of advanced pay for crew members who would sail on the caravels. Absolute monarchs held absolute powers, and *Niña* and *Pinta* were to be outfitted within ten days. Perhaps thinking the Palos officials could be cowed into giving him a third caravel, Columbus's demands for

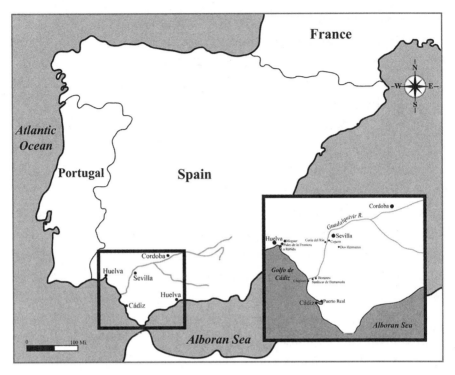

Figure 1. The South of Spain important in the Age of Exploration.

it fell on deaf ears. He then chartered *Santa María* from its owner. The flagship of the expedition that Columbus himself would captain was larger than the other caravels, but not by much.

Details of equipping and provisioning the three vessels are wholly lacking, but it took ten weeks instead of ten days to get ready for sea. The delay was not excessive and ultimately proved fortunate. A June departure would have run the risk of encountering a West Indies hurricane at the height of season. Columbus also carried three other royal letters that assisted his preparations. Collectively, they required all persons in the southern Spanish province of Andalusia, especially timber merchants, carpenters, bakers, and provision dealers, to furnish Columbus with everything he needed at reasonable prices. Furthermore, such items could not be taxed. Finally, they granted suspension of all civil and criminal prosecutions against anyone agreeing to sail with the mariner. The last provision no doubt spawned the oft-repeated canard that Columbus emptied the jails of

Andalusia to obtain crew members for his three ships. Some recruits may have spent time behind bars, but they of necessity had to be capable sailors given what lay ahead at sea.

Since all officers and men for the enterprise were paid by the Crown, more is known about them than the ships they sailed on. Columbus, not well known in Palos and surrounding regions and a foreigner to boot, proved inept as a recruiter of men willing to sail into the great unknown. Two brothers, Martín Alonso Pinzón and Vicente Yáñez Pinzón, were essential to that end. The former took command of *Pinta* as captain and master; the latter, of *Niña*. The Pinzón brothers were prominent Paleños, and perhaps that smoothed a few feathers of the local citizenry because they captained the two expropriated caravels. When fully staffed with captains, officers, and cabin boys, the crew numbered ninety aboard the three vessels. Oddly, no priest sailed on the initial voyage of the enterprise. Last to go aboard the three ships were kegs of fresh water from a fountain near the Church of St. George at Palos. Every crew member then had to confess their sins, receive absolution, and take communion. Finally, they boarded the vessels and set sails for the first voyage of Columbus.

Columbus planned a stop in the Canaries, partly conquered and occupied by Spaniards in the 1480s, and then set a westerly course. His experience while sailing from Portugal in the 1470s and 1480s led him to believe that once out of Canary calms he would encounter favorable winds. It was his good luck that the northeast trade winds would carry his fleet all the way to the Americas, which he did not know existed. Columbus also assumed that Japan with its promise of riches was on a parallel latitude from his point of departure at Las Palmas, Grand Canary. After clearing the port and sails filled with wind, Columbus kept on his chosen latitude by astrolabe sightings of the North Star. Thirty-three days later, he exulted over the words *"Tierra! Tierra!"* shouted by Rodrigo de Triana abroad *Pinta*.

On October 12, the three caravels anchored safely off San Salvador, a landmass in the Bahamas later renamed Watling's Island. [**Figure 2**] Columbus and selected shipmates went ashore by boats launched from all three ships. The natives encountered were similar to those inhabiting the four major Caribbean Islands in that they spoke Taíno/Arawakan languages, which greatly interested Columbus— and believing then and until the day he died that he had encountered people

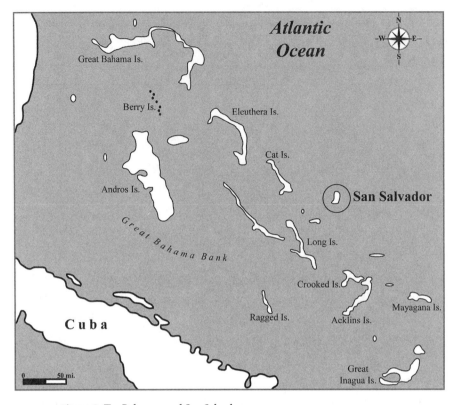

Figure 2. The Bahamas and San Salvador.

living on an outlying island near India, he called them *Indios*. Their ancestors had migrated to the Caribbean islands from South America, and they eventually occupied Española (which contains the present-day countries of Haiti and the Dominican Republic), Cuba, Jamaica, Puerto Rico, and the Bahamas. Perhaps he can be forgiven for unknowingly giving the native people a name that would confound scholars and others for centuries on how best to distinguish American Indians from the inhabitants of India. Far more important, however, the natives of San Salvador had met folk from Europe like they had never seen before—strange bearded men who came in floating houses and spoke an unintelligible language. Problems with communication loomed large. Unfortunately, we will never know what the natives thought of the white strangers because their tongue was incomprehensible to the Spaniards and not recorded. Contrariwise, Columbus had a lot to say about the natives he encountered.

The people the Admiral saw were completely naked. He decided to win their friendship because he believed their lives would be better if they converted to the Catholic faith and clothed themselves. To win favor, Columbus awarded red caps, glass beads, and other trinkets of slight value. The Indians received all items with great pleasure and soon adorned their necks with beads. Those still on shore were excited and waded toward Spaniards bearing colorful parrots and skeins of cotton. They were also rewarded with beads and small brass bells. Contacts increased as nearly all boat occupants came ashore. At that juncture, the Admiral recorded how the natives appeared to him—their bodies handsome yet naked as the day of birth, faces good and attractive, hair coarse and straight as a horse's tail—with bangs in front but at back a hank allowed to grow long and never cut. The Indians bore no arms and knew nothing of them. Because Columbus thought it would please God, he later sent six natives to board the ships so that they might learn Spanish, act as interpreters, and receive instruction in the Catholic faith.

On the following day, boats filled with Spaniards landed on a different beach. Again, the Admiral described the natives who met them as friendly with well-formed and handsome bodies. Those Indians had dugout canoes carved from tree trunks large enough to carry more than forty men and still move wonderfully fast when propelled by paddles that resembled baker's peels. If the canoes capsized, the Indians were all good swimmers. They righted the vessel, re-boarded, and bailed water with hollowed out calabashes tethered within. The Indians again presented spun cotton as gifts but did not use it for clothing. Finally, Columbus described the islanders as incredibly generous and anxious to give anything they had in exchange for trifles. Unfortunately, these guileless and generous Indians would arouse the worst traits of cupidity and brutality in many Europeans, and even the Admiral's apparent humanity was politically motivated. The hospitality of the mostly Taíno-speaking Indians of San Salvador would make them easy targets for enslavement.

Forty-eight hours after landing on the Bahamian island known to its native inhabitants as Guanahaní, named for then extinct iguanas, the three caravels lifted anchors and sailed in search of Japan. Columbus owned a copy of Marco Polo's *Travels* and it contained a description of Japan as an island with houses roofed in the finest gold, and accessories that included dinner plates thick in gold.

Pearls likewise existed in abundance. Guanahaní obviously was not Japan. The fleet next stopped at an island since identified as Rum Cay. Natives there offered the precious liquid, fresh water—always rare on many Caribbean islands because they had no rivers and all water came from pools of rain or wells. Indeed, the Indians on Rum Cay took casks from the three ships into their large canoes and returned them brimming with water. The natives were so obliging in every regard that Columbus commented: "Nothing was lacking but to know the language and to give them orders." His observation again denotes the Spaniards' cupidity as they entertained notions of growing rich by directing the labor of docile natives. But these Indians likewise had little gold. For the first time, however, the Europeans on Rum Cay saw patches of cultivated Indian corn, which became commonplace as the three vessels navigated through the Bahamas.

An important invention of the Bahamian Indians and other natives deserves mention—the hammock. As Spaniards sought fresh water on one island after another, one party described the beds of natives as "like nets of cotton." But the weaving of *hamacas* differed from nets in that it employed lengthwise thick threads joined periodically by cross-woven connectors. When supported on both ends by heavy woven cotton or hemp twine attached to supporting poles, or perhaps as slings supported between two trees a short distance apart, both made for comfortable resting or sleeping above ground. What sailor or backyard aficionado seeking rest or relaxation has not at one time or another appreciated a hammock?

As *Santa María* and its accompanying caravels moved southward from the Bahamas, they approached Cuba's north coast in *Oriente* Province. In late October, Spaniards explored a stretch of coast from the Río Mares to the Bay of Naranjo. Their first landing found no trace of human beings except for fish nets, bone fishhooks, harpoons, and "a dog that didn't bark." The canine had been domesticated by Taínos for eating purposes. Its sole vocalization was a grunt not a bark—making it totally useless as a home guardian, but that was not its purpose.

Anxious to explore the interior of an island, Columbus had men row him up the nearby Río Gibara, and along its shoreline he welcomed the sight of tall green grasses, amaranth, and palms different from Africa. The Admiral, perhaps unusually sensitive for a man of the sea, loved seeing greenery and hearing birds sing. Natural beauty, however, he could not take back to Spain. So he briefly continued searching elsewhere in eastern Cuba, which he renamed "Juana" after the daughter of the Catholic Monarchs and later heir apparent to the Spanish throne. Ultimately, Columbus viewed his encounter in Juana as little more than a frustrating delay. Nothing short of finding the Great Khan and Japan would truly satisfy him or his monarchs—a quest he continued for the rest of his life, and one that would have a profound influence on the attention he paid to governance of lands discovered. Over the course of three months in late 1492, a change came about in Columbus. He knew that settlement by Europeans and the introduction of commercial plants and livestock would be necessary to turn these newly discovered islands into profitable enterprises, especially since he had seen little evidence of gold. Soon thereafter, Columbus began to envision governing the islands that he had discovered according to the trading-post model, in which European and colonial goods were exchanged in the Atlantic islands off Africa such as in settled regions of the Canaries.

By December 5, the Columbus expedition had reached the eastern tip of Cuba, still believing that any landform so huge must be Japan. Sailing east, on the next day the fleet reached a large island Columbus named Española, later called Hispaniola. The Admiral went ashore hoping to find enough gold before his return voyage to please his royal sponsors. He found none. Meanwhile, search parties dispatched to the interior returned with reports of people who were more handsome and better built than those on the other islands. Determined to see for himself, Columbus recorded his impressions on December 16. The inhabitants on Española were completely naked and indeed the most handsome he had seen. They were also very white, and should they go about clothed to protect themselves from the sun the natives would look as white as the people of Spain. Columbus then described Española as the most beautiful of the island paradises he had visited. And he added—the natives are "plump and . . . not weak like the others."

At this point in his exploration, the Admiral had become thoroughly convinced that colonization and settlement of the West Indies islands must follow the exact policies of the Portuguese and Castilians on the Atlantic islands. In a message written to his sovereign sponsors, he wrote that lands he had encountered were "greatly good and fertile, especially this island of Hispaniola, and no one could believe it if he has not seen it." He added that nothing was lacking there except settlement and ordering the Indians to do whatever his Highnesses may wish. The Admiral further observed that he had seen three sailors come ashore with nothing but good intentions and confront a crowd of Indians. All had fled in fright, "because they are so cowardly that a thousand of them could not stand against those three men." The natives were therefore only fit to be ordered about and made to work, plant, and do whatever asked of them that might be needed. What lay in store, predicted the Admiral, "are constructed towns wherein the natives can be taught our Spanish customs and to go about clothed." All so stated by the Admiral was nevertheless an interim plan because he had not given up hope of finding gold mines that could easily be worked with mining technology, which as he noted was well beyond the skill of naked islanders.

While the expedition was exploring eastern Cuba, Martín Alonso Pinzón had sailed off on his own in *Pinta* and without Columbus's permission—a matter that greatly vexed the Admiral who insisted on controlling all matters. The incident was but one of several that spelled trouble between the headstrong Pinzón and Columbus, because the former thought the latter took too many chances. As Christmas approached, men of *Santa María* and *Niña* were in a celebratory mood. Surely, they would soon be headed home, but disaster loomed when the flagship went aground on a bank off the northern coast of Española. Remarkably, Columbus reported the incident laconically in his diary. He may well have done so to shield himself from blame because much of what went wrong can be laid at his feet.

Several routine precautions in caring for the ship had been relaxed, perhaps because of the holiday spirit. If so, it set the stage for tragedy. Columbus had allowed sailors to survey Caracol Bay and take soundings—something he had always done before—rather than checking things himself. Then error compounded error on Christmas Eve when the ship's cabin boy instead of an experienced helmsman had control of the tiller. That mistake was not Columbus's due to sailing protocol. The chartered ship's master and owner Juan de la Cosa bore responsibility for allowing the helm to be in the hands of a juvenile.

The *Santa María* went aground suddenly. The youngster's cry of anguish woke Columbus who rushed to try to save the ship. In haste, crew members launched a boat but failed to take a tow line. They cowardly rowed for the safety of *Niña*, whose officers rightly refused to let them board. When Columbus saw the boat return, he ordered the mainmast cut down and thrown overboard in a desperate measure to lighten the vessel. But it was too little too late. As the tide ran out, the ship stood higher and higher in the water; and then the planking broke apart. Columbus ordered the flagship abandoned and took his crew aboard the *Niña* where they a waited daybreak.

In the light of day, nothing could be done but salvage the wrecked ship. Columbus knew a local ruler nearby, and a landing party carried a message to him that sought his help. The chieftain, named Guacanagarí, immediately sent people in large canoes to assist with the unloading and moving of items ashore. He also donated shelters to protect goods and equipment on land. Once accomplished, there was no choice but to leave a portion of the fleet's crew on Española because not all could travel home on *Niña*. Although the Indians had been invariably helpful and kind, Columbus knew those left behind would be in mortal danger if the natives turned on them. From *Niña,* he wanted to make an impression. So he ordered a demonstration of European weaponry by firing Lombard cannons and a muzzle-loading gun. The thirty-nine mariners left behind would have a crude fort and some cover from the sun and weather, but their safety over months ahead depended far more on the good will of the Indians and the sustenance they would provide for European castaways.

On January 4, 1493, Columbus headed home along the north coast of Española, which he had convinced himself was in fact Cipango—as the Spanish then called Japan. Two days later, a lookout saw *Pinta* sailing toward them. The reconciliation of the Admiral and Martín Pinzón was tense. Columbus apparently hid his anger so as not to endanger their return voyage. The trip home was troubled by weather and ships that did not sail well—*Niña* lacked ballast because of so many heavy items left ashore on Española; *Pinta* had a faulty mainmast that hampered precise sailing. Despite these difficulties, both vessels returned to Palos on March 13—the same harbor they had departed on August 3 the year before.

Columbus's triumphal return and his journey over land from Palos to Barcelona where he reported to his Catholic Sovereigns at court are not pertinent to this study. For his extended stay in Barcelona, the Admiral brought with him small amounts of gold and gemstones collected in the Indies, seven Taíno companions then six-thousand miles from home, and tales of innumerable unexplored islands. The monarchs authorized and financed another voyage to leave Spain as soon as possible. Its preparations are important to understanding the Spaniards' return to Española and their troubled settlement of that island.

The Sovereigns ordered Juan Rodríguez de Fonseca, the Queen's occasional confessor and Archdeacon of Seville, to plan Columbus's second voyage in his home archdeaconship. Those not familiar with the geography of Spain are reminded that Seville is not a coastal city. It lies fifty miles up Spain's largest navigable river, the Río Guadalquivir. The Guadalquivir empties into the far eastern Atlantic Ocean at Sanlúcar de Barrameda, located a short distance northwest of the coastal port of Cádiz. More important, Seville would become the designated port for departures and arrivals of vessels engaged in Spain's increasing contacts with the Americas. The city held a monopoly that would last well over two centuries. Situated on the left bank of the Río Guadalquivir, Seville—starting in the 1490s and extending into the first decades of the 1700s—would become the very nerve center of administering all matters related to the Indies.

Fonseca was a masterful organizer of Columbus's second voyage. Within five months he assembled a fleet of seventeen vessels and equipped them with sea stores, extra gear, and arms. He likewise accumulated necessary food items for an extended voyage, and the cleric also recruited fifteen-hundred men. The Archdeacon collected seeds for plantings, domestic animals, and tools for a proposed mining-agricultural colony whose purpose was to transplant Spanish civilization to the Indies. Furthermore, these intricate preparations were done in an era when the best means of conveyance were two-wheeled carts drawn by oxen. Fonseca's enormous task received aid, as did Columbus on the first voyage at Palos, on orders from the royal Sovereigns Ferdinand and Isabella. Officials in nearby cities, towns, and villages received directives to grant every request f or purchasing necessary provisions—yet they were expressly forbidden to assess any tax or duty. From the royal armory came powder, cannons, and other military equipment. Payments to seamen, soldiers, and artisans provided reasonable wages for all. Finally, all other vessels not so chartered or attached to the new fleet were forbidden by royal decree "to sail to the said islands and mainland of the Indies without our license and command."

Columbus's second voyage involved the troublesome task of acquiring and loading almost the entire menagerie of domesticated animals found on farms and ranches. Into the holds of vessels went horses, cattle, sheep, goats, and crates of chickens. The difficulty of transporting horses across the Atlantic without the animals breaking a leg will be addressed later in this study when the Spanish conquest encountered armed native resistance and used war horses to suppress it. But in all instances, livestock in the holds of vessels added to the unpleasantness and stink of oceanic travel.

Seville continued to serve as the initial port for outfitting and provisioning the seventeen vessels. When loaded, the ships sailed down the Guadalquivir for final assemblage at Cádiz. When Columbus, who had been away from Seville while basking in Barcelona's sunshine, first saw the fleet he would command at its final point of departure, he found it far from ready. Some ships' stores were still delayed in delivery. The Admiral also expressed displeasure over the lack of shallow-draft vessels useful for exploring coastlines and probing rivers. Columbus's complaints directed at Fonseca were not reasonable given the mariner's total absence from Seville, where the ships were built and assembled. And it was also not a good idea to publicly berate Fonseca, especially given the Archdeacon's grim inclination to hold an unrelenting grudge for anyone who dared to criticize him.

The makeup of the completed armada in ships and men is little known, other than the Admiral's flagship—again named *Santa María*. It was authorized by the Crown at 200 tons and was clearly larger than the original ship of the same name. Unlike the first voyage, priests were among the fifteen-hundred men, but women were again excluded. Also different was how many of the new ship captains viewed Columbus. He enjoyed great authority and reputation by reason of his discovery, and he had solid support from many veteran shipmates under his command. Despite that well-deserved reputation, Columbus still suffered lack of respect because he was a foreigner—a circumstance that later weakened his command as governor and viceroy of the Indies.

Sailing day, September 25, 1493, came more than a month later than the departure date of the first voyage, August 3, 1492. But it buoyed the Admiral's spirits when his sons Diego and Ferdinand were on hand at Cádiz to wish their father *buen viaje*. On October 2, 1493, the fleet made the port at Gomera on Grand

Canary. While there, someone brought eight live pigs on board. Those swine, better equipped than rabbits in multiplying their numbers, formed the foundation of all swine in the Indies. When the fifteen ships, delayed ten days by a prolonged calm, left port on October 13 for the Indies, Columbus did not set a course to sail directly to Española, never mind the urgency of checking on the thirty-nine Spaniards left at La Navidad—named "the Nativity" because it was established at Christmas 1492. Instead, he hoped to explore new islands along the way. There are few details of this ocean passage since it was uneventful, primarily because it began so late in the year. If the fleet had left the Canaries by September 1, as the Admiral had hoped, it could hardly have avoided a hurricane before reaching the islands.

With the fleet on its way to the Indies but not reaching them until November 11, this interval provides a good opportunity to summarize what had been learned on the First Voyage. On San Salvador, the only domesticated creatures under the control of Taíno Indians were parrots and dogs. Some of the natives bore scars on their naked bodies, and in sign language those afflicted communicated they had fought off unidentified native slavers in large ocean-going canoes who had come to capture them; not all had been paradise before European contact. The Spaniards saw only men on the coast, which suggests a division of labor whereby males protected the coast while females remained farther inland.

On the extreme northeastern coast of Cuba, Spaniards found not only domesticated parrots but also the yellow non-barking hound dog that was bred for food. The Taínos raised Indian corn and amaranth as grain crops. Their non-food plants included cotton, tobacco, and hemp, the last used for cordage. Some Indians in Cuba and elsewhere slept in hammocks, previously unknown to Europeans. Again, only men were observed along the northern coastline. When Columbus ordered men to row him up a river, he observed tall grasses on the shorelines and a variety of songbirds.

On the third major island encountered on the first voyage and named Española, Columbus and a small party had explored inland. There they first saw native women who were as naked as the men. Of interest to Columbus, these Indians were whiter than those previously seen, which pleased him. He thought with protection from the sun, followed by being properly clothed, they might in time pass as Spaniards. Overall, the people and land on the third major island, then only partially explored, most favorably impressed the Europeans. It was also the only island in which Spaniards saw a somewhat hierarchical arrangement of native society wherein a chieftain could order his subjects to assist in salvage operations on the wrecked *Santa María*. Therefore, Española would likely have been Spaniards' choice for occupation and extended settlement in any event. But the wreck of the flagship, the necessity of leaving thirty-nine men behind, and the improvised colony at La Navidad provided the decisive elements. Española would not only become the first fully Spanish colonized major island in the Caribbean, but it would also be the only one for well over a decade. That island would first test whether Europeans with their superior material culture and their passion for gold and glory could co-exist with the less than completely innocent and guileless Taínos, and thereby avoid a demographic disaster.

The Indian population of the West Indies islands at the moment of European contact is estimated by historians at about five million. Where demographers have made systematic studies of pre-1492 Indian population on the mainland, especially in Central Mexico, the results have indicated human densities that are perhaps amazing to the reading public. Twenty-five million inhabitants in the heartland of New Spain (colonial Mexico) is a number accepted by many scholars. Others find that number inflated, but few would deny population density in that specific region of the Americas. Therefore, in this study, I have accepted that five million mostly Taíno and a much lesser number of Arawak natives faced contact with Spaniards over the next twenty-three years, 1493 to 1516, with terrible consequences.

As mentioned, Columbus intended to explore other islands en route to Española in the fall of 1493. The Admiral kept no log on his second voyage, but that did not stop members of the expedition from writing their own accounts in letters sent to Spain and the Catholic Sovereigns. Those firsthand accounts provide marked contrast to the Admiral's sanguine and hyperbolic reports sent to the Crown. Unlike Columbus, they had no reason to embellish what they saw. One of the fullest of those accounts comes to us from Diego Álvarez Chanca, a physician from Seville who sailed with royal appointment as the fleet's doctor.

On a small island identified only as Santa María de Galante but likely near Guadeloupe, Dr. Chanca reported on Spaniards who visited a deserted village.

Within the confines of a house, secure from animal predators, they found gnawed on human arms and leg bones—presumed to be the remains of a cannibal feast. On the next stop, an island that was christened *Santa María de Guadalupe* when the fleet landed there on November 4, Dr. Chanca reported the seizure of number of natives who had fled to the Europeans for deliverance from cannibalistic Caribs. The women captives were especially grateful to have been rescued and secretly pointed out to the Europeans which of the islanders were in fact Caribs themselves and which were not. Thereafter, Dr. Chanca and others made distinctions when reporting on other *Indios* as natives and on Caribs as cannibals.

Dr. Chanca was horrified by what he and his colleagues learned from women they had rescued. They described the Caribs as bestial, and the physician was especially appalled at how those Indians treated conquered peoples. The Caribs valued young and handsome women, and a lone member of the tribe might claim as many as twenty of them as his concubines. Those unfortunates received treatment that seemed incredibly savage to the Europeans. Male children given birth by the captive women to Carib men were eaten, because they only reared those born to Carib mothers. Boys found among captives were castrated and raised for food, because their flesh was so good that there was nothing like it in the world. Indeed, the arms and leg bones found in Carib houses were so thoroughly gnawed that not a morsel of flesh remained. To the disgust of Dr. Chanca and others, in one house they found the neck of a man cooking in a pot. Among those who came fleeing to the safety of Europeans to avoid that fate were three boys, all castrated. The matter-of-fact accounts of Dr. Chanca to Spanish authorities in Seville, supported by other firsthand observers, leave little doubt of their authenticity.

Leaving Guadeloupe, the fleet sailed north, to the west of what are now called the Leeward Islands. The Admiral, always given to self-promotion, named an island Saint Christopher, now Saint Kitts. At another isle, Columbus named Santa Cruz—known later after its French occupation as Saint Croix. There an incident with Caribs turned into a deadly fight. A war canoe, containing several men and two women, approached. On board as well were two Indian captives. The Europeans gave chase in a ship's boat, and the Caribs responded with a fusillade of arrows that wounded several men, one of whom later died. The enraged Europeans responded with concentrated musket fire, killing everyone except one woman.

This marked the first recorded skirmish between American Indians and Europeans in the West Indies and it foreshadowed the shape of things to come. When other lethal exchanges occurred, the outcome depended on which side had the most power. As the Spaniards would soon discover, it was the Indians who enjoyed the upper hand on Española to the peril of the thirty-nine mariners left at La Navidad. They would learn this after passing through a chain of islands Columbus named in Spanish the "Eleven Thousand Virgins," to commemorate the legend of Saint Ursula, the Roman British Christian saint and her group of holy virgins who died on October 21, 383. They of course were later named the Virgin Islands. The fleet then continued toward Española. En route on November 19, the fleet sailed along the southern coast of Puerto Rico. Spaniards estimated the island at being as large as Sicily, but the wind was so favorable the Admiral did not stop to investigate its harbors.

On November 22, the ships reached a large island, which the Indian guides who had accompanied Columbus to Spain and back declared was Española. Because the Admiral had only seen the mountainous region of Española on his first voyage, he found it difficult to believe that the flat expanse of land he saw was part of the same landmass. But he was later persuaded on reaching Caracol Bay, where the *Santa María* had run aground eleven months prior. In the meantime, Columbus explored other parts of the island as possible sites for settlement, because he knew the land around La Navidad was poorly situated for long-term occupation. On one of the forays, a search party came upon three badly decomposed bodies. One of the corpses showed evidence of having grown a beard; and since the Europeans had never seen a bearded Indian, those reconnoitering the land concluded that the victim had wandered away from La Navidad and been killed by Indians—it was not a good portent.

Soon afterward, as the flotilla coasted toward the bay where the original *Santa María* had been lost, several canoes bearing Indians approached the ships and the occupants asked to speak to the Admiral. Crew members directed them to his flagship, where they were permitted to board. When satisfied that the man who appeared before them was Columbus, a spokesman for the natives announced that they were emissaries of Guacanagarí, the chieftain who had sent men and canoes to help salvage European gear on Columbus's flagship the previous December.

When asked about the thirty-nine Europeans left at La Navidad, Guacanagarí's emissaries stated that they were fine, except for those who had died of sickness and others who had gotten into fatal disagreements with fellow Indians over their demands for gold and women. As it turned out, the two categories of dead Spaniards included the entire garrison.

Believing Columbus might hold him responsible for so many who had died, the chieftain was terrified and stayed in bed while feigning a leg wound. He need not have worried. Columbus no doubt remembered the kindnesses of Guacanagarí who had also helped build a shelter and fort for the thirty-nine castaways. He accepted the loss of Spanish lives, but he was even more determined to find a suitable place for a colony on Española. Taking the fleet back east along the north coast of Española proved difficult due to steady trade winds—it took twenty-five days to make about thirty-two miles to windward. Columbus picked a site where he believed gold could be mined and broke ground for Isabela—named in honor of the Queen. He chose poorly, but animals on the ships were dying, and many onboard the seventeen vessels clamored to touch land. Isabela rose but far from high on a flat plain a mile from the nearest fresh water. Nevertheless, the Admiral boasted of founding the first town in the Indies, which he laid out on a classic grid of streets. One of his seamen recorded a less glorious reality: "Here we made two-hundred houses, which are as small as hunting cabins back home and are roofed with grass."

The European settlers at Isabela soon fell ill. Dr. Chanca ascribed their sickness to three reasonable causes: half rations during the voyage because no one could be sure when they would find land; the settlers already weakened had been forced to labor at building the new town; and they had experienced a sudden change in climate. But the overall cause of people becoming sick seems to have been due to malnutrition. Imported seeds had not had time to germinate and produce cereal grains. Columbus responded in the short run by ordering a flour mill built and the remaining seeds ground for food. Dr. Chanca did note that the local fish were good, even better than in Europe, but the oppressive heat made it necessary that catches be eaten immediately, or they spoiled. More recent theories have suggested that the settlers developed Reiter's syndrome—caused by a tropical bacillus initially manifesting dysentery, arthritic conditions, inflammation of the eyes, even blindness, and penile discharge. Typically, Reiter's is spread by unsanitary food handling.

Columbus further responded to the dire conditions at Isabela by sending Alonso de Ojeda (perhaps early on more commonly spelled Hojeda) and forty men to reconnoiter other regions of Española in early January 1494. Don Alonso had captained one of the caravels on the second voyage, and he had earned a favorable reputation at the royal court as a client of a powerful duke. Ojeda returned in a month from a successful expedition to the interior bearing large nuggets of gold. Columbus was sorely tempted to collect more of the precious metal and send it to the King and Queen, but it was more important to send most of the fleet back to Spain for additional supplies. Along with the returning ships came a lengthy report of conditions on Española written by Columbus for the Catholic Sovereigns and carried to Spain by his capable emissary Antonio de Torres.

As usual, the Admiral was careful to present the best possible scenario of matters on Española to his royal sponsors. From its shores, spices could be seen in abundance. Even better were Ojeda's reports from the interior where he had seen rivers full of gold. But despite the lure of accessible riches from streams and rivers, mines would be necessary to extract the maximum amount of gold in the future. Columbus, therefore, implored the King and Queen to recruit miners, especially from the mercury mines at Almadén, and then send them to his supervision on Española. Without doubt, the most experienced miners in Spain were those employed at the famous—and infamous , due to the dangers of handling cinnabar and the potential for mercury poisoning—mines in La Mancha province. In stressing the need for miners and mining technology in the Indies, the Admiral signaled to the Royal Monarchs that they should not expect quick returns on their investment.

Not surprisingly, given the total annihilation of the original garrison at La Navidad, Columbus retreated somewhat from his earlier reports to the Catholic Monarchs on the tractability of the Indians. Even though he still called the natives "very simple and without malice," the Admiral admitted having ordered a wall constructed around the new settlement. A strong fort would also be necessary to secure the vast amounts of gold the island would yield prior to it being loaded on ships leaving for Spain. If Europeans remained vigilant, as the Admiral assured

Ferdinand and Isabella, the natives would never attempt an assault. In so writing, Columbus insisted that lack of watchfulness had doomed the garrison at La Navidad. That comment was at best half-truth because evidence of a frontal attack by Indians was lacking. Instead, the mariners were killed one by one because of their repeated demands for gold and concubines. There were limits to the Indians' docility, and as the outsiders disrupted their way of life, violence occurred.

The Admiral's report to his Sovereigns mentioned that Spanish colonists continued to fall ill, which he attributed to a change in air and water. The settlers' sicknesses, however, had prevented him from sending more gold to Spain. He followed by assuring the royal monarchs there was nothing to worry about. The colonists' health would soon improve when Spanish food he was requesting arrived. He also stated that the land around Isabela was so rich that the wheat and vines he brought with him would soon flourish, so there would be no need to import wine and bread from rich agricultural regions in Spain like Andalusia. But that lay in the future, so in the interim he asked the monarchs to send wine, wheat, biscuits, and salted meat. Among other items requested were raisins, almonds, honey, and rice. Those were Spanish foodstuffs recommended for the sick because they were easy to digest. Columbus also asked for domestic animals that included sheep, lambs, calves, young heifers, and male and female asses, as well as mares. Finally, with the Torres fleet sent to Spain were more than twenty Indians, presumably Caribs. They were sold as slaves when the ships reached Seville. The Admiral believed that with the refinements of life in Spain, the Caribs might abandon their abominable custom of eating human flesh.

The list of things Columbus needed from Spain, which would make life more bearable and profitable at Isabela, spoke to the precarious nature of the Europeans' lives at the first settlement in the Indies. Their circumstances assuredly must have been dire. Picture well over a thousand Spaniards living in huts on a stark plain that grew not a single tree for shade. The tropical climate of the Caribbean isles was so hot and oppressive that the native inhabitants, as seen from coastlines, did not wear a single item of clothing throughout the year. Likewise, Spaniards on the few forays and expeditions that penetrated the interiors of Cuba and Española saw only naked men and women. Aside from the unrelenting heat, a drink of water was a mile from Isabela. Since every settler who sailed to the Indies dreamed of acquiring riches there, morale at Isabela was no doubt low. Perhaps worse, there were no women from Spain until 1498 when Columbus was authorized to recruit one woman for every ten men emigrants. Meanwhile, libidinous men seeking sex on Española were aroused by naked Indian women. Those encounters were certain to cause trouble—as had previously been demonstrated at La Navidad.

The fleet captained by Antonio de Torres, bearing a laundry list of items sought by Columbus to secure the settlement of Española, reached Seville in late spring 1494. Ferdinand and Isabella were then in residence at the port city. Despite the Admiral's rhetorical efforts to present a favorable impression of his great enterprise of the Indies, unsettling news from the islands had aroused suspicions in the minds of his royal patrons. They did not blame the sickness of settlers or the lack of domestic animals in the colony on Columbus; instead, the King and Queen pointed to his overall mismanagement of the expedition that had departed the previous year. For example, the Sovereigns had ordered the Admiral to recruit twenty armed troopers and their equipment from the local militia to maintain discipline in the colony. The troopers had arrived well mounted and armed, but Columbus had never inspected them before sailing. He later realized the militiamen had sold their fine horses and purchased nags for the voyage, thereby pocketing the difference in price. Many other men-at-arms had done the same in selling good weapons and replacing them with inferior ones. Some had even sold muskets, crossbows, powder, and shot while replacing them with nothing. The reader may remember that Columbus had basked in the sunlight of Barcelona while preparations for the second voyage were underway in Seville and Cádiz, and he arrived shortly before embarkation. Later, when questioned about his laxity in inspection, the Admiral's weak excuse was: "I did not see to it, because I was a little indisposed." Time after time, Columbus was inattentive as a colonial administrator, and the suspicions of his royal sponsors in this regard slowly increased.

Whatever the long-term doubts of his sponsors, the royal couple responded generously to Columbus's requests—with a few exceptions. The monarchs chose not to comment on the Admiral's plan to sell Indian slaves in Spain to pay for the livestock and draft animals needed on Española. Isabella was especially concerned about the unjust enslavement of her new subjects, so she ordered

Columbus to fight the Caribs when necessary, but to concentrate on converting them to Catholicism.

While Antonio de Torres sailed from Spain on the resupply mission, Columbus led five-hundred men into the interior of Española. They explored in hopes of finding gold but returned to Isabela with very little of it; and at that juncture, the Admiral again decided to go exploring at sea. By his own admission, the responsibilities of administration bored him, as did the largely fruitless inland forays that yielded few rewards. Increasingly, as was his custom, he left his brother Diego in charge. The small fleet commanded by the Admiral sailed from Isabela on April 24, 1494. It consisted of three ships, including the faithful *Niña*, which had sailed again on the second voyage. The principal route of discovery was along the south coast of Cuba, interrupted initially by a side trip to and from Jamaica. In all, the three vessels coasted Cuba for 335 leagues, well over a thousand miles. No one on the fleet had heard of an island so huge, thereby lending the belief that Cuba must be mainland. But finding little wealth, the vessels returned to Española. Although Columbus had suffered exhaustion and extreme fatigue to the point of having to be carried ashore, good news awaited. His brother Bartolomé had arrived a month or so earlier. From France where he had lived for a time, don Bartolomé had previously traveled to Spain with intent to sail on the second voyage, but he arrived too late. Ferdinand and Isabella nonetheless ordered Juan de Fonseca in Seville to equip him with two or three caravels loaded with necessities for Isabela and sent him on his way. He reached Española with the much-needed supplies on June 24, 1494, to the delight of his brothers who had not seen him in years.

During the Admiral's absence at sea, his brother Diego had proven an even less competent administrator than Columbus himself. Discontent had run so high at Isabela that dozens of disillusioned settlers seized two or three caravels and sailed home to Spain without permission. By then the route back to Spain was well enough known to make a transatlantic voyage without having the experience of a Columbus or the Pinzones. That fact alone had encouraged desertions at Isabela, and there was worse to come.

Before the end of 1494, Antonio de Torres returned from Spain bringing yet another relief fleet filled with supplies for the Isabella settlement. With Torres came a request from the Catholic Monarchs asking Columbus to return to Spain and advise them on negotiations with Portugal over moving the demarcation line of 1494 as determined by the Treaty of Tordesillas, which had divided the two colonial empires. Columbus declined but perhaps should have accepted. It is quite possible the Sovereigns had offered an honorable way to remove the Admiral from administrative tasks that seemed beyond his skills. A few years later, they would not be so considerate of his feelings.

In February 1495, Torres set out for Spain once again. Prior to his departure, Columbus sought ways to convince his patrons that his colony could turn a profit. Significant amounts of gold had not been recovered, so the Admiral decided to send them human cargo as chattel slaves. He justified taking such action because the sale of captured rebels in the Canary Islands who were at war with Spaniards there served as precedent. But a legality that had great significance for the future of Spain in America was about to come into play. Subjects of the King and Queen, whether in the Canaries or on Española, were protected against enslavement unless they were at war with Spain. But in a conflict defined as a just war by Spain—explained below in chapter 3—Indians could be seized and enslaved with impunity. However, that concept had not been formalized by Castilian law. So, the Catholic Sovereigns had declared a moratorium on slaving until the matter could be settled, but Columbus did not know that.

The Admiral and his men marched through the island on a slaving expedition supported by men armed with muskets and lances on horses, with dogs trained for warfare—and in doing so captured sixteen-hundred Indians who offered resistance. Of that number, only five-hundred-fifty would fit on the vessels Torres had prepared to leave for Spain. Columbus awarded six-hundred-fifty as slaves to settlers at Isabela and released the remaining four-hundred. Those spared slavery fled in terror, including many women with infants at their breasts. To run faster and avoid being captured again, the women placed their babies on the ground and left them to their fate. Those avoiding slavery did not stop until they had separated themselves from Isabela by seven or eight days.

The Indian population on Española was already declining precipitously due to disease and fatalities in battle, and Columbus's slaving expeditions made the situation even worse. During 1495 there was growing hostility between Indians and Europeans over who owned lands on Española. For example, in March of that year, the governor fought and won a pitched battle in the interior of the island. To reward his men and preserve battlefield gains, he began for the first time in the Indies a system of forced labor whereby Indians were assigned to specific settlers and obliged to work for them under the whip. Columbus also ordered the construction of several forts to protect European interests. By the beginning of 1496, the native population of Española had been reduced to bitter but largely subservient obedience.

Back in Spain, a growing number of those who opposed Columbus enjoyed spreading stories about his deeds and mismanagement, and the Sovereigns began to listen. Among the Admiral's most vocal critics were former settlers returning from the second voyage. Some had gone home on one of Torres's two relief fleets, while others returned on the caravels that had brought Bartolomé Colón to Española. Still other disgruntled persons informed the King and Queen that the entire enterprise was a joke because there was no gold on Española and expenditures of the Crown would never be recovered. Without doubt some of those who railed against Columbus and his brothers were incensed at having to take orders from foreigners. But there was more than that to blame on Columbus. He had made himself the target of condemnation by overselling the bounty of the islands, as well as the passivity and good will of their inhabitants.

There were also contrasting views of the inhabitants among those who had previously been on-scene European observers. All had condemned the Caribs as bestial cannibals, but many failed to differentiate them from the much more tractable Taínos. That assessment reflected the racial superiority harbored by the Europeans toward the naked humanity that had appeared before them. It also presaged the "Great Debate" that lay ahead during the Spanish conquest of the Indies on the true nature of the Indians. A Spanish settler on Española recorded his view of them: "They live like beasts, [and] they have intercourse openly whenever the feeling moves them, and aside from brothers and sisters, all the rest are common property. From what we have seen in all the islands where we have been, both the Indians and the cannibals are great sodomites, not knowing, I suppose, whether they are doing good or evil."

Despite worrisome reports coming from returned colonists, the Catholic Monarchs were intent on rectifying the need for domestic livestock on Española. On April 9, 1495, they ordered Fonseca to send six mares, four male and two female asses, four calves and two heifers, eighty sows, plus sheep and rabbits. The mares and jackasses reflected the need for steady and reliable draft animals. To lend protection of the settlers and their possessions, dozens of mastiffs trained in warfare would join the expedition. The royal couple also instructed Fonseca to send mining engineers, farmers, vegetable gardeners, iron workers, coopers, and crossbow makers. Finally, skilled fishermen and several well-constructed fishing boats built in Seville completed the list of specified items. The care that Ferdinand and Isabella took to the make the colony successful and self-supporting as soon as possible reflected their continuing support for the Columbian enterprise in the Indies.

That said, the Sovereigns could not completely ignore the litany of complaints about Columbus that had reached their ears. They appointed Juan Aguado, a Crown official who had sailed on the second voyage, to investigate. Don Juan had returned with Torres in February 1495. Among his other duties, the royal agent was charged with ensuring the fair distribution of all items sent to the colony. Of interest, the King and Queen told Aguado to do nothing about slaving or the slave trade pending the recommendations of a royal commission composed of theologians, canon lawyers, and royal appointees.

In October 1495, Aguado arrived on Española armed with a commission to investigate the charges made against Columbus and his brother, Diego. The commissioner was appalled at what he found: high death rate among natives and the number of colonists severely reduced by disease and desertion. It appeared to Aguado that many settlers when given the opportunity had chosen to go home to Spain on any ship returning there. Perhaps shaken by the intensity of Aguado's investigation, Columbus decided to return to Spain but would leave his brother Bartolomé in charge of the colony by appointing him *adelantado*. This designation for a Spanish colonial official would be used until the end of the sixteenth century. It carried high prestige and denoted a Spanish official, usually a governor, on the frontier of Spain in America—just as the possessor of that title had been used during the expanding frontier during the centuries-long Reconquest. Ordinarily, the right of appointment as *adelantado* resided with the Crown, but Ferdinand

and Isabella temporarily overlooked the Admiral's presumption in awarding it to his brother, although they would later confirm the title to preserve the royal prerogative.

On March 10, 1496, Columbus set out on his second return to Spain. He took only two ships, the faithful *Niña*, then making its second roundtrip, and a cobbled together caravel using parts salvaged from two disabled vessels. The Admiral chose a more direct route east from Isabela and to the south of his first return in 1493. His choice of route was a mistake because he had to fight headwinds during much of a troubled voyage. *Niña* and its companion caravel after two months at sea reached Cádiz on June 11, 1496. The Admiral's crewmen were ill, their "faces the color of saffron." The former governor and viceroy of Española would soon face a reception far different from his triumphal return three years earlier as the political atmosphere in Spain had changed. Nonetheless, Columbus would prove useful to his patrons for several more years.

NOTE BENE

English equivalents for distance, measurement, weight, and monetary units.

League of land: 3.0 miles in 16th century.

Vara: about 33 inches.

Pulgada: about one inch.

Arroba: twenty-five pounds.

Fanega: 1.6 bushels.

Maravedí: coin and smallest unit of Spanish currency.

Gold peso: 450 maravedís.

Silver peso: 272 maravedís. Also known as "piece of eight," consisting of eight reales,
    each valued at 34 maravedís.

Castellano or ducat: 375 maravedís.

CHAPTER 2

Columbus's Voyages Three and Four, and Retirement

Immediately on disembarking at Cádiz on June 11, 1496, Columbus wrote to Ferdinand and Isabella to inform them of his arrival and eagerness to appear at court. The King and Queen, attending to diplomatic matters with France and arranging the marriages of two children, were then in northern Castile. While awaiting their response, the Admiral helped organize a small fleet dispatched to Española under the captaincy of Peralonso Niño. He then traveled up the Río Guadalquivir to Seville for a happy reunion with son Diego—younger son Hernando was then absent from Seville while serving as page to Prince Juan, the only son of Ferdinand and Isabella. At court, there was much on the mind of the royal couple besides France and marital issues involving their children. Foremost was the near success of the Portuguese in rounding the tip of Africa and reaching India, and final preparations were then underway in the rival nation for outfitting Vasco da Gama. Elsewhere, Henry VII of England had employed another Italian adventurer named Jacobo Caboto (John Cabot) who sought a northern Atlantic passage to Japan. This was surely not the time to dismiss Columbus who had demonstrated by sailing west from the Canaries that he had established Spanish presence on islands in the Indies still believed to be outliers of the Orient.

Returning to family matters of the Catholic Monarchs, Princess Juana would soon sail to Flanders and marry Philip the Handsome, heir apparent to Hapsburg possessions. The Queen was then separated from Ferdinand, who had temporarily returned to Catalonia to deal with a crisis there, and as a kindness to her Columbus wrote a letter offering advice for her daughter's safe journey from the Bay of Biscay to Flanders. The Queen responded graciously, thanking the Admiral for his consideration and expertise. In early fall 1496, Columbus traveled overland to the royal court at Burgos to report on his accomplishments and seek support for a Third Voyage to the Indies. The Admiral, dressed in humble attire, came bearing gifts from Española.

Always clever as supplicant on his own behalf, Columbus chose not to appear as Lord Admiral of the Ocean Seas by wearing brass insignia. Instead, he came dressed like a Franciscan friar: same brown-colored clothing cut like the order's habit, fastened at the waist with a cord sash. His choice of attire suggested abject poverty and self-abnegation. Almost certain to please the *"muy católica"* Queen Isabella with his faux religious garb, Columbus "was at his persuasive best." Then came gifts from Española, which the Admiral presented to her Majesty: "masks, belts, collars, and many other things made of cotton," but little gold. Nonetheless, the Queen accepted all items with royal enthusiasm.

Matters changed when Columbus asked the Queen to provide funds for his proposed third voyage. She told him that it had taken every peso of the Crown's resources to pay for the upcoming wedding of Prince Juan and Princess Margarita of Austria, as well as for the defense of Catalonia from France, which had drawn Ferdinand away from court. Isabella informed Columbus that the cost of preparing his proposed third voyage to the Indies had to come from the gold Peralonso Niño was supposed to bring on his return voyage from Española. That was bad news for the Admiral because he knew little gold had been found on the settlement island. In fact, as Columbus had observed from firsthand experience, the only thing of real value on Española was its people and the potential for profits by selling them into slavery. That commerce, however, had been placed on hold pending the adjudication of the matter of Indian enslavement and the Spanish understanding of just war. That weighty issue, however, would not be set forth in writing until 1513, and even at that time was far from settled.

While Columbus languished at Burgos, Peralonso Niño returned to Cádiz on October 29, 1496, but thereafter handled correspondence poorly with the Queen. Niño sought immediate recompense for what he claimed was a great amount of gold collected without specifying its actual value. His request was hardly diplomatic, given the financially stressed Crown, and the Isabella expressed her annoyance with him. If Niño had a great quantity of gold, she needed it to remove the financial pinch she found herself in. It was therefore imperative that the mariner appear at court with gold in hand. Instead, Niño peevishly returned to his home in Moguer near Huelva, and he did not travel to court as the Queen had requested until the end of December. [*See* **Figure 1**] The gold he delivered was also much less than the Crown had hoped for. Columbus was likewise irritated because he was delayed in getting answers from his brother Bartolomé on conditions in Española, which had been sent to him in care of don Peralonso. What especially irritated the Crown was the large number of slaves Niño had brought to Spain in the hope of selling them. Furthermore, the small amount of gold then found on the settlement island reflected poorly on Columbus's claims of its riches. Nevertheless, faced with competition from Portugal and England, the Catholic Monarchs were obliged to retain Columbus's services, but they had to place his expedition on hold until political and family matters had been resolved to their satisfaction.

It seems that Columbus, a man who greatly favored exploration over administration, was not adept at waiting. As things turned out, he had good reason to be concerned about what was happening on Española. Columbus, as noted, had left Bartolomé in charge as *adelantado* when he chose to return to Spain during the Aguado inspection. Conditions even then for European settlers were at a critical impasse, and they deteriorated more rapidly under a tribute arrangement forced on the dwindling Indian population, initially by Columbus and later by his brother. Appropriately labeled a "ghastly system" by the Admiral's critics, the Columbus brother saw it as a necessary means of acquiring gold to send to Spain.

All natives fourteen years and up had to submit a small but fixed amount of gold every three months or face severe punishment for failing to do so. This was especially difficult if not impossible to accomplish because there were no mines, and the natives had not been taught how to pan for gold. Indians who lived in areas where gold could not be found along streambeds had to submit one *arroba* (twenty-five pounds) of spun cotton in lieu of trimonthly payments in gold. The system, according to one critic, "was burdensome, irrational, impossible, and abominable."

When first contacted by Spaniards on Española, the Indians had some gold trinkets acquired over long periods of time as personal or family treasures, and the natives valued them because they were shiny and attractive. However, all such items had long since been stripped away by trade or confiscation. At that time, the only profitable way to acquire gold was by washing it out of sand or gravel in the beds of small streams. That required unremitting labor without survey knowledge of where there was even the remotest possibility of finding a nugget. None of this was known to the frantic Indians who had to roam the land constantly while hoping by chance to find a bit of gold. If unsuccessful, they faced harsh punishment under the whip. Unable to meet their tribute quotas, some Indians fled to the mountains where they were hunted with dogs, while others turned on their Christian overseers and killed them. Retaliations by Spaniards led not just to the punishing specific offenders but to the wiping out entire villages where remission of gold was in arrears.

Ethnologists have estimated the pre-Spanish contact population of Española at 500,000—and that number was for one of the more densely peopled major islands in the Caribbean. One third of the Indians had died by 1496. By 1508, when Spaniards began settlements on Puerto Rico and Jamaica, native inhabitants remaining on Española stood at only 60,000. Such was the fate of the largely gentle and almost defenseless people who happened to have potential as slaves, women as concubines, and the small possessions Europeans coveted. The garrulous old conquistador and writer Bernal Díaz del Castillo who figures importantly later in this study was once asked why he left Spain for the Indies. His reply had stunning honesty: "I came to serve God and get rich," but perhaps not in that order.

It was nonetheless strange that after a year and a half of colonization and settlement on an island noted for its rich soil and abundant rainfall Spaniards on Española were still dependent on food and other necessities imported from Spain. Michele de Cuneo, an observer on the scene, explained why: "Although the soil is very black and good . . . [settlers] have not yet found the way or the time to sow; the reason is that nobody wants to live in these countries." Although Columbus had planned permanent occupation of Española, which would lead to a colony where Hispanic culture and Christianity could take root, the settlers themselves wanted first and foremost to get rich quick and return home to spend it. That attitude prevailed for many on the major Caribbean islands where everyone they saw was naked and the climate tropical. It seems Columbus himself had come to that conclusion. He should return to Spain, seek support for a Third Voyage, and continue his search for Japan and the mainland of Asia wherein untold riches could be found. His delay at Burgos meant that matters on Española would continue to spiral downward unless circumstances improved at Isabela. And that did happen.

Just before Columbus had sailed to Spain, colonists searching for gold elsewhere on Española had found promising signs of it near the southeastern coast of the island. They reported their discovery to the Admiral, and he barely had time to name the region San Cristóbal before boarding *Niña*. His brother Bartolomé, newly named *adelantado* but not yet confirmed by the Crown, devoted considerable time and energy to the new locale by building a series of forts as waystations between it and Isabela. In exploring further, Spaniards discovered an excellent harbor at the mouth of a river, surrounded by good arable land. They named the port city Santo Domingo, and it would later become the Crown's most important administrative municipality in the Indies for a quarter of a century.

Bartolomé Columbus directed his attention to the more promising region of Santo Domingo by stripping Isabela of any useful equipment and supplies he found movable. That angered the settlers at Isabela who had come to depend on the Admiral's recently instituted tribute payments in gold or cotton. Discontent escalated into rebellion against the authority of the Columbus brothers. An uprising led by Francisco Roldán, whom Columbus had placed in charge of Isabela before sailing back to Spain. Don Francisco began arming settlers and recruiting Indian allies by promising an end to the hated tribute system. The Roldán rebellion escalated and Bartolomé Columbus could not suppress it. The revolt was unique in that it used the Indian allies of one European faction against another that had no native assistance, and the standoff continued for two and a half years. During that time, the enraged *adelantado* Bartolomé Columbus lashed out at all Indians by capturing the two principal chieftains on the island and sending them and others to Spain as slaves. But he could not reinstitute tribute payments by the Indians, nor could he suppress the Roldán rebellion, which continued even after Columbus returned to Española on his third voyage.

Back in Spain, the royal wedding of Prince Juan and Margarita of Austria took place in early April 1497. Ferdinand and Isabella then turned their attention to Columbus and plans for his third voyage. They reconfirmed his titles as admiral, viceroy, and governor of his discoveries in the Indies. Those were exclusive rights granted to no other Spaniard, but the Crown's generosity did not extend to funding the proposed new voyage. Matters were also different in that Juan Rodríguez de Fonseca, the great organizer in Seville, no longer lived in the city because he had been appointed bishop of Badajoz in extreme southwestern Castile. The Sovereigns appointed Antonio de Torres in the bishop's stead. Torres, a close friend of Columbus, was familiar with travel to and from Española. His demands on the Crown nevertheless soon soured the monarchs, and they withdrew his commission—followed by their reappointing Fonseca and ordering him to return to Seville. This meant still more delays in organizing the third voyage because the paperwork commissioning Torres had to be redrawn. That complication, as it turned out, was minor compared to Fonseca's role in dealing with the Admiral. The two men had never gotten along well, and their disagreements meant even further postponements, but one matter was resolved: the Catholic Monarchs officially confirmed Bartolomé Colón's appointment as *adelantado*—after the fact, since he had already assumed the post.

The Crown and Fonseca followed with an important decision that would affect all future administrators of royal commissions in the Indies. Those empowered would be issued thorough and detailed instructions on what they could and could not do. The new directives were regarded as the best means of ensuring absolute monarchical control over lands some five-thousand miles across a great ocean. This pleased Bishop Fonseca, who was adamant that the chain of command flow in only one direction—from the divinely empowered Crown down through its formal appointees. Some two decades later, these strictures might well place a conquistador named Hernando Cortés's head under the executioner's axe. In the meantime, it meant Christopher Columbus must follow new rules that governed his third voyage.

A list of instructions given Columbus by the Catholic Monarchs in the summer of 1497 is presented here, because they became the norm for all administrators appointed in the Indies. The Admiral could recruit a maximum of 330 people. Included were forty mounted and armed troopers, one-hundred men-at-arms, thirty sailors, thirty apprentice sailors, twenty gold workers, fifty farmers, ten vegetable gardeners, twenty artisans of varying skills, and thirty women. The last recruitment was the first authorization for Castilian women to sail with men to the Indies, and it established the ratio of one female emigrant for every ten males that prevailed for several years. Additionally, the royal couple spelled out the tools needed for a self-sustaining colony: hoes, spades, pickaxes, sledgehammers, and crowbars. Also included were millstones and other equipment so settlers could mill their own flour. Further, the completed list enumerated twenty yokes of draft animals. The A-to-Z list of things commanded by Ferdinand and Isabella included how to handle gold discovered in the Indies, which they suspected had been underreported in the past with the intent of defrauding the Crown of its one-fifth share. In the future, all precious metals must be coined into Granadan *excelentes* (value not specified). Among the three-hundred and thirty people recruited were men skilled in minting coinage, with the commandment that they bring with them dies and other instruments needed to cast coins.

The Catholic Sovereigns ordered Columbus, and by extension later administrators in the Indies who succeeded him, to work toward converting the Indians to Catholicism. That called for the recruitment of priests to serve the spiritual needs of Indians and Spaniards alike. Not surprisingly, given its future widespread use in the Indies, the Crown approved the tribute system begun on Española by Columbus. It became the forerunner of a complex institution called *repartimiento*, or encomienda. Initially, both had the same meaning, but the first eventually evolved into something quite different from the second—called forced labor for wages. Encomienda would become widespread in the islands. And in a following chapter, I will try in a few sentences to describe an institution addressed in book-length studies. For now, encomienda and *repartimiento* had origins that reprised medieval Castilian rulers' attempts to resettle and defend lands taken from the Muslims during the long Reconquest (ca. 720–1492). It is mentioned here because *repartimiento* in its original meaning would become a significant departure from the trading-post system that Columbus and the Crown had first set up on Española, and it served to underpin the Spanish Empire's settlement and control of the Americas.

In the later months of 1497, tragedy struck the royal family and delayed final preparations for Columbus's third voyage. Prince Juan, the heir of Ferdinand and Isabella, died (according to legend from excessive lovemaking in the first months of marriage) on October 4 leaving Margarita of Austria a pregnant widow. The best hope for an undisputed successor to the thrones of Aragon and Castile lay with her unborn child. At the end of the year, doña Margarita delivered a premature and stillborn daughter. That set off a year of mourning at the royal court and further delayed departure of Columbus's third voyage.

The Crown finally provided six vessels under the command of the Admiral. Two of them were readied sooner than the others and sent ahead to the Canaries to await the remaining four. When all had arrived, they were divided into two contingents. The first contained a *nao*, a medium-size sailing vessel often used to carry supplies and domestic animals, and two caravels for Columbus's use in exploring. The second grouping of vessels carried provisions and men and women headed for Española. Recruiting passengers had nonetheless been difficult because news from the island had been little other than bad. As inducement, the Crown offered to pardon all prisoners not then guilty of committing major crimes defined as treason, heresy, smuggling, counterfeiting, and sodomy—oddly, however, offenders charged with such "lesser offenses" as murder were free to leave Spain. Ten men having been arrested for commission of homicide would join the other two-hundred and twenty emigrants en route to the settlement island.

The last four ships outfitted at Seville sailed down the Río Guadalquivir to Sanlúcar de Barrameda in May 1498, and on the thirtieth of the month the third voyage of Columbus began. The fleet as planned separated at Gomera in the Canaries. Three vessels sailed directly to Española, while the Admiral took an equal number farther to the south by way of the Cape Verde Islands. In choosing a different route to the Indies, Columbus had embraced a bizarre theory that gold matured best under the most direct rays of the sun. To him it meant the richest deposits of that precious metal were likely found near the equator, and that belief led the Admiral to continue sailing south until he sighted the continent of South America on the coast of present-day Venezuela where the huge delta of the Río Orinoco touched the Atlantic Ocean. Instead of recognizing the existence of a great undiscovered continental landmass, Columbus saw the outpouring of the Orinoco's waters as discharging from the earthly paradise of the Garden of Eden. While that may seem strange to modern readers, to Columbus and his contemporaries Holy Scriptures were as much a source of knowledge about the existing natural world as they were religious texts. However, finding no gold in the Río Orinoco, Columbus next sailed along a jutting peninsula atop the continent immediately west of Trinidad, which he named Paria. Again, he found no gold. From Paria the Admiral led the three vessels with unerring accuracy to the new capital of Española at Santo Domingo, where he arrived on August 31. Given what he soon saw, he might well have been better off by being a worse navigator and missing the island completely, thereby remaining lost forever.

At Española, Columbus found chaos and crisis. Some colonists, including those recently arrived on the three supply ships, had committed mutiny, seized one of the ships, and demanded the right to sail it back to Spain—others were bitter at the pittance they received from the tribute system. Neither Bartolomé nor Diego Colón had been able to restore order, and Columbus himself had little luck in accomplishing that. Worse, at Isabela the rebellion led by Francisco Roldán remained unchecked and ongoing. Columbus gave permission to disgruntled settlers who had had enough of misery and disappointment to leave the colony, take one slave with them, and seek passage to Spain. But in writing the Crown the Admiral continued to exaggerate favorable conditions in the colony, and he was even optimistic about ending the Roldán revolt. Along with his reports to the Catholic Monarchs came three-hundred disillusioned settlers and an equal number of slaves they intended to sell in Spain. But Queen Isabella would not allow enslavement of her subjects, and she ordered the slaves freed.

With usual hyperbole, Columbus described Española where Indians were disappearing like darkness at dawn, where settlers were demanding return passage to Spain, and where no one had yet made a profit in a land he described as "most beautiful and the most fertile under heaven, in which there is gold and copper and many kinds of spices." The Admiral also claimed the island would prosper when the capital returned to Isabela. Even the queen knew her namesake town was poorly located without a viable port or nearby source of fresh water. She also knew that Bartolomé Colón had sent everything movable to Santo Domingo, which had an excellent harbor and nearby prospects of gold. Both monarchs had heard more than enough of Columbus's exaggerated accounts of how things were going on Española, and it should be remembered that they had been at pains to send what they thought would have make the island a self-supporting colony with supplies, draft animals, and new settlers including ten women.

Ferdinand and Isabella decided to send an inspector general to Española. They designated Francisco de Bobadilla and armed him with extraordinary powers to restore order. Don Francisco had excellent credentials. He was commander of the military order of Calatrava, an association of knights who took modified monastic vows and dedicated themselves to fighting and eliminating the infidel. Bobadilla could also claim years of experience. In Spain, knights of Calatrava were landowners with proven skills in the direction and management of agricultural workers. As some historians have pointed out, the selection of Bobadilla with his talents and résumé was a clear indication that Ferdinand and Isabella had begun to lose faith in Columbus. Further evidence may be seen when the royal couple began licensing other voyages of discovery, thereby ending the exclusive rights they had granted to the Admiral. The newly commissioned explorers included Vicente Yáñez Pinzón, Alonso de Ojeda, Juan de la Cosa, and Amerigo Vespucci. Those mariners for the most part concentrated their efforts along the coastal regions of South America. The last would eventually lend his name to the entire hemisphere, thereby denying that honor to Columbus.

While the commissioning and investing of Bobadilla occupied the Catholic Monarchs, on Española Columbus had made some progress in solving problems that plagued the settlement island, but the policies he initiated went beyond his orders and were bound to displease his royal sponsors. The queen had given the Admiral permission to make land grants if the grantees would agree to live on their property, build a house, and farm the land. Columbus offered this to the Roldán-led rebels at Isabela but went well beyond the scope of his orders. He agreed the malcontents could also command the services of an Indian chieftain (called a cacique) and his people. The grantees could then move their subject people away from where they lived and demand of them whatever they wished. That settlement was again called *repartimiento*. During the centuries-long Reconquista, *repartimiento* had been a land grant designed to hold newly won territory and control the Muslims who lived on it by demanding their labor, but Isabella had not specified its use on Española. As a technical point in Spanish contact on the major islands of the Caribbean and especially later in New Spain (colonial Mexico), encomienda was initially the same as *repartimiento*, but it was not regarded as a land grant.

It was Columbus himself in settling with Roldán and his supporters who created the foundations for *repartimiento*/encomienda that would result in a devastating pattern of Spanish overlords controlling almost every facet of the lives of Indian vassals. The resulting demographic disaster reduced an estimated five million Indians on the Caribbean islands by approximately 96 percent in less than twenty years.

When Bobadilla arrived at Santo Domingo, he had to wait for a favorable tide to enter the harbor. But even from a distance he could see seven corpses on the gibbet and would soon learn five more were sentenced to join them. Clearly, this was clearly not the idyllic colony portrayed in glowing terms by Columbus in the letters he had sent to the Catholic Monarchs. When the visitor general stepped ashore, he took immediate action by seizing control of Santo Domingo. He confiscated Columbus's goods, arrested Diego Colón, and ordered the Admiral, who was away from the capital, to surrender as well. Identical orders were sent to the *adelantado* don Bartolomé, who was likewise absent on assignment elsewhere. The Columbus brothers complied, and in October 1500 Bobadilla sent the three of them bound in chains back to Spain. The captain of the vessel bearing the brothers offered to remove their chains once at sea, but Columbus stubbornly refused. He wanted to arrive in Spain as a prisoner unjustly accused of crimes, despite all he had accomplished for the greater glory of Spain in the Indies.

Historian Samuel Eliot Morison wrote that Bobadilla's proceedings were "outrageous," but he also acknowledged that Columbus had been a failure as governor of Española. He was weak when he should have been strong and ruthless at the wrong time. For example, when supplies intended for all settlers arrived from Spain, the Admiral was biased in his distributing them—rewarding his stalwarts while denying fair treatment to those whom he regarded as lazy and dishonest. Such partisanship had caused great rancor, especially as meted out by a foreigner. Perhaps a Spaniard dealing with other Spaniards could have done better, yet no one might have succeeded in ruling hundreds of impatient Castilian adventurers whose primary interests were getting rich without work and then returning to Spain.

While at sea, Columbus penned a letter to the sister of his friend Antonio de Torres. Doña Juana had been former governess of Prince Juan and was well respected at court. This was clever strategy by the Admiral because he did not know whether his arrest and confinement had been ordered by the Catholic Monarchs. If Columbus had addressed a letter that voiced discontent to her Majesty the Queen, it might appear he was criticizing the actions of someone who had consistently been his friend and advocate. On the other hand, he correctly assumed that doña Juana would share the letter with Queen Isabella if she thought it appropriate to advancing his cause, which she in fact did. A portion of the letter is quoted below because it sums up Columbus's sense of outrage and injustice. Furthermore, his complaints were not without merit: "They judge me . . . not as a governor who had gone to Sicily or to a city or town under a regular government, where the laws can be observed *in toto* without fear of losing all, and I am suffering grave injury. I should be judged as a captain who went from Spain to the Indies to conquer a people numerous and warlike, whose manners and religion are very different from ours, who live in sierras . . . without settlements, and where by divine will I have placed under the sovereignty of the King and Queen, our lords."

Once again Columbus would turn supplicant for funding a fourth voyage to the Indies as his final quest. Queen Isabella was upset that he had suffered the indignity of being bound in fetters during the ocean voyage, but she cautiously waited six weeks before ordering his release and appearance before her. The royal court was then at Granada where Columbus's First Voyage had been authorized eight years prior. The Admiral, the *adelantado*, and don Diego presented themselves on December 17, 1500, at the beautifully tiled Alhambra palace, its fountains and fragrant gardens fed by water channeled from the nearby Sierra Nevada.

While Columbus may have found his surroundings delightful, Ferdinand and Isabella remained friendly but evasive. Something more urgent or promising seemed to always hold their attention rather than the faraway Indies. Months passed in the second year of the new century as the Admiral fretted at court, and during that time Pedro Cabral, a Portuguese mariner, had discovered Brazil;

several other mariners including Amerigo Vespucci had also sailed under Crown approval. Through all delays it must have become obvious to Columbus that it was hopeless for him to hope for complete exoneration and the restoration of his rights and privileges. It was also preposterous for him to believe that he and his heirs could be governors and viceroys forever in the Indies with the right to tithe all trade, as specified in the 1492 Capitulations of Santa Fe. Spanish legal experts pointed out that the generous royal concessions of the Catholic Monarchs were contingent on the Admiral's successful performance, and he had not been able to demonstrate that in the lone colony of Española. The Crown told Columbus he could keep his prized titles of Governor, Viceroy, and Admiral of the Ocean Seas, but they would carry no actual authority.

Then, on September 3, 1501, all hope of an administrative assignment in the Indies evaporated for Columbus. The Sovereigns appointed Nicolás de Ovando as supreme justice of all islands and mainlands in the Indies—the only exceptions being those the royal couple had recently granted to Vicente Yáñez Pinzón and Alonso de Ojeda. Ovando would remain in power for eight years. Since concessions made to the Admiral in 1492 also included rights for his heirs in perpetuity, his older son Diego could claim those privileges as Second Admiral of the Ocean Seas as well as other titles. But don Diego experienced limited success in appeals to that effect, which continued until his death in the 1520s. Meanwhile, Ovando sailed from Cádiz on February 13, 1502, with an enormous fleet of thirty-two ships, including twenty-four caravels. On board were twenty-five-hundred mariners, women colonists, men-at-arms, vast supplies, as well as a full complement of domestic livestock. Not onboard due to an ill-advised affair with a married woman that had ended badly for him in Seville was eighteen-year-old Hernando Cortés. He had been granted passage to Española by his distant relative and fleet commander Nicolás de Ovando. Cortés's misadventures on the eve of the fleet's departure will be recounted in a following chapter.

As Ovando, the first truly effective administrator in the Indies, sailed toward Española, the Catholic Monarchs wanted him to have adequate time there before allowing Columbus to sail. So, they waited until May before discussing conditions with Columbus for his Fourth Voyage. During that interval and continuing throughout 1502, Ferdinand and Isabella realized that a bureaucratic structure in Spain was needed to govern faraway territories. Columbus, himself, had demonstrated that distance across a vast ocean from royal authority had tempted men like him "to slip the restraints of law and loyalty." Starting in September, the Sovereigns appointed men of proven loyalty and gave them titles that were important throughout the sixteenth century and beyond. Those bureaucratic positions were occupied by proven defenders of royal absolutism, and they were often lumped together under the title of "Treasury Officials." The *veedor de fundiciones* was the gold smelter and marker; the *factor,* manager of crown properties; the *tesorero,* treasurer; and the *contador,* accountant. Likewise appointed was an *alcalde mayor,* who would become chief justice of the Indies. Those positions were all in place on Española before the end of 1502.

Meanwhile, Columbus, with approval for his fourth voyage, left Granada for Seville in October 1501. The Sovereigns had provided money to outfit four caravels, and salaries for one-hundred and thirty-five men and cabin boys. The mariner's twelve-year-old son Hernando would sail with him and write an account of his experiences. This collection of sailors contained numerous youngsters in their early teens, perhaps because Columbus was on a tight budget, and the youths were more affordable than experienced seamen. Shortage of funds also affected the quality of vessels the Admiral purchased, and that would contribute to crises in the months ahead.

The fourth voyage left port in Seville on April 3, 1502, under Bartolomé Columbus's command. It sailed down the Guadalquivir to Cádiz where the Admiral and young Hernando came aboard. More than a month passed in making final preparations, and on May 9 the fleet put to sea for the Canary Islands. From there, the ocean crossing left at night on May 25. Columbus's instructions from the Catholic Monarchs forbade him to land at Santo Domingo where disagreements might occur with Nicolás de Ovando and his staff. However, Columbus was authorized to send an agent ashore to retrieve his possessions, a right granted by the royal couple at Granada. The items had been confiscated by Bobadilla prior to his sending the Admiral home in chains. This was no small concession, since Columbus had amassed gold on Española amounting to 12,000 gold pesos.

The fourth voyage reached the island of Martinique on June 15. After three days' rest there, it continued along the south coast of Puerto Rico before anchoring off Santo Domingo on June 24. Again, Columbus was slipping restraints clearly imposed on him by Ferdinand and Isabella because he was only authorized to stop at Santo Domingo on his return voyage to Spain. But the Admiral had good reason for disobedience.

Columbus wanted to send letters to Spain with a fleet that was soon to depart. He also needed to buy a replacement vessel for the caravel *Santiago*, which had given him nothing but trouble at sea. The Admiral complained the ship was a "a crank and dull sailing vessel." In any event, the *Santiago* was unsuitable for further exploration. But more important, Columbus sought refuge for his fleet in Santo Domingo harbor from what he sensed was an approaching hurricane, and he probably knew storm signs better than anyone else. Governor Ovando had assembled thirty ships for departure to Seville. Although don Nicolás refused Columbus's request for anchorage in the harbor, his agent did reclaim the twelve-thousand gold pesos and consign it for transport on one of the soon-to-depart ships. Columbus meanwhile strongly advised Ovando to delay sending the fleet until the approaching storm had blown over.

The governor treated the Admiral's advice with disdain and mockery by reading his letter to an audience of sycophants who howled with laughter—the Admiral was an old fool to be mocked as a prophet and soothsayer. The Seville-bound fleet left as scheduled and was strung out at sea along the track of the incoming storm when it struck. Over five-hundred lives were lost, including Columbus's friend Antonio de Torres and his enemy Bobadilla. Nineteen other ships went down with all on board. The cargo intended for the Catholic Monarchs and merchants in Seville included 200,000 castellanos in gold. Remarkably, the vessel carrying Columbus's 12,000 gold pesos made it safely to Seville. Before the hurricane struck, Columbus had found a cove along a shore west of Santo Domingo for his caravels, and they safely rode out the storm, although strong wind gusts caused the carvels to slip anchors and be driven to sea. Yet all escaped destruction. That led the Admiral's enemies to insist he had raised the storm "by magic art." The city of Santo Domingo built of wood and thatch was leveled.

Because Columbus had sailed west of Santo Domingo in seeking shelter for his fleet, he found it difficult to sail against the prevailing wind and return to the destroyed capital. So replacing the largely unseaworthy *Santiago* was not possible.

He continued westward along the north coast of Jamaica before landing briefly near the southeast point of Cuba. From there he anchored off an island named Las Pozas, because his men found "wells" of pooled fresh water by digging in the sand. Columbus then sailed southwest until he reached the coast of Honduras without recognizing he had reached the mainland of Central America. Continuing south along the Mosquito Coast brought his ships offshore from present-day Costa Rica and Panama.

By then the poor quality of vessels acquired in Seville caused serious difficulties due to "ship worms" that had riddled the hulls of the caravels. The vermiform creatures resembled worms only in appearance because they were bivalve mollusks that thrived in sea water and had an appetite for wood. At some point, Columbus chose the two most seaworthy ships and abandoned the *Santiago* and *Vizcaína*. All personnel and supplies came aboard the remaining two caravels that were taking on water at an alarming rate and required continuous use of the bilge pumps. Even so, the Admiral continued to search for the elusive and non-existent strait to Japan and the Orient.

Columbus did encounter a sea-going canoe that was an interesting example of Indian naval architecture. It was an enormous dugout long as a galley and eight-feet wide. A crew of twenty-five included paddlers as well as several women and children. At midpoint on the canoe a waterproof awning of palm leaves served to block sun and rain. Those bearing arms had two-handed wooden swords, their edges imbedded with flint or obsidian chips. The canoe's occupants wore dyed cotton shawls that bespoke a level of cultural attainments thus far not seen elsewhere in the Indies by Europeans. The origin of these Indians was likely Yucatan because their weaponry and clothing reflected natives with an advanced culture.

The two remaining caravels on May 1, 1503, began a long beat due north toward the coast of Cuba. From there the ships turned east toward Española, fighting winds and currents all the way. By then the vessels' hulls resembled sieves, insofar as they took on water beyond the bilge pumps' capacity to expel it. Columbus knew the vessels, with water rising nearly to the decks, would never make it to Santo Domingo. He turned southward toward the coast of Jamaica. As they approached the island, the Admiral aligned the caravels side by side and drove them ashore.

His mariners strung hawsers to bind the vessels together and blocked their hulls in upright positions. The beached ships became shelter and home for Columbus and many of his crew of more than a hundred men and youths over the next eight months.

The Admiral and the other ship captain took stock of their options for rescue. They could not count on a vessel passing Jamaica by chance. Their best hope was to seek aid by contacting Spaniards on Española, but through a series of mishaps, all boats on the original four caravels had been lost. Accordingly, an ocean-going Indian canoe seemed the only remaining possibility of carrying word of their plight to Governor Ovando. For the crossing to Española, the marooned Spaniards selected two suitable Indian canoes staffed by ten Jamaican paddlers and six Europeans. Their captain was Diego Méndez de Segura, the fleet's chief clerk, accompanied by Bartolomeo de Fieschi, a Genoese mariner. Upon landing anywhere on Española, Méndez would travel to Santo Domingo and alert Ovando to the castaways' situation, while Fieschi and the Jamaican rowers would return with news that a rescue vessel would soon arrive for them. The hopeful Europeans remaining on Jamaica watched as the two canoes paddled away and disappeared to the north. They would learn nothing about the success or failure of the canoers for eight months. The waiting would prove stressful, and it served to undermine discipline among the marooned shipmates.

Shortly after January 1504, the malcontented Porras brothers—Francisco and Diego, the latter of the two had been captain of one of the roped-together caravels—led a mutiny. They seized all ten Indian canoes Columbus had collected and paddled off with fellow mutineers and captive natives toward Española. Their efforts came to naught, forcing the Porras brothers to return to the stranded caravels and make peace with Columbus who had little choice but to accept them. By then relations between Columbus's partisans and the local natives had soured, because of the Europeans' constant demands for food once their ships' supplies were exhausted. The Indians, good at bargaining, had not stopped providing vital food but demanded higher and higher prices for it.

At that point, Columbus demonstrated his advantages as a European possessed with vastly superior knowledge of lunar events. The Admiral knew an eclipse was imminent from the astronomical tables he carried for navigation. He invited the local Indian chiefs to meet with him on the day before the eclipse. The ensuing trick was Columbus at his cunning best. He told the gathering that he and his men were Christians, servants of a powerful God in heaven "who punished the wicked and rewarded the good." His God had not permitted the Porras brothers to reach Española because they were evil, and his God was angry with the Indian chieftains for charging too much for food. On that very night, continued the Admiral, God would show his displeasure with the Indians by eating the moon. He, however, could restore the moon but only if the chieftains changed their ways.

What followed as darkness fell was best described by Columbus's young son Hernando: "At the rising of the moon the eclipse began, and the higher it rose the more complete the eclipse became, at which the Indians grew so frightened that with great howling and lamentation they came running to the ships with provisions praying the Admiral to intercede with God . . . and promising they would diligently supply all [the Christians'] needs in the future." Columbus told the Indians he would withdraw to his quarters and speak with his God. He waited there while "the Indians cried all the time for his help." When the crescent phase of the eclipse had finished, Columbus emerged from his cabin and told the Indians he had appealed to God who heard his prayers. The Indians would see God's anger pass away as the moon reappeared. Hernando Colón continued: "from that time forward they were diligent in providing us with all we needed and were loud in praise of the Christian God."

Eight months after Méndez and Fieschi had departed, a caravel sent by Ovando arrived. The captain conveyed the governor's best wishes and presented much appreciated gifts of bacon and wine. However, Ovando did not have at that time a ship large enough to carry all of them from Jamaica to Española, but a second vessel would follow. With rescue imminent, Columbus was eventually able to resolve matters with a few rebels who had disavowed his leadership. And when Diego Méndez arrived with a caravel, all castaways left for Santo Domingo. As they sailed, don Diego explained to Columbus why rescue efforts in his behalf and that of his crew had taken so long. He and Fieschi had reached Española in good time by canoes, but Ovando was not in Santo Domingo. Instead, he was campaigning against Indian rebels in a different part of the island, and the governor ordered

Méndez to join him there. Seven months had subsequently elapsed before Méndez could travel to the capital and organize a rescue effort and send it to Jamaica.

From Santo Domingo, Méndez dispatched a strange letter that Columbus had drafted in Jamaica to the Catholic Monarchs in Spain. Written when the Admiral was in the depths of despair—he feared he would die among the castaways at Jamaica—the letter revealed a man possessed by religious visions and grandiose plans for the re-conquest of Jerusalem. The religious overtones were not likely to concern extremely devout Queen Isabella, but the rambling and incoherence of the Columbus's writing worried her. The Admiral complained bitterly of poverty when it was clear to her that he had 12,000 gold pesos securely deposited in Seville. He begged the royal couple to restore all his titles and honors out respect for his sacrifices and accomplishments, but "his delusions of grandeur and self-definition as God's chosen instrument" on earth went too far. Columbus claimed to hear voices that compared him with heroes in the Bible. And since 1501, Columbus had adopted a cryptic signature that identified him as the "Christ-bearer." In short, he increasingly saw himself as an instrument directed by the hand of God.

There is little doubt Columbus was suffering from ill health. He had sharp pain in his lower extremities, as well as inflammation of his eyes that prevented reading. Modern scholars have attributed his physical deterioration to gout, arthritis, or Reiter's syndrome—joint pain or swelling caused by infection elsewhere in the body. It is possible the man's multiple ailments contributed to his confused state of mind. Whatever the case, Columbus's letter written from Jamaica did not inspire the Catholic Monarchs to permit the author of such incoherence to remain in charge of affairs in the Indies.

In Santo Domingo, Columbus had Méndez's caravel repaired, and he chartered a second in preparation for his voyage to Spain. Most of those who had sailed with the Admiral decided to remain on Española and seek their fortunes there. Only Columbus, his family, and his close associates chose to sail toward home. Even so, bad luck continued to plague the small group of mariners. Barely out of port, the mainmast on the chartered caravel split. Columbus sent it back to Santo Domingo and continued with only one ship. The mainmast of this ship split as well, splintering into four pieces and rendered useless. The Admiral and Bartolomé improvised a mast from a lateen yardarm and made it to Sanlúcar de Barrameda at the mouth of the Río Guadalquivir on November 7, 1504. Columbus would never sail again.

The Admiral traveled upriver to Seville where he rested at home. He waited there for days hoping to receive an invitation to court from Isabella, but she was gravely ill. The Queen died on November 26. Some biographers of Columbus have suggested that with the passing of his great patroness and friend, King Ferdinand turned a cold shoulder toward the Admiral. But even gravely ill Isabella knew better than to restore all the rights and privileges that had been bestowed on Columbus before his first voyage. Allowing the mariner to reassume full rights as governor, viceroy, and admiral in perpetuity would result in weakening royal control over new and promising colonies across a vast ocean. As noted earlier, legal experts in Spain had insisted that Columbus had forfeited his exclusive rights by failing to establish even one successful colony on Española.

Columbus had also irritated the Queen by his continued efforts to profit from the sale of Indian slaves in Spain. She considered the natives subjects of the Crown and therefore protected from enslavement other than under explicit circumstances and not-yet-spelled-out formalities. Those circumstances, as we shall see, would soon come about. In truth, Isabella had slowly come to accept that Columbus was an incompetent administrator—as indeed he was. The Admiral had also been guilty of disobedience that could not be abided in an absolutist framework of governance. Without doubt, increasingly influential Bishop Fonseca who plainly disliked Columbus had influenced the Queen's negative assessment of the man. As Columbus scholars William D. Phillips, Jr., and Karla Rahn Phillips have remarked: "No government would have allowed Columbus's privileges to stand, once it became clear how much was at stake."

Columbus nevertheless spent the last two years of his life lobbying for full restoration of his titles and privileges, as well as the right to pass them on to his son Diego. He was successful in passing on the title Second Admiral of the Ocean Sea, but as events played out in Spain and the Indies that position meant little. Diego Columbus, like his father, fell victim to the Crown's realization that broad movements in settlement and colonization of new-found lands would soon be too great in scope for any one individual to handle—no matter how competent that person.

Other events in Spain likewise did not work out to Columbus's advantage. Several of Ferdinand and Isabella's children who lived to adulthood suffered death and misfortune of biblical proportions. Their two eldest children, Princess Isabella and Prince Juan, were both dead by 1498. Right of succession to the Crown of Castile then passed to their third child and second daughter, Juana, married to Prince Philip the Handsome, heir to the Habsburg dynasty. Their arrival in Spain from Flanders shortly after 1500 as future Philip I and Juana of Castile was marked by the untimely death of Philip in September 1506. The already psychologically unbalanced Juana—even her mother Queen Isabella had acknowledged Juana's instability of mood and temperament—meant that Fonseca's influence over affairs in the Indies would be even greater in the future. Again, the bishop was no friend of Columbus as he petitioned the Crown for reversal of lost favors. [**Figure 3**]

Figure 3. Columbus Monument, Plaza de Colón
in Barcelona. Photo credit and permission
to publish, Montse Vilahur Gies.

Columbus died unhappy but in the company of his sons at Valladolid on May 20, 1506. He was never poor, although his pride remained wounded. Perhaps it was best that he never lived long enough to realize how far away Japan and Asia were from his explorations in the Caribbean. He had observed the continent of South America off the coast of present-day Venezuela on his third voyage; on the fourth voyage, he had viewed the coasts of present-day Honduras, Nicaragua, Costa Rica, and Panama. He can hardly be blamed for failing to recognize the landmasses of the Western Hemisphere when they did not appear on any maps. But he nonetheless had discovered a world unknown to Europeans. "And he had set in motion a chain of events that, even in his lifetime, had begun to alter human history on both sides of the Atlantic."

Columbus's younger son Hernando would secure the Columbus family legacy in a library he founded by buying books with his father's fortune, and by preserving his personal and treasured volumes. Known as the Biblioteca Colombina, it is housed within Seville's enormous Gothic Cathedral. The library contains more than 15,000 volumes. Of those almost two-thousand books (*incunabula*) were printed between 1453 and 1500. It has been my good fortune to have had a guided tour of the Biblioteca. If one has reading knowledge of Spanish and acquires some facility in paleography, it is a unique experience to read in Columbus's own hand marginalia comments he made in *Marco Polo* and other books essential to formulating his great enterprise of the Indies.

CHAPTER 3

Hernando Cortés and the Spanish Struggle for Justice

While Columbus sailed on his Fourth Voyage, an important administrative change for control of the Spanish Indies took place in Seville. In January 1503, the Crown ordered Bishop Juan Rodríguez de Fonseca to set up the *Casa de Contratación* (House of Trade). Among the Casa's multiple functions was an obligation to supervise emigration, transport, and trade with Spain's about-to-expand American empire. The House of Trade would increase its exclusive powers over the next twenty-one years until joined by a newly created Royal Council of the Indies. For example, the Casa registered the name of everyone who wished to emigrate from Spain to the Indies. And it was not easy to qualify for exiting rights. One had to present family records through three generations confirming that he or she was not a "New Christian"—a recent convert from Judaism to Christianity. Such persons, by avoiding exile in 1492, had been allowed to keep their property but were long thereafter viewed with suspicion, and the Crown demanded "cleanness of blood" for those traveling to the colonies. The Casa was also the official repository of all maps and navigation charts and licensed pilots leaving Spain on expeditions to the Indies. Finally, the House of Trade was the highest court in settling maritime disputes. But most importantly, the Casa designated Seville as the only authorized port of departure for or arrival from the Indies. That restriction would prove both advantageous and cumbersome during the more than two centuries that Seville's exclusive rights remained intact.

The biggest problem lay with the silt-created sandbar at Sanlúcar de Barrameda near the mouth of the Río Guadalquivir. Ships returning to Spain from the Indies with heavy laden cargo such as dyewoods and bullion had difficulty clearing the sandbar. So at least some material had to be off loaded at times and then reloaded after the vessel's draft cleared the sandbar. Even then, ships had to sail against the river's current for fifty miles to reach Seville. When winds were unfavorable, teams of mules hitched to vessels with heavy draglines helped haul ships upstream to their destination. Maintaining Seville as an inland port was good for reasons of security, but another factor that favored Seville was a powerful merchant guild there with great influence at Court. It profited immensely by having a monopoly on merchandise that arrived from the colonies.

Those seeking opportunity and wealth in the Indies relocated from the interior regions of Spain to Seville for passage across the Atlantic because there was no point in going elsewhere. As mentioned earlier, the year 1502 found teenager Hernando Cortés there as he awaited passage to Española on the huge fleet assembled for fray Nicolás de Ovando by Bishop Fonseca. But an amorous misadventure with a married woman caused Cortés to miss the boat.

At this juncture, a profile of what little is known with any degree of certainly about the early life of the most famous Spanish conquistador in North America seems in order. My slight advantage in writing about Cortés comes from having had Professor France V. Scholes as my mentor at the University of New Mexico. Scholes at one time likely knew more about Cortés than any other scholar. As mentioned in the introduction, I have more than ninety handwritten letters from Scholes. During our discussions my mentor occasionally shared insights into the life of the man named Fernando Cortés at birth.

My mentor died in 1979, and with him went his extensive knowledge of the great conquistador. Then in 1993, Sir Hugh Thomas with the aid of only one researcher at the great Archive of the Indies in Seville published what I think is the most complete archival-based study of Cortés in English. My profile of Cortés often depends on the scholarly research and writing of Thomas. But first things ought to come first. Even though the man always signed his name as Fernando, and even though there is a very dated biography of him entitled *The Rise of Fernando Cortés*—hereinafter, the most famous Spanish conquistador in North America will be referred to as Hernando Cortés.

Cortés's parents lived in the hamlet of Medellín in the far western Spanish province of Extremadura, and there is disagreement among historians and others on the birth year of their son—with several insisting incorrectly and with near certainty on 1485. In Medellín, however, an inscription on a baptismal font in a reconstructed chapel records that a child named Fernando Cortés received the rite of baptism there in 1484. His parents were Martín Cortés and Catalina Pizarro Altamirano. Don Martín fought in several battles as an infantryman, because he could not afford a horse. Those battles, however, were not part of the fighting that took place during the Reconquista. Instead, the conflicts were between families who fought for control of castles, grazing lands, and water rights. Medellín was a region of Spain bordering Portugal, disputed by adherents of the Catholic Monarchs and Portuguese-backed candidates. Beyond towns in Extremadura, commission of murder and robbery was commonplace. The more powerful nobles lived in small castles or well-defended houses. As a reminder of such turbulent times, young Cortés grew up in the shadow of a castle whose ruins still dominate the skyline above Medellín. Its owner in his youth was the formidable doña Beatriz Pacheco, Countess of Medellín.

Well before his birth, Cortés's grandparents had lived in the somewhat larger town of Trujillo, the birthplace of future conquistador of Peru, Francisco Pizarro. This explains the Pizarro contribution to the surname of Cortés's mother, and circumstances made don Hernando and don Francisco second cousins. Trujillo was located about forty miles from Medellín and beset by even greater violence. In Trujillo bitterness divided the town's two prominent families, the Pizarros and Altimiranos. Their feuds led to insults, beatings, and even murder. As Sir Hugh Thomas has observed, marriage between these families "would have been as provocative as one between Capulets and Montagues." Looking for more peaceful circumstances, Cortés's grandparents left Trujillo and relocated to Medellín. It is important to remember that Hernando Cortés's mother Catalina was the daughter of a successful lawyer, Diego Alfón Altamirano, and his family connection with the Altamiranos would significantly aid him in post-conquest New Spain.

With apologies for this prolix genealogy of Cortés's mother, his father's family history is equally complex. Martín Cortés was born out of wedlock to María

Cortés and Rodrigo Pérez de Monroy. What matters is the reminder that family in those times was often all important, and that the surname Cortés came from his grandmother—although that was not unusual in Spain. Through the Monroys, Hernando Cortés was a relative of the first royal governor of Española, fray Nicolás de Ovando. And still later in New Spain, don Hernando would receive favors from a relative named Altamirano in family matters, including finding a temporary home for his exceedingly prominent daughter also born out of wedlock. [**Figure 4**]

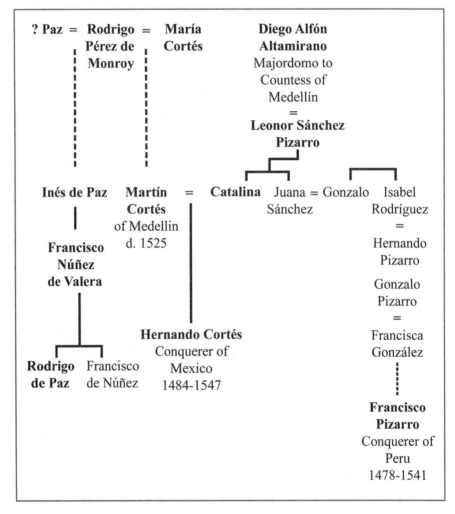

Figure 4. Cortés and His Relations. Adapted from Thomas, *Conquest*, Appendices, np.

In childhood, Hernando Cortés profited from being an only child. His mother and father poured love and affection into their son, and it gave him self-confidence that lasted throughout his life. Cortés was also a fine athlete, and he would become a skilled horseman. But education really set young Hernando apart from other future conquistadors, and again family mattered. When he was twelve, his parents sent him to live with an aunt named Inés de Paz, his father's half-sister, and her husband Francisco Núñez de Valera in Salamanca. Don Francisco was a prominent notary with more legal work and writing than he could handle; accordingly, nephew Hernán, as his family called him, became a copyist for his wealthy and demanding uncle. The future conquistador of New Spain learned to write Castilian with facility as demonstrated later in letters he sent to the King. He also learned Latin, because many of the legal codes of Spain were written in that language, and as a copyist he was exposed daily to Latin words and phrases. Again, those who knew Cortés later in life averred that he spoke Latin like a priest, and as a good Latinist.

Cortés's facility in Latin has led to conjecture, and even claims, that he attended classes in Salamanca's famous university, widely regarded as one of the best in Europe—along with universities in Oxford, Paris, and Bologna. But there is not a shred of evidence that Cortés attended classes at the University of Salamanca. He never mentioned schooling in his extensive writing; and on a personal note, Professor Scholes asked me during one my research trips in Spain to check on the possibility of matriculation records at the university—which I did. The university's registrar informed me that there are no records of student attendees until the first years of the 1500s. It seems in the final analysis that Cortés had a facility for learning Castilian and Latin. There are also many examples of individuals with multilingual talents who did not acquire languages beyond their birth-tongue by attending classes.

There is circumstantial evidence that Cortés learned to swim in the Río Tormes that divides Salamanca. With certainly, there is no river near his birth city Medellín, and don Hernando's ability to swim would later save him from drowning in a canoeing accident in Cuba. It also seems that Cortés learned to ride a charger in Salamanca. His uncle was rich enough to own two horses and he and his nephew probably enjoying riding for recreation. Finally, in a rare informal letter that has survived, Cortés mentioned the "kindness and endearment" of his Aunt Inés de Paz. She was like a second mother to him at a formative time in his life. These examples illustrate how important Cortés's family was in building his sense of worth and self-confidence. To compare him with his functionally illiterate cousin Francisco Pizarro would be like comparing night and day.

At the age of fourteen, Cortés left the comfort and security of his aunt and uncle's home in Salamanca. It is reasonable to assume he also left Salamanca at that time, but that is conjecture. Not a shred of written information remains regarding where Cortés lived or what he did over the next three years. But if he decided to relocate to a city more important than Salamanca, it probably would have been Valladolid. That city in the late 1400s was closest to serving as the de facto capital of Castile. Ferdinand and Isabella had married there in 1469. Valladolid had imposing new buildings, including the Dominican College of San Gregorio. At the city also took place the marriage of Princess Juana by proxy to the feckless and philandering Philip the Handsome. Wherever Cortés lived for about three years, he likely earned a living while serving as copyist for a notary. He appears to have acquired enough money to buy a horse; he developed a passion for gambling that lasted throughout his life; and he probably enjoyed favors from the *señoritas* of the night.

In the first year of the new century, one can pick up the paper trail of Cortés upon his return to Medellín and the brief time he spent there with his parents. It was not a happy reunion. His father and mother had not seen him for almost five years. He had left home as an innocent twelve-year-old but returned a more worldly-wise teenager. What caused the greatest rift, however, was the disappointment of Cortés's parents that their son had not studied law, or at least prepared himself to enter royal service in some capacity. Instead, young Hernán made it clear that he intended to seek adventure outside Spain. He would perhaps travel to Italy and join the Spanish army there, or he would find a way to sail to the Indies. When Cortés left his parents in spring 1501, he did so without their blessings. He would never again see his father.

Cortés's first goal was to reach Seville, but it was not wise to ride alone in Spain. Roads between towns and cities were unsafe because brigands and highwaymen preyed on unarmed travelers, despite the existence of a rural constabulary operating as the *acordada* that had authority to hang highwaymen without trial from the nearest tree. Cortés first traveled south to the Roman-founded city of Mérida, where he apparently joined a group of merchants headed to the port city. In Seville, Cortés decided on adventure in the Indies instead of campaigning in Italy under the army command of Spain's then most famous general, the "Great Captain" Gonzalo Fernández de Córdoba. It was probably an easy choice for young Hernando.

By the turn of the century, Columbus's three voyages seemed to have brought him to the verge of reaching Japan, and Spanish explorers would then be within reach of Asia's riches. Mariners had explored enough to recognize that the major Caribbean islands held little promise of great wealth, but their imaginations fueled chimeric visions of unlimited prospects beyond. Many Spaniards were influenced by the writings of St. Augustine, who had devoted an entire chapter of *The City of God* to the question of whether descendants of Adam and Noah had produced monstrous and bizarre offspring in distant lands. Nearly all literate conquistadors as well as those who perhaps knew someone with reading facility enjoyed stories from chivalric romance novels—the most famous being *Amadis de Gaula*. The less literate saw medieval churches that sprouted griffins, gargoyles, and mixtures of man and beast. Where did these creatures come from if not the minds of clergymen who influenced church architects? Accordingly, beyond every mountain and horizon Spaniards in America would look for mythical and fabulous creatures—enormous giants, white-haired boys, bearded women, humans with tails, headless folk with an eye in their navel, Amazon women, and trumpet-blowing apes. Somewhere was the city of El Dorado where gold was so plentiful it was used to pave streets. A persistent legend held sway for decades contended that during the Muslim conquest of Portugal, seven Catholic bishops had fled by ships across the Atlantic Ocean, and those high clergymen had founded the Seven Cities of Cíbola. And even the state of California gets its name from a chapter in *The Adventures of Esplandían*, first published in 1510. It told the tale of Queen Calafia and her island filled with gold.

Hernando Cortés was in Seville well before he was granted passage to Española with fray Nicolás de Ovando's enormous fleet, because campaigning in Italy held little promise for him when compared to the Indies and its potential for wealth. All he had to do was stay out of trouble for a brief time, but he failed to do that. The teenager entered an affair with a married woman whose husband was conveniently away from Seville on business for several days at a time. On one occasion, the husband's trip was unexpectedly cut short and he returned home sooner than expected. The cuckolded husband found young Hernando in a "compromised situation" with his wife. Cortés fled through a window and retreated along a poorly constructed wall that collapsed under his weight. He fell amidst a shower of stones and mortar and severely injured his back but managed to escape. His injury required weeks to heal, during which he missed the fleet's departure—and once again, Cortés disappeared from written records for nearly two years. This was a time when Cortés probably traveled about Spain on horseback, apparently first to Valencia, and then elsewhere. It seems he had little difficulty finding work as a copyist for notaries. Less than two years later, he was back in Seville seeking passage to Española. In the interim, Cortés likely earned maravedís as a copyist and lived frugally enough to buy a serviceable sword and chain mail shirt—essentials for a would-be conquistador in the Indies.

It is not certain when Cortés found passage to Española, but it appears to have been in early 1506. While visiting wharves along the Guadalquivir, young Hernando found a ship captain named Antonio Quintero from Palos who would accept him aboard the nao *Trinidad*. It would join three vessels leaving Sanlúcar de Barrameda for Las Palmas in the Canary Islands, a favorite stop before departure to the Indies. It was prudent for vessels crossing the Atlantic Ocean to travel as members of a small fleet of at least three or four ships. There was safety in numbers should a ship become disabled, and a single ship had little chance of warding off corsairs or vessels belonging to a hostile nation, since Spain was often at war with France. Those considerations aside, passengers aboard a nao that transported animals in the hold faced at least a month-long horror at sea.

Spaniards were often stoic about lack of personal cleanliness and accustomed to discomfort, but one unhappy passenger recorded what life was like aboard a ship that crossed a great ocean. His experiences were doubtless much the same as Cortés's and others on *Trinidad*. The ship would have seemed like a narrow prison. Sleeping quarters were on deck planking in all manner of weather. Relieving one's self daily meant hanging over the side, always dangerous even in calm waters.

Passengers had to get by on half rations, because time at sea was always uncertain due to weather conditions. Smells from below deck became intolerable as animals urinated and defecated in the bilge water. The lowest crewmembers labored half-naked at the pumps three or four times a day, which stirred the stench. Thirst was constant because water was apportioned by a mate one cup at a time from kegs. After days at sea the biscuits rotted, and everything smelled of rat urine. Meat was often salt-cured bacon that exacerbated thirst, and no one could bathe at any time.

Horses were the most difficult and valuable animals transported in the hold. The animals traveled in suspended canvas slings with reinforced grommets that kept them from breaking a leg. Mariners attached the sling to large block and tackle descending from an overhead beam. In calm waters, crewmembers lowered the chargers until their hooves barely touched flooring to keep up the animals' leg strength. When attached to a boom this same apparatus could lower or raise a horse into or out of the hold. The boom on deck rotated enough to allow horses to be loaded or unloaded over the side of a vessel.

After a month-long Atlantic Ocean crossing without mishap, Cortés disembarked at Santo Domingo, again likely in early 1506. By then he was about twenty-one years old, and since he was a descendant of old Christian families it is appropriate to refer to him as a hidalgo. This title, the lowest rung in the ladder of those who claimed status as *gente decente* (respectful people), or lesser nobles, carried the honorific *don* before one's given name. The title *hidalgo*, a contraction of *hijo de algo* (son of something), was important because it permanently separated them from untitled commoners. And since Cortés's distant relative Nicolás de Ovando was governor of Española, don Hernando found himself in a more favorable situation than many other immigrants on the island.

Soon after setting foot in Santo Domingo, Cortés grandly remarked that "he had only arrived to be weighed down with gold." To people he met, the new arrival on Española stated that he wanted to operate a mine. A stranger on hearing don Hernando's plans reminded him that mining was unrelenting hard labor without guaranteed results. However, when Cortés asked to speak with the governor, he learned from his secretary Francisco de Lizaur that Ovando was out of the city and occupied elsewhere with administrative duties. Nevertheless, by Cortes's admission he had found a valuable friend in the governor's secretary.

When word from his secretary reached Governor Ovando and informed him that Cortés had arrived in Santo Domingo, he ordered his relative, a Monroy, to go on an expedition to Xaragua in the western part of the island. This was about three years after the rebellion led by Queen Anacoana and her chieftains had been crushed by Diego Méndez and Diego Velázquez. Perhaps the reader will remember that this revolt had prevented Méndez from reaching Santo Domingo for several months and his sending a vessel to Jamaica to rescue Columbus and his mariners. In any event, it seems Ovando wanted to remind Cortés that revolts by Indians labeled as pagans had to be punished with an iron fist. It was also at Xaragua where Queen Anacoana, the widow of the deceased native rebel Coanabo, was hanged in 1503. That lesson was not lost on Cortés, but it may have been unnecessary.

To understand Cortés and his actions more completely as a conquistador and captain general of men-at-arms, it is important to note that somewhere along the way to his reaching twenty-one years of age, don Hernando had become one of the most fiercely militant Catholics of the conquest era. It is a demonstrable fact in his life that he did not hesitate to kill pagans in the name of Christ. This fact helps explain but certainly does not justify his orders to slaughter Indians by the score, if not by the hundreds, in the name of religion without compunction. It seems Cortés like many of his fellow countrymen believed Indians who did not know the Christian God were beyond the pale of redemption and salvation. Their very existence as pagans was intolerable to him. Time and time again during the conquest era, even the Mercedarian friar Bartolomé de Olmedo, who accompanied Cortés on the conquest of New Spain, counseled the Conqueror to be more moderate in his view of those who did not know God; it was advice he often chose to reject.

Nevertheless, Cortés's time in Xaragua brought the benefit of meeting Diego Velázquez, the future governor of Cuba who later would have great influence on don Hernando's life. Upon his return to Santo Domingo, a settler named Gonzalo de Guzmán hired Cortés as supervisor of his sugar mill, but that employment was far from his liking. He quit after a few weeks and appealed to Ovando for a more suitable appointment. The governor responded by choosing Cortés as notary of Azúa de Compostela, a new settlement about twenty leagues west of Santo Domingo near a sheltered bay. Cortés held this position for an extended time, during which he also profited from his lifelong passion for gambling. The future Conqueror was a cardsharp whose specialty was cheating with marked decks of playing cards. I will comment further on that vice of don Hernando's during the conquest of New Spain, when he teamed with two of the Alvarado brothers in cheating their own men-at-arms at simple card games. Meanwhile, Cortés chafed at working as a notary in Azúa de Compostela—because had he wished to do that for the rest of his life, he might as well have stayed in Spain. However, Cortés knew there was no point in his asking for a rich encomienda in Española due to the great die-off of Indians that had occurred there since 1493.

Because the institution known as encomienda would be the settlement pattern in the future colonization of Cuba, Jamaica, and Puerto Rico, it is necessary to discuss its intent, how it functioned, and the resultant devastating impact it had on the native population of those islands. At the heart of encomienda was the Crown's determination to exercise benign supremacy over the Pope in important matters of faith. The privileges that made this possible had come from papal accords in the late 1400s and early 1500s that Rome came to regret, but it was too late to undo them. Without doubt, Spain had impressed the papacy because of its commitment to pursue the Reconquista to completion and thereby reclaim all lands previously controlled by Muslims, the last of which remained in Granada for nearly eight centuries. As an example of state supremacy, the Spanish Inquisition was headed by Spain's monarchs but operated under the umbrella of papal approval. That papal concession dated from1478. Then, in the 1490s, the Crown through concordats with the Holy See received the right to collect tithes to the benefit of the Catholic faith, and even further the Crown gained the right to nominate three candidates for important bishoprics and archbishoprics, and the Pope had to appoint one. This negotiated supremacy of state over church was termed *patronato real*, or royal patronage. It burdened the Crown with the solemn obligation to convert New World natives in Spanish realms to Catholicism.

The question was how to convert several million Indians on the remaining major Caribbean islands of Cuba, Jamaica, and Puerto Rico to Catholicism? In theory, the answer was by encomienda, or *repartimiento*. A varying number of Indians classified as free vassals of the Crown were assigned to the supervision and control of an encomendero. Indians in the West Indies islands possessed little exploitable wealth, so their primary obligation was to work for their Spanish overseers at tasks assigned by them. Work might involve such things as caring for livestock, tending crops and gardens, mining or panning for gold, and performing household duties. The encomendero, as a lay person, was charged with Christianizing and Hispanicizing native dependents. The encomendero was also obligated to serve the King with arms and a horse, should he possess one, by campaigning against Indian-led rebellions.

To say that encomienda did not perform as planned by the Crown is classic understatement. One of the lesser-known aspects of the New Deal in the United States centuries later and during the later 1930s was recording the WPA Slave Narratives, recollections of former slaves, all of whom were well advanced in age. One interviewee was asked how long his workday was. His reply, "from 'can see' to 'can't see,'" likely described the workday of encomienda Indians who worked in pit mines or panned for gold in steams. In their quest for gold, encomenderos worked Indians to the point of exhaustion or death. They also fed Crown vassals poorly and frequently did not care for them if they became ill. Other encomenderos remarked that they were not interested or capable of teaching catechism to pagan Indians who did not understand Spanish. And disease took its toll. Of course, how encomenderos treated their native charges varied some from one Spaniard to another. But there is no denying the overall devastating impact of encomienda on native population in the Caribbean islands.

In 1511 the Crown appointed Diego Velázquez as governor of Cuba and ordered him to bring two to three million Taíno/Arawak natives under Spanish control. Indians there were to be Christianized and Hispanicized—by the sword if necessary. Recruiting volunteers on Española, where the Indian population had already declined by more than 70 percent, was not a problem for Governor Velázquez; and among his volunteers was Hernando Cortés who gladly gave up his position as notary of Azúa de Compostela. Initially, don Hernando had no status in Cuba other than as one of the men-at-arms serving under the governor. But Velázquez knew Cortés from their meeting at Xaragua in 1506. He also knew that the future Conqueror was a relative and favorite of Governor Nicolás de Ovando. Shortly after the occupation of Cuba got underway Cortés became Velázquez's personal secretary. With his knowledge of Spanish and Latin and skills as a writer, don Hernando was in position to prosper, and he would attain that objective.

Cuba was first renamed Juana, followed by Fernandina. It was an enormous island when compared to Española, Puerto Rico, and Jamaica. Along either its north or south coast, if a ship sailed along its inlets and bays it stretched for more than 1,200 miles. The island was so huge Columbus thought it was mainland, but Juan de la Cosa, an excellent mariner and talented cartographer, depicted its insular configuration on a map he drew as early as 1502—never mind that the Admiral refused to accept the map's accuracy.

Cortés saw no military action in Cuba, nor did he command men-at-arms. He was present when the Indian rebel Hatuey was captured and condemned to public execution by burning at the stake for having killed Spaniards. Hatuey had previously been a rebel chieftain on Española but escaped to Cuba about the time Queen Anacoana was hanged. Not surprisingly, some Cubans regard Hatuey as the island's first martyr. There is an account of his final moments before execution that bears repeating. Hatuey hated Spaniards and by extension their religion. Prior to being burned alive, he was asked by Padre José Hernández if he wished to accept baptism as a Catholic, whereupon he could go to heaven—in which case he would be strangled prior to his body being consumed by fire. Hatuey asked if there were Spaniards in heaven, and when assured that that would indeed be the case, stated that he preferred not to go there.

Cortés bore no sympathy for the condemned man, because Hatuey's deep-seated hatred of Catholicism and belief in pagan gods could not be tolerated. Worthy of mention, young Bartolomé de las Casas, who would later become the great defender of Indians, was then an encomendero in Cuba with an attitude like Cortes's regarding paganism. But as don Hernando observed, with the death of Hatuey there were no more rebellions in Cuba that might have cost the lives of Christians. Even more important in Cortés's preparation as a would-be conquistador was his conviction that capturing, controlling, or executing Indian chieftains in the Indies was good strategy, because the natives were then deprived of leadership, inspiration, and organization. He probably believed that in the long run seizing and controlling rebel chieftains would save Spanish lives.

Prior to Diego Velázquez's tenure as governor of Cuba, the governance of Española had undergone changes of its own. In 1509, fray Nicolás de Ovando's governorship of the island ended. At that point, Diego Columbus aggressively claimed all titles and privileges bestowed on his deceased father by the Capitulations of Santa Fe. Since the Catholic Monarchs had granted those rights in perpetuity, don Diego had a persuasive argument. As mentioned, however, the Crown had already disavowed the concept of concessions in perpetuity, because Columbus had failed to demonstrate competence as governor of a single island. Still, King Ferdinand decided to honor Diego Columbus by appointing him as Ovando's successor and governor in Santo Domingo. He could call himself Second Admiral of the Ocean Seas if he wished, but his right to one eighth of all gold, gems, and spices from the Indies was abrogated. This infuriated don Diego, and he often was absent from his post as governor while traveling to Spain and lobbying on his own behalf. Years later, in 1513, the Crown created the Audiencia of Santo Domingo, the highest judicial body in the Indies, thereby stripping Diego Columbus of his powers as magistrate and inciting him even further. Thereafter he was gone from Santo Domingo so often that the Crown appointed a trio of Hieronymite friars to act as interim executives with full administrative powers in don Diego's absence.

But those administrative changes paled in significance beside a sermon preached in a straw-thatched church on the Sunday before Christmas in 1511. A Dominican friar named Antonio de Montesinos changed the entire conversation and dynamic regarding the treatment of Indians held in encomienda with these words: "In order to make your sins against the Indians known to you, I have come up on this pulpit. I who am a voice of Christ crying in the wilderness of this island, and therefore it behooves you to listen . . . with all your heart and senses so that you may hear it; for this is going to be the strangest voice that ever you heard, the harshest and hardest and most awful and most dangerous that ever you expected to hear . . . . This voice says that you are in mortal sin, that you live and die in it, for the cruelty and tyranny you use in dealing with these innocent people. Tell me by what right and justice do you keep these Indians in such cruel and horrible servitude? . . . Why do you keep them so oppressed and weary, not giving them enough to eat nor taking care of them in their illness? For with the excessive work you demand of them they fall ill and die, or rather you kill them with your demand to exact and acquire gold every day. And what care do you take that they should be instructed in religion? . . . Are these not men? Have they not rational souls? Are you not bound to love them as you love yourself? . . . Be certain that, in such state at this, you can no more be saved than the Moors or Turks."

The wealthiest people, titled or called *gente decente*, were outraged but no one was converted on hearing the sermon. How dare a priest say their souls had no more chance of salvation than those of a Turk or Muslim? The colonists gathered at the house of Diego Columbus to protest the scandalous homily delivered by Montesinos. From there a delegation descended on the vicar, Pedro de Córdoba. He assured them that on the following Sunday the offending priest would apologize and preach on the same subject. The delegates left, assuming they had won their point.

On the following Sunday, important people crowded the small church and expectantly waited as Montesinos mounted the pulpit. His first words were these: "Suffer me a little, and I will show thee that I have yet to speak on God's behalf." Montesinos, far from apologizing, belabored the colonists with even more passion that before. He concluded that he as a priest would not receive them for confession until they changed their evil ways, nor could they expect salvation any more than could highway robbers. The priest defiantly ended by telling those offended in the congregation that they could write in protest to whomever they chose. Several of those offended did write to King Ferdinand, who read their protests on March 20, 1512. Three days later, the Dominican Order's Superior in Spain under influence of the King wrote to the Provincial in Española. The high church official warned his Dominican brethren that if any of them again preached such inflammatory words, they would be sent to Spain on the first available ship for punishment by their Superior. Furthermore, no more members of their order would be allowed to sail to the Indies. That ended the impasse for a brief time, but the Spanish struggle for justice in the Americas had just begun.

It is easy to understand the anger of encomenderos on Española. They were convinced of their clothed superiority over naked natives; they were Europeans and Christians amid pagans; they had a superior material culture that included ships that could sail across a great ocean; they had horses and mastiffs for combat; they had armor, steel, and gunpowder; they had muskets, crossbows, and cannons as weapons; and they were masters of vassals awarded to them by Crown-appointed agents.

The dispute over treatment of Indian vassals held in encomienda that had arisen with Montesinos's fiery sermons did not end with threats from the Dominican Superior in Spain and the order's Provincial on Española. The Franciscans sent Alonso del Espinal to Spain to speak for their order on behalf of the Indians, and the Dominicans entrusted none other than Montesinos himself to do the same. Both priests gained an audience with the King, and their list of Indian grievances against encomenderos so bewildered Ferdinand that he ordered a group of theologians and high Crown officials to deliberate and draw up laws that governed the conduct of encomenderos. At the same time, this panel of experts concluded that idleness was injurious to the Indians, and that servitude was necessary "to curb their vicious inclinations and compel them to industry."

The assembled learned men did agree that the Indians were free vassals of the Crown with the right to receive humane treatment. At the same time, however, the Indians needed to be in close contact with Spaniards to complete their conversion to Catholicism. Accordingly, the encomienda system was viewed as essentially sound. Needed, however, was a comprehensive code known as the Laws of Burgos, which were set forth on December 27, 1512, and then revised before being issued in 1513. The laws are far too numerous to quote. In all, they attempted to set up an ideal relationship between an encomendero and his Indian vassals. For example, they obliged the former to teach the Creed, prayers, and how to confess. They enjoined the master of vassals to make sure children born to the Indians were baptized within eight days following birth. There were specific instructions on how long an Indian could be worked in a mine, how they should marry and procreate, and each town had to have two inspectors to see that an encomendero faithfully carried out the laws in accord with their intent. Perhaps Law 24 serves as representative of the troublesome nature of the Laws of Burgos. It "prohibited Spaniards from calling an Indian a 'dog,' or any other name unless that, too, is his real name." Law 24 also banned encomenderos from beating Indians with whips or clubs. Obviously, such offenses were at times commonplace, otherwise why pass laws to prevent them? In any event, inspectors could not be everywhere on an island the size of Cuba, and if present they were subject to bribes to look elsewhere or ignore any observed mistreatment of an Indian. But the laws reflect the intent of the King and his counselors to ameliorate or eliminate the worst abuses associated with encomienda.

As for encomienda itself as the primary institution of Spanish Indian policy both in the Caribbean islands and later in New Spain, it existed in Mexico with its huge native population—albeit with important changes—throughout the colonial era. However, it did not end even then. Independent Mexico in 1821 continued paying a stipend to descendants of Moctezuma II's son, don Pedro of Tula, from his encomienda there, which had been awarded in perpetuity in the 1520s. Those stipends would continue until the early 1930s in Mexico.

If the Laws of Burgos proved ineffective in protecting Indians, and they did, their intent was nonetheless more just than that of the Spaniards who tenuously employed just war theory to justify their enslavement of Indians. This theory, which will be explained below, had perplexed Ferdinand and especially Isabella ever since Columbus turned slaver as a means of turning a profit on Española. Thereafter, they had employed the best legal minds in Spain to address the issue.

Matters, however, did not come to head until summer 1513. Martín Fernández de Enciso, who later wrote the first book on America to be published in Spain, insisted on a gathering of important officials at the Dominican monastery of San Pablo in Valladolid to address Indian slavery. Those present included the friars of San Pablo, the King's confessor, and Lope Conchillos, Secretary of the Royal Council. Enciso began the discussion by insisting that God had assigned the Indies to Spain, just as Jews had received their Promised Land. Why had God chosen Spain? Because asserted Enciso, the Indians in the New World were guilty of idolatry. His argument that Spain as God's instrument on Earth had as its solemn obligation the necessity of stamping out by root, branch, and twig those who worshipped idols. This reasoning appealed to many Spaniards, including Hernando Cortés, and it helps explain their militancy in dealing with New World natives during the conquest of the Indies.

After some discussion, the high theologians of San Pablo accepted Enciso's theory with the proviso that Indians who peaceably gave over their lands to the King's representatives be allowed to live on it as vassals. But in all cases and in all new lands, a manifesto, or Requirement, had to be read to the Indians by an interpreter before hostilities could legally take place. The Requirement consisted of approximately eight-hundred words, or about three pages of double-spaced text. It began with a brief history of the world since creation and the establishment of the Papacy. It next mentioned the donation of Pope Alexander VI, which divided the world beyond Europe to Spain and Portugal in both the Americas and Asia in 1494. Therefore, the King and then Queen Juana became superior lords of all islands and mainlands with the responsibility of preaching the faith to all those within them. Should the native occupants submit peaceably, as the Requirement mandated, it was well and acceptable. If not, learned Spaniards spelled out the punishment that would follow: "We shall take you and your wives and your children, and shall make slaves of them, and as such shall sell and dispose of them as their Highnesses may command; and we shall take away your goods, and do all the harm and damage that we can, as to vassals who do not obey, and refuse to receive their lord, and resist and contradict him. . . . The deaths and losses which shall accrue from this are your fault, and not that of their Highnesses, or ours, nor of the cavaliers who come with us."

With a nod to legality, the Requirement requested a notary give testament in writing that due process had been observed in the reading of the manifesto. In addition, while searching for other means of justification for enslaving Indians, some Spaniards turned to Aristotle. They welcomed the Greek philosopher's insistence that some humans are born as "natural slaves" to make life easier and more comfortable for those not deserving of sweat and hard labor. The doctrine was a popular one.

Encomienda and reading of the Requirement both served in the permanent settlement of the two remaining major islands in the Caribbean—Puerto Rico and Jamaica. Perhaps the reader will recall that Columbus sailed along the south coast of Puerto Rico on his second voyage while returning to Española. But the early history of the island cannot reasonably be separated from Juan Ponce de León, who was described as a "gentleman" on the 1493 voyage. On Española, Ponce partnered with Juan de Esquivel, the future governor of Jamaica, and the two men set up holdings on the eastern part of the island at Salvación de Higuey. They prospered as ships bound for Spain stopped there to take on cassava bread.

In 1508 Ponce crossed the narrow Mona Passage to Puerto Rico, where he initially was well received by Taíno Indians. The subsequent conquest and occupation of the island was easily achieved, thanks in part to Ponce's red-haired and black-eyed mastiff named Becerillo, who became famous for his alleged ability to smell the difference between friendly and hostile Indians. The latter soon appeared because of Governor Ponce's barbarities. The mistreated Taínos revolted and eventually drew support from their traditional enemies, Caribs on nearby Santa Cruz Island—but both were no match for mounted and armed conquistadors. Following the failed rebellion, Ponce awarded encomiendas and did well financially. But like Columbus, he soon tired of administration and returned to Spain where he persuaded King Ferdinand to grant him a license to seek out one of the persistent legends repeated in the always popular chivalric romance novels: a fountain whose waters when drunk made one permanently youthful. The Fountain of Youth was believed to be in what was then regarded as an "island" known as Florida.

In planning stages for a voyage to Florida, no one compares favorably with Antón de Aliminos. His understanding of Caribbean waters, currents, coastlines over the next six or seven years was remarkable. Indeed, historian Robert S. Weddle remarked that Alaminos "truly was the Gulf's pilot of discovery." Born in Palos around 1475, Aliminos sailed on Columbus's final voyage—despite claims by some historians than he sailed on the second voyage—and he later served as chief pilot for Ponce when he sailed to the coast of Florida. As preparations got underway in Puerto Rico for Ponce's attempt to discover the Fountain of Youth, Governor Ponce worked his encomienda Indians to death as they panned for gold in steams, carried heavy loads of supplies and equipment to his ships, or scrambled for food because cultivated crop lands on the island were being ravaged by great herds of wild cattle.

Ponce's three vessels finally sailed from Puerto Rico to Florida on March 4, 1513, by way of San Salvador. They left the first island explored by Europeans around March 25, and on March 27, Easter Sunday, they sighted what they believed to be an island beautifully adorned with spring flowers—thus the words *Pascua Florida* in Spanish for the Easter festival. It is assumed that Ponce's ship and the two companion vessels landed on the east coast of Florida to near present-day Daytona Beach. More importantly, while in Florida, Alaminos was apparently the first on record to note the existence of the Gulf Steam current, widely used thereafter along with the Bahama Channel by Spanish ships returning to Seville.

There is no doubt Ponce's expedition later rounded the southern tip of Florida and sailed up its west coast, perhaps as far as Charlotte Harbor. From there, it began the return voyage to Puerto Rico. En route the 1513 expedition reached the coast of Yucatan, the first Spaniards on record to have observed that mainland. The three vessels returned to Puerto Rico in early 1514, but those on board had failed to find the youth-preserving fountain known as Bimini. Soon after, Ponce again sailed to Spain, eager to claim Florida before a rival conquistador might claim the honor. In Spain, King Ferdinand readily agreed and bestowed on him the title of *adelantado* of Bimini and the "island of Florida." Back in Puerto Rico, Ponce would earn notoriety as one of the cruelest Spanish conquistadors and administrators because of his brutal treatment of native people. Things were no better on the remote part of Puerto Rico claimed by Miguel Díaz de Aux, Ponce's only serious rival for control of the entire island. In 1521 at the head of a colonizing expedition, Ponce returned to Florida. Near where he had first landed, would-be settlers began constructing buildings, during which they were attacked by Indians. Perhaps with poetic justice, given his record of native abuse in Puerto Rico, *adelantado* Ponce received a serious thigh wound that caused him to withdraw to Cuba. On reaching port there, he died in July 1521 at the age of forty-seven. It would fall to later explorers to establish that the island of Florida was in fact a peninsula.

As mentioned, during the time Ponce lived on Española he had partnered with Juan de Esquivel, the future governor and conquistador of Jamaica. While serving as governor, Esquivel managed with alacrity to overwork and eliminate a large percentage of the native population before conveniently dying himself. Anxious to succeed Esquivel and his two interim successors, who had done little to improve on don Juan's "sterling" record, Francisco de Garay, perhaps the richest man on Española, was in Spain when news of Esquivel's demise reached there. Garay was an opportunist who would later become one of Hernando Cortés's most persistent competitors in the conquest of New Spain.

Garay had sailed on Columbus's second voyage in 1493. He was always loyal to the Admiral, perhaps in part because he was related to Diego Columbus's wife,

María de Toledo, a niece of the powerful Duke of Alba. Christopher Columbus appointed Garay as notary of Santo Domingo, where he also received an encomienda and profited from stock raising and mining. His business partner and longtime associate was Miguel Díaz de Aux, who had given up making his fortune in Puerto Rico following the near total demise of Indians there. One day as a young Indian slave girl on Garay's mining property sat idly poking a stick in the mud, she uncovered a gleaming object that was an enormous gold nugget valued at 36,000 gold pesos—the equivalent of 60,000 one-ounce silver pesos. This enormous wealth claimed by Garay made him a prime candidate to succeed Esquivel as King Ferdinand's protector of royal property on Jamaica and he became the island's second royal governor. When Garay returned to Española, he and Díaz soon relocated to Jamaica with the approval of Diego Columbus in 1509.

While still on Española, Garay had also become famous for his success in raising cattle and swine. The latter were descendants of those eight live pigs loaded on a vessel at Las Palmas that sailed on Columbus's First Voyage in 1492. Garay later claimed that it took five-thousand natives to manage his livestock and pigs. The ability of feral hogs to increase greatly their numbers is a phenomenon still familiar to Americans in some parts of the United States in the twenty-first century. At point here, however, Garay and Díaz transferred hundreds of pigs from Española to Jamaica where the island became famous with pirates better known as buccaneers. The word in English derives from the French *boucanier*, and it from *boucan*. It relates to freebooters who later came ashore on Jamaica, killed hogs, and roasted their meat on a frame called *boucan*. Francisco de Garay thus had good fortune on Española, but that would not be the case later when he became Cortés's extended rival in the Conquest of Mexico.

CHAPTER 4

Cuba and the Voyages of Córdoba and Grijalva

Following the occupation and settlement of Puerto Rico and Jamaica, events in Cuba from 1513 to 1519 are essential to understanding developments that led to the conquest of New Spain, as colonial Mexico was known for more than three centuries. While serving as secretary to Diego Velázquez, Hernando Cortés accompanied the governor as he toured the huge island, awarded encomiendas to colonists, and searched for the best places to found towns. Afterward, don Diego agreed that Hernando Cortés could take up residence in Asunción de Baracoa, the first capital of Cuba. Once there, the future Conqueror set up a foundry and established a small hospital that provided shelter, food, and comfort to orphaned children and elderly folk who were unable to work or care for themselves. Cortés drafted letters Velázquez sent to the Crown and handled other matters requiring written correspondence. Again, don Hernando benefited from having been placed on the path to education by his parents and an uncle in Salamanca, and his writing skills would consistently set him apart from other conquistador captains. Cortés also had an advantage through family ties that would serve him in the conquest of Mexico and beyond. Likewise, don Hernando's ability to converse almost daily with the governor of Cuba had its value. Velázquez liked Cortés, appreciated his learning and skills, awarded him with a shared encomienda, and appointed him notary of Asunción de Baracoa.

Cortés and Juan Suárez, a colonist from Granada, became co-encomenderos. This seemed a routine arrangement at the time, but it would lead to troubles that would plague don Hernando for years. For the time being, however, the future Conqueror was on the road to success. For example, he claimed to have founded the first cattle ranch in Cuba. Although ranching was not to his liking, he would profit from managing what seemed omnipresent in the islands—herds of swine. Cortés sold salted pork and bacon to captains and passengers on ships leaving Cuba for Spain. Apart from his half-interest in an encomienda, Cortés acquired ownership of land that had potential for gold panning by his vassals in a nearby stream. He also used Indian workers to construct what he described as his hacienda or living quarters. Once completed, Cortés took a young Indian woman as his mistress— only, of course, after she was baptized as a Christian. The concubine bore don Hernando's first child, a short-lived daughter named Leonor Pizarro, whom Governor Velázquez accepted as his godchild.

Just when matters were going well for Cortés, he got into a dispute with Velázquez that at first did not end well. A group of unhappy encomenderos asked him to speak on their behalf with the governor to the end of receiving more Indian vassals. Cortés carried their complaints to don Diego, who was sensitive to any criticism. To don Hernando's astonishment, Velázquez dismissed him as his secretary, clapped him in irons, and ordered him sent to Santo Domingo for trial as a dissident colonist. The governor then changed his mind, apologized, and reappointed Cortés as his secretary, but he was adamant about not awarding more encomienda vassals to anyone. The incident sheds light on the mercurial temperament of Velázquez, and the next disagreement between the two men ended far worse for Cortés.

In the interim, the future Conqueror made a near-fatal mistake one night by deciding to visit by canoe one of his properties that lay across a body of water called the Bocas de Bany. The canoe somehow capsized, and when don Hernando surfaced the canoe had vanished in the darkness and he became disoriented. Treading water while trying to get his bearings, Cortés spotted a campfire on a shore about half-a-mile distant. He swam toward the light and found a fire tended by Spaniards who were fishing. As mentioned, Cortés had likely learned to swim in the Río Tormes while living in Salamanca, and that ability probably saved his life. The man's athleticism and physical strength would repeatedly serve him well. After his escape from drowning in the Bocas de Bany, however, he would face a second and more serious dispute with Governor Velázquez. This incident had long-term consequences related to don Hernando's romantic escapades, followed by his breech of promise to a woman.

About a year after his trouble with the governor as a representative of encomenderos unhappy over the number of vassals assigned to them, the second clash of Cortés and Velázquez began innocently and remotely. Don Hernando's fellow encomendero Juan Suárez's mother and three sisters lived in Santo Domingo. The women had departed Granada to serve as ladies-in-waiting to the wife of Diego Columbus. They later gave up that employment and traveled to Cuba in the train of Velázquez's bride, the ill-fated María de Cuéllar, who would die within a week of the wedding. Doña María's death left the women without employment, and Juan Suárez invited them to live with him at his residence, which was near Cortés's hacienda. Cortés courted one of the Suárez sisters named Catalina and seduced her after a promise of marriage, which he later was reticent to honor. Doña Catalina had no property and not even enough money to appropriately dress herself. Indeed, her brother Juan at auction had bought some apparel of the departed María de Cuéllar and given it to his sister. So obviously, doña Catalina brought no dowry into a marriage with Cortés, and that irritated him. Nevertheless, the spurned woman went to Governor Velázquez and asked him to force don Hernando to marry her as he had promised. When Cortés refused the match, the governor ordered him sent him to jail where he shared confinement with thieves, murderers, and common criminals for a short time.

Most likely, Cortés bribed a jailor and sought safety in a church. Enraged, the governor sent the town constable, Juan Escudero, into the chapel where he violated ecclesiastical sanctuary by arresting don Hernando and placing him in irons. The constable then frog-marched his captive back to jail. Along the way, Escudero insulted Cortés, whom he probably envied, and cursed him. Cortés, however, was not a good person to have as one's enemy. The future Conqueror apparently never forgot or forgave the slightest insult, and he was ruthless in punishing those who dared to cross him. Escudero would later rue this incident. Cortés likely bribed another jailor, escaped in disguise, married Catalina, and soon returned to the favor of Governor Velázquez, who was even a witness at don Hernando and doña Catalina's wedding.

Cortés was seemingly happy with his wife, and they got along well for as long as he remained in Cuba. Marital accord would later change and end badly for doña Catalina, but that lay years ahead, and after the conquest of Mexico. Notably, Diego Velázquez had again demonstrated lack of firm resolve. His inconstancy was not lost on Cortés, who was made of sterner stuff. In assessing Cortés's strengths, it is also important to note that not only did he write well but also spoke well. His oratory in inspiring men to overcome adversity had not yet come into play. The garrulous conquistador Bernal Díaz del Castillo, who decades later wrote so engagingly on the conquest of Mexico, often stated that he marveled at the Conqueror's ability to inspire men with "honeyed words." Those who knew Cortés firsthand, even those critical of him, remarked that he worked hard and commented that there was no better hacienda in Cuba than his. Nonetheless, Cortés had not yet commanded men in a battle, so his abilities as captain general of men-at-arms in fighting Indians remained unproven.

Like Velázquez, Cortés moved his residence from Asunción de Baracoa to Santiago when it became the new capital of Cuba in 1515. Located on the southeast shore of the island about 110 miles from its most eastern point, Santiago became the center of important events during the years 1515 to 1519. Not least of these was the emergence of Bartolomé de las Casas as the great defender of Indians and an accomplished historian of Spain in America. Las Casas had arrived on Española with Ovando in 1502. He participated in quelling native uprisings and he accepted an encomienda for his services. Las Casas also held few religious scruples against the mistreatment of Indians or their enslavement, even after he became a priest in 1510. From available evidence, he was just as exploitive and harsh as others. When Diego Velázquez left Española to conquer and settle Cuba in 1511, Las Casas readily agreed to join him. He even seems to have been present when Hatuey was burned at the stake in 1512 but offered no opposition to it.

Something life-altering nonetheless struck Las Casas around 1514. He broke ties with Velázquez, returned to Spain in 1515, and entered the Dominican Order in the following year. For the next fifty years, 1516–1566, Las Casas never faltered in advocating justice for Indians. In Spain, initially armed with nothing but his voice, he endlessly badgered whoever was monarch with an unchanging message: his beloved Indians were rational human beings with souls like Spaniards, and they must peaceably be converted to Catholicism. By the time Las Casas had become a Dominican cleric in 1516, the Indian population in the major islands of the Caribbean had been reduced by an estimated and shocking 96 percent from pre-European contact. At that time, Spaniards in the Indies began to import black slaves from Africa as a source of replacement labor. Initially, Las Casas favored that approach because it helped save the lives of remaining Indians from overwork. However, he later apologized for his error and declared the same rights for blacks as fellow human beings. To appreciate the differing attitudes Las Casas faced in Spain over his view of New World Indians, not until 1537 did Pope Paul VI issue a papal bull that declared Indians rational human beings worthy of salvation. Unfortunately, that papal pronouncement did not apply to blacks held in slavery. Finally, Las Casas also used his pen as a historian to write the history of the Indies. In English translation, his *Short Account of the Destructions of the Indians* was a powerful indictment of fellow Spaniards' record in the destruction of American Indians. If one looks at documented events in the Spanish conquest of the Indies, researchers could, if they chose, pen another and then another *Brevísima Relación de la Destrucción de las Indias*, almost without end. How else could one explain the near extermination of the Indian population in the Caribbean islands by 1516?

To answer that question more completely, let us look at the spectacular failure of the Laws of Burgos, already mentioned, and the ridiculousness of the Requirement. The fundamental problem with the laws of 1512–1513 was that they were based on the false assumption that encomenderos would put the health and well-being of their Indian vassals before their quest for riches. To again quote Bernal Díaz del Castillo: "I came to the Indies to serve God and get rich." What then could have been more unlikely than gold-hungry Spaniards taking time to teach Catholic catechism to their encomienda vassals? As for the Requirement, how could interpreters know an Indian language before occupying their homeland on an island or mainland unknown to Spaniards? And even if they did know an Indian tongue, how were they to make understood world history in two sentences, the creation of the papacy, and the importance of Pope Alexander VI's donation of the world outside Europe to the Spanish and Portuguese in 1494? Las Casas summed up the Requirement in words to this effect—Spaniards read it to rocks and mountains, mumbled it in their beards; and then if the Indians did not immediately submit, they could be enslaved in a "just war." The great Dominican defender of Indians admitted that when he read the Requirement, "he did not know whether to laugh or cry." Still, how many nations would have suspended conquests for two years as Spain did in 1517–1519 by forbidding further occupation of Indian lands without the express permission of Hieronymite friars in Santo Domingo, acting in the absence of Governor Diego Columbus who was in Spain?

The shortage of labor and quest for gold led to an exploratory expedition that left Cuba in 1517 on the first preliminary voyage that antedated the conquest of Mexico. As early as 1514, Diego Velázquez had written to King Ferdinand to inform him of rumors repeated by some Indian chiefs who lived near the western end of Cuba. In the past, other natives had arrived there by traveling for about six days in canoes from "other lands beyond." If true, these other natives were likely Mayas. In any event, Spaniards by this time had explored long enough to know that there was little wealth on islands to the east of Cuba, so why not explore to the west? To that purpose, three wealthy friends of the governor offered to buy and provision two naos. Their spokesman was Francisco Hernández de Córdoba who asked the governor if he would join them by equipping a shallow-draft brigantine, which was needed for exploring coastlines, as well as entering the mouths of rivers. Velázquez agreed and further contributed by recruiting the services of Antón de Alaminos, the most experienced pilot in the Indies. He also received permission from the Hieronymite friars at Santo Domingo to carry out an exploratory expedition if there would be no attempt to enter, stay, or colonize new lands. That was because a moratorium on new settlements had been enacted due to the near extermination of Indians elsewhere. That restriction had been decreed by King Ferdinand, and his Majesty's commandments were enforced by the three friars in Santo Domingo. Of great significance, a passenger on one of the naos was Bernal Díaz del Castillo, the future chronicler and historian. Díaz had previously been a colonist in Panama, but from 1517 onward he seemingly witnessed almost every occurrence leading up to and including the conquest of Mexico.

The three ships left Santiago on February 8, 1517. They first sailed east and then rounded the eastern point of Cuba. Afterward, the explorers followed the long north coast of the island but stopped at the west end of it to take on wood and water. At that juncture, Alaminos persuaded Hernández de Córdoba to head due west. The chief pilot remembered seeing the coast of an "island" when he had sailed with Juan Ponce de León in 1513, and he thought it might contain riches. After six days and sailing approximately 200 miles, a distance and time consistent with native rumors, mariners on the three vessels spotted an island later named "*La Isla de Mujeres*" (The Isle of Women.) [**Figure 5**]

The Spaniards continued sailing due west, and they next encountered what they believed to be a mainland that was, in fact, Yucatan. As they approached it, they were met by five canoes, possibly with sails, filled with Mayas. The canoes were huge craft made from the hollowed trunks of Ceiba trees, each capable of carrying up to 150 people. More important, the Indians were dressed in cotton shirts, loincloths, and sandals made of deerskin. Imagine the amazement of Europeans who were accustomed to seeing only Indians who often wore nothing. Other aspects of the Mayas' appearance were not so appealing. Their faces and bodies were painted or tattooed, and their earlobes were shredded from bloodletting sacrifices. Spaniards were mistaken in claiming the Mayas practiced circumcision, due to their misunderstanding of the natives' practice of drawing blood from their penises to honor gods. Some thirty Indians were welcomed aboard Hernández's flagship where they received gifts of glass beads, hawk bells, cured bacon, and cassava bread, made from the root of a plant indigenous to the Caribbean and from which comes tapioca. Cassava bread was a staple on all sea expeditions. Greatly pleased, the Mayas and their five canoes returned the way they had come. On the

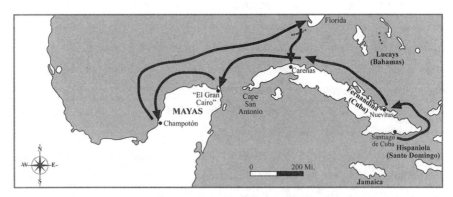

Figure 5. Journey of Hernández de Córdoba (1517). Adapted from Thomas, *Conquest*, 86-87.

following day, twelve large canoes carrying a chief and many people approached the anchored ships. At that point, Hernández de Córdoba, the captains of the other two vessels, and Antón de Aliminos realized that they "had reached new land rather than something well known."

The Spaniards first went ashore on the northeast corner of the Yucatan peninsula near a town they named *El Gran Cairo* because of its stone houses, the first such construction any of them had seen in the Indies. Landing in boats, seemingly at the invitation of Mayas, the Spaniards had prudently armed themselves with muskets and crossbows. Once everyone was on land, Hernández de Córdoba ordered a scribe to read the Requirement to uncomprehending but apparently friendly Indians, and the Spanish captain then claimed the land for the Crown. All went well for the Spaniards until native guides led them into a forested area where they were immediately attacked by Mayas. Wearing cotton-quilted armor, they had bows and arrows, spears, and slingshots as weapons. Fifteen Spaniards were injured, but an equal number of Indians died from musket and crossbow fire. Later, the Europeans cautiously entered the town where they were treated as guests for a few days, while enjoying feasts of corn, wild game, fish stews, and pepper sauces. But they stayed too long and wore out their welcome—something Spaniards were good at doing.

Especially irritating to the Mayas was the Spaniards' incessant demands for water, always scarce in Yucatan because of its karst topography characterized by soluble limestone or dolomite, which in places created sinkholes and even underground rivers. After having been denied water and further sustenance, the Hernández expeditioners returned to their ships. They took with them small discs of gold and silver, other objects of gold and copper, and some pottery. Their human cargo included two cross-eyed (regarded as desirable in appearance) Indians nicknamed "Old Melchor" and "Little Julián" as potential interpreters, always useful in the Caribbean from the era of Christopher Columbus.

The small fleet then sailed west along the north coast of Yucatan until it curved southward. There the vessels encountered troublesome headwinds and finally anchored offshore of the present-day town of Champotón. Once again, the Spaniards were impressed by houses of stone and fields of cultivated corn. But their presence also attracted Mayas painted in black and white, and since the Indians also bore weapons, the Spaniards assumed the black and white was war paint—a correct conclusion. However, the Indians did not attack but instead asked if the strangers had come from the direction of the rising sun—probably meaning from the Caribbean. When assured that was indeed the case, the Mayas might well have concluded that these strangers and others like them had been responsible for committing terrible atrocities over the past twenty years. Nevertheless, the Spaniards settled down for the night with their backs to the sea, in violation of the restrictions on the license to explore that the friars in Santo Domingo had granted them. Those commandments forbade them to spend even a night on lands occupied by natives in the hope of eliminating contacts, which in the past had resulted in the deaths of so many Indians.

At dawn with terrible ululated war cries, Mayas armed with stone-headed axes, bows and arrows, wooden spears with fire-hardened points, obsidian-edged swords, and stones propelled by sling shots attacked the Spaniards. In a few minutes, twenty Spaniards lay dead with many more wounded. In trying to protect his men, Hernández de Córdoba received more than thirty wounds, some of which would prove fatal. In almost blind panic, Spaniards swamped their landing boats, causing occupants to swim, drown, or become captives.

All who survived were desperately short of drinking water. Despite the urgency of returning to Cuba with many wounded and dying men, water needs came first. Fortunately, Antón de Aliminos, who was also wounded, remembered a freshet at the mouth of a river located on the extreme southwest coast of Florida. After sailing there and refilling water kegs, the vessels sailed almost due south to the port of Carenas (future Havana) on the north coast of Cuba. The flagship bearing its dying captain struggled back to Santiago where Diego Velázquez received Francisco Hernández de Córdoba and heard his report. Shortly thereafter, don Francisco died of wounds in the home of a friend. But the gold and other items brought to Santiago by the 1517 expedition, as well as enthusiastic accounts of contacts with an Indian people far more advanced than ever before seen by Spaniards in the Caribbean, spurred the efforts of Diego Velázquez to send a follow-up expedition to Yucatan in 1518. In the interim, Pedro de Alvarado—who would come closest to being labeled the Achilles of Spanish conquistadors in the Indies—stepped off a ship in Santiago, Cuba.

Pedro de Alvarado was one of those rare individuals in history who seems larger than life. Born in Badajoz in far southwest Spain around 1486, he was younger than Cortés by only a couple of years, but he was taller than the Conqueror and more physically imposing. Alvarado's appearance was strikingly different from many conquistadors in that he had reddish blond hair and probably blue eyes that were often friendly but likely turned hard as agates in anger. Later in the conquest of Mexico, the Aztecs would give don Pedro a nickname that reflected his unusual appearance—*Tonatiuh*, meaning "Child of the Sun." It was not necessarily a compliment, and like the sun, if an Indian stood too close to Alvarado for an extended moment could get fatally burned. The word "charismatic" is perhaps overused, but it seems appropriate in describing Pedro de Alvarado. His imposing physical presence, his exploits in battles with Indians, his grace and charm, his athleticism, his horsemanship regarded by contemporaries as likely the best, and his inclination to violence all set don Pedro apart from other captains of men-at-arms.

Alvarado's father was wealthy enough to own a high-spirited stallion apparently named Guerrero, or "warrior." Perhaps the elder Alvarado told his son Pedro that if he could bring the charger's willful nature under his control, he could become an accomplished *caballero*. That he did, and it later earned him high praise from fellow conquistadors. Great horsemen learned to loop connected reins over a charger's neck, which left either hand free to wield lance or sword.

Pedro de Alvarado was an eldest son, and it appears that his three brothers— Jorge, Gonzalo, and Gómez—were born in descending order of birth. However, only Jorge is mentioned as important in the conquest of New Spain. While still at home in Badajoz, don Pedro's uncle, Diego de Alvarado, died as grandmaster of the prestigious Order of Santiago and bequeathed nephew Pedro his white cloak adorned with a red cross. Don Pedro, who liked fine clothing, wore this attractive apparel with great pride.

Seeking more opportunity than life offered at Badajoz, Pedro de Alvarado with his three brothers in tow traveled to Seville and arrived there around 1515. While awaiting passage to the Indies, don Pedro and one of his brothers climbed the Giralda, just like tourists do today. The Giralda is the signature tower and minaret that dominates the skyline of the old city with its impressive height of about 340 feet. Both tower and minaret were begun and completed in the second half of the twelfth century. When don Pedro and his sibling climbed the Giralda, it was under repair and scaffolding extended for some feet over one side of the tower. On a dare from his brother, don Pedro walked to the end of it, turned around, and walked back to safety. He seemingly did not know fear.

In 1516 the Alvarado brothers took passage to Santo Domingo and stayed there for about two years before dropping out of the written record. But news of gold brought to Santiago by the Hernández de Córdoba expedition caused them to resurface and move to Cuba in early 1518. As preparations got underway for a follow-up expedition later that year, Pedro de Alvarado convinced Diego Velázquez, without a shred of truth, that he was an experienced ship captain. So, of course, newly arrived in Cuba, don Pedro would captain one of the vessels.

Velázquez understood the importance of the Hernández de Córdoba expedition, so he lost little time in sending a friend to Santo Domingo to seek a license from the Hieronymite friars for another exploratory expedition to the new-found land. Although natives there had not allowed the Spaniards to go into the interior, it almost certainly contained riches based on what could be observed in the coastal town of Champotón. Velázquez also dispatched another friend to Spain to ask the Crown for his appointment as *adelantado* of Yucatan, but that title was a long time coming for reasons that are essential to our understanding of the complexities of events in Spain and beyond during the years 1516–1521.

In 1516, King Ferdinand died, and his immediate heir Princess Juana, the widow of Philip the Handsome, had already demonstrated serious psychological instability. Her condition was so severe that her father sent her to the town and castle of Tordesillas where she in effect was confined but far from out of consideration until she died half a century later in 1556. With the death of her father, Juana's son Charles, who had lived in Flanders (present-day Belgium) for the first sixteen years of his life, received orders to come to Spain and rule there but only if he could acquire the permission of his mother, then unfortunately known as *Juana la Loca*, or Joanna the Mad.

When Charles first set foot in Spain in 1516, he was an awkward teenager surrounded by his rapacious Flemish and Burgundian tutors and advisers. Worse, an eyewitness commenting on Charles's appearance noted that "aside from looking like an idiot, the young monarch spoke not one word of Castilian." Another observer remarked that Charles's enormous lower jaw, infamous with the Hapsburgs, caused the royal mouth to gape so openly a fly could have winged in and out unimpeded. No one, however, should underestimate this teenage king. Three years later in 1519, his grandfather and Holy Roman Emperor Maximilian I died. His intended heir Philip the Handsome was dead, so Charles I of Spain also became Charles V of the Holy Roman Empire. A point of interest here is opposition touched off by Charles's arrival in Spain. Fueled by the hatred of his arrogant advisers, a complicated internal uprising known as the Revolt of the Comuneros (1519–1521) beset Spain for almost two years. That conflict need not concern us, except to point out that there was so much confusion and unrest at the highest levels of Spanish government that little of importance got done quickly, if at all. In May 1520, when Charles I sailed from Spain to claim the title Charles V, Spain suffered civil war, albeit of limited scope, and Martin Luther's posting of his Ninety-Five Theses on Wittenberg Castle's door in 1517 complicated matters even more. In the absence of Charles I, Bishop Juan de Fonseca became extremely powerful, to his obvious delight. The high cleric was no friend of Hernando Cortés or any other conquistador. However, as will be explained below, the chaotic situation in Spain during those same crucial years (1519–1521) probably saved Cortés's neck from the chopping block.

Back in Santiago, Cuba, preparations went forward in equipping the 1518 expedition to Yucatan, and then beyond its limits to fringes of the still unknown Aztec Empire. Diego Velázquez had easily won quick approval from the friars in Santo Domingo for his second expedition. Once again, the acting executives for the Indies during the absence of Governor Diego Columbus forbade any settlement of islands or mainlands. That probably pleased Velázquez, given that he had appealed to Spain for appointment as *adelantado* of Yucatan, which if granted would ensure him exclusive rights there.

By contrast, there was no doubt about Velázquez's choice for overall commander. He chose his nephew Juan de Grijalva, who was about twenty-eight when he accepted command. Don Juan was quite young when he first sailed to Española in 1508, and he had accompanied his uncle when he undertook the conquest and occupation of Cuba in 1511. Like many men-at-arms, Grijalva received an encomienda for his assistance with arms and mount. To support the second expedition's sailing from Santiago, Velázquez purchased four ships, two naos, one caravel, and a brigantine, but he left provisioning the vessels as the responsibility of the ship captains. That was hardly an onerous obligation, given that onboard victuals were usually little more than cassava bread and salted bacon. Oddly, both naos were confusingly and redundantly named *San Sebastián*. But there was no uncertainty in the governor's choice of Antón de Alaminos as chief pilot. Aside from Grijalva, the other ship captains were Pedro de Alvarado, Francisco de Montejo, and Alonso de Ávila—the last three were all hidalgos. Not to be overlooked—sailing again was the future chronicler and historian Bernal Díaz del Castillo, as well as the youthful interpreter Little Julián—Old Melchor, perhaps accurately named, had died in Santiago.

The four vessels rounded the eastern tip of Cuba and left the island's shore at its western point on the north coast toward the end of April, and within a week, men onboard were the first Spaniards to set foot on the island of Cozumel, which is about thirty miles in length and twelve miles at its maximum width. The people on Cozumel spoke the same Maya dialect as natives on the Yucatecan mainland. This was of little consequence to the Grijalva-led expedition but would later become especially important to Cortés in the conquest of Mexico. [**Figure 6**]

From an initial landfall on Cozumel, Grijalva's ship and three companion vessels sailed to a different part of the island where the commander landed with

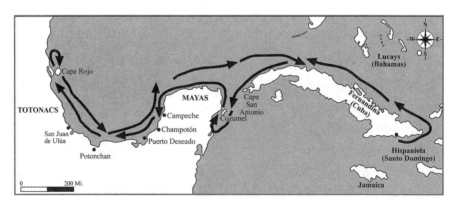

Figure 6. Journey of Juan Grijalva (1518). Adapted from Thomas, *Conquest*, 102-103.

a hundred men. They found stone houses and streets likewise paved with stones. Much impressed, Chaplain Juan Díaz commented that the buildings were so well constructed "that they might have been built by Spaniards"—this was obvious high praise for native building skills.

At this second site, several Spaniards climbed a white pyramid, and Grijalva had his standard bearer, Bernardino Vázquez de Tapia, raise the flag of Castile. The notary, Diego de Godoy, then read the Requirement, although there were no Indians to hear it because they had wisely fled to the interior as the ships approached. With no Indians to confront, fray Juan Díaz led ten conquistadors on a brief excursion to the interior of Cozumel. They found well-built villages and some farms that contained managed honeybees. The Spaniards returned to the ships bearing honeycombs that were much appreciated.

On May 7, Grijalva and his company stopped at a third location on Cozumel near a river. There the expedition commander and his companions filled their water kegs and took on food and some rodents called "edible rats." They next sailed toward *El Gran Cairo* and followed the route of Hernández de Córdoba along the northeast and north coasts of Yucatan. The four ships then turned south and anchored near the town of Champotón where Hernández and many of his men had suffered misfortune and death. The mariners led by Grijalva came ashore in boats but were armed with two small cannons and several muskets. Grijalva demanded gold, but the Mayas said they had none. The Indians were nevertheless insistent that their visitors leave, and some of them, remembering the outcome of battle the previous year, were confident of winning should there be fighting. But Grijalva, advantaged by knowledge of Hernández's mistakes, told the Indians that he and his men planned to spend the night on land despite being outnumbered by nearly three-thousand armed Mayas.

When dawn came, Mayas wearing black and white colors of war approached the Spaniards, and a chieftain placed a torch in front of them. Through Julián the translator the cacique sent this message: "Behold this torch which we will light and place between our armies.

If you do not leave before the torch . . . [has] burned, you will all die. We do not want you as guests." As the torch flamed out, a pitched battle commenced. Grijalva had positioned one of the cannons atop a nearby pyramid. It opened fire with pieces of metal probably cut from worn-out horseshoes that cut a path through Indian's ranks. When the second cannon fired, it was an agreed upon signal for Spaniards armed with muskets to join the fray. Other Spaniards armed with swords also weighed in, forcing the Mayas to withdraw.

On the next day, Grijalva sent a message conveyed by Julián to the Maya leaders. If they would provide him with wood and water, he would return to his ships and leave. This second battle at Champotón had been costly for Mayas and Spaniards alike. Forty of the latter including Grijalva had been wounded, and one expeditionary was killed. The Mayas decided to provide the requested wood and water, and Grijalva kept his word by withdrawing to the ships and continuing to explore the coast of Yucatan, the first to do so beyond Champotón. It is not known whether the Mayas had used poisoned arrows in this battle, but fourteen wounded Spaniards would later die aboard the ships.

The next stop for the Grijalva expedition was at a narrow opening into a large lagoon and an excellent harbor. The explorers called it "*Puerto Deseado*," the Desired Port, because they had previously not been able to find one that suited their needs. Grijalva allowed his men to stay on shore for two weeks. That provided an opportunity to careen (clean and caulk with oakum holes in the hull caused by mollusks) a ship that badly needed it. The area inland from Puerto Deseado contained hundreds of rabbits, which the crossbowmen enjoyed shooting and eating in preference to the "edible rats." The expeditioners had also brought along a female greyhound that was adept at catching rabbits. The dog enjoyed the chase so much that she wandered inland and could not be found when the ships lifted anchors. A year later, the Cortés expedition also stopped at Puerto Deseado and reclaimed the greyhound that was still catching "edible rabbits."

Puerto Deseado lay within lands of Yucatan where the Maya dialect was Chontal, and Julián could not understand it. The Spaniards responded by capturing four Indians who spoke the Chontal tongue and began teaching them Spanish. One of the captives was especially adept at learning Castilian. He was named Pedro Barba, after the godfather of one of Grijalva's captains. With the four Indians on board, the Grijalva expedition moved on in early June to the Río Tabasco, which they named the Río Grijalva—a name it has since retained. The current of the river carried such a large volume of fresh water that it was drinkable for some distance at sea, which permitted the Spaniards to refill their water kegs.

To the delight of the Spaniards, many Indians headed by their chief approached in canoes, and several carried gilded shields. They asked Grijalva what he wanted, and he replied that he wished to trade. The chief was welcomed aboard the flagship, and he paid homage to Grijalva by ordering his followers to adorn the captain in breastplate and bracelets of gold. The commander responded by having his men dress the cacique in Spanish clothing, topped by a velvet cap. More cordialities followed but not more gold. In fact, this region near the foothills of Chiapas produced no gold, so all such metal possessed by these Chontal Mayas had been acquired by trade with other natives.

Of interest, it seems that Grijalva was the first Spanish captain to use double translators. He spoke to Julián, who by then knew some Spanish; and Julián in turn spoke to Pedro Barba, who talked and understood both Yucatecan and Chontal Maya. Later, Cortés would employ a more famous double team of translators that gave him tremendous advantage throughout the conquest of Mexico. In fact, beginning with Columbus, Spaniards understood the strategic value of communication with native peoples. Nevertheless, there was always this question: what was translated and understood since Spaniards did not know Indian languages? For example, years later in the conquest of Peru, Francisco Pizarro had a native translator named Felipillo, or "Little Philip," who knew some Spanish and Quechua, the language of the Incas. He was asked to translate the concept of the Holy Trinity. Here, like with many of the Catholic faith, Felipillo has sympathy in trying to accept Catholic doctrine—he allegedly said: "As best he understood, there were three Gods and one, and that made four."

Grijalva continued sailing for a few days and arrived at the mouth of the Río Tonalá. The expeditioners were then at a region called Coatzacoalcos. This area of Mexico is also known as Tabasco, a land that produced cacao beans for chocolate drinks. The beans were so valuable they served as the currency of the Aztec empire. The region also produced tanned jaguar pelts, beautifully decorated tortoise shells, and green stone known locally as *chalchihuite* (turquoise). The stones, which came from mountains in Chiapas, were much valued by the Aztecs who traded gold, copper, and obsidian for them.

At that juncture, Pedro de Alvarado, who disliked taking directions from anyone and was especially unhappy with Grijalva's cautious decisions as commander, sailed off on his own and entered the Río Papaloapan on the caravel he captained. This understandably irritated Grijalva, but don Pedro later defended himself by claiming his ship needed careening. While anchored in the river for several days, Alvarado was aware that Indians on shore had kept him under surveillance. The natives were probably traveling merchants who also served as spies for the Aztec Emperor Moctezuma. Later, the Spanish would learn that these native observers had reported in words to this effect—strange, bearded men speaking an unintelligible language had come in a "floating house."

After a few days, Alvarado sailed down the river and caught up with the fleet but did not apologize to Grijalva for his actions. Nonetheless, the combined fleet of four ships next arrived off the coast of present-day Veracruz and dropped anchors. Nearby was an island, and a few Spaniards approached it by boat. They found two temples and the first evidence of human sacrifice. Four Indians, two adults and two children, had been dead for some time. One of the adults was missing arms and legs. There were also skulls, bones, and dried blood on the walls of a partially enclosed temple. The dual temples had likely been constructed to honor the Aztec deities, Huitzilopochtli and Tezcatlipoca. Before leaving, Spaniards named this isle, "*La Isla de Sacrificios.*"

While anchored in the great harbor that fronts the present-day city of Veracruz, Indians on shore began waving white banners and motioning for the Spaniards to come and join them. Grijalva sent Captain Francisco de Montejo in a ship boat with Julián and Pedro Barba to learn what the natives wanted. But neither interpreter could understand a single word of Nahuatl, the language spoken by Aztecs. In sign language, the Indians indicated that they wished to speak to the Spanish commander on one of the naos. At that time, Grijalva along with a few mariners went ashore. The commander was warmly welcomed by a local chief, and he was invited into a hut covered with freshly cut fronds. Grijalva received sweet-smelling incense and tortillas to eat. There followed gifts of cotton cloaks of varying colors. In every manner, the Aztecs treated the Spaniards with great respect—in marked contrast to their reception by the Mayas on Yucatan. Before departing his Aztec hosts, Grijalva noticed a small island that fronts the port city of Veracruz and gave it the enduring name of San Juan de Ulúa. Since present-day Veracruz was not founded until the late 1590s, Spaniards throughout most of the sixteenth century referenced the site as San Juan de Ulúa.

During the cordialities between the Grijalva mariners and the Aztecs, a snow-covered peak could be seen in Mexico's distant interior. When the Spaniards asked about it, they were told that it was called Orizaba, or "the Mountain of the Star." Pedro de Alvarado was especially interested and expressed hope of exploring more on the mainland, but Grijalva would not allow it. Instead, the four vessels moved up the coast of Mexico and encountered other natives who called themselves Totonacs. These were proud people, and they were probably among the most reluctant of all Indians in Mexico to accept their status as tributaries of the Aztecs. The Mexica could have conquered the Totonacs but instead demanded onerous tribute payments that included rich cotton cloaks, warrior costumes, cacao beans, young men for religious sacrifices, young women for violation and enslavement, and decorative feathers from local birds. As for the Totonacs themselves, they were impressed with the ships and weapons of the Spaniards and perhaps saw them as potential allies in fighting the despised Aztecs.

Impressed at having been so well received by the Totonacs, other ship captains joined Alvarado in suggesting that they should set up a colony among those natives. Likewise, mariners of lesser rank joined the discussion by pointing out that they were unpaid volunteers who had joined the expedition in the hope of eventual profit. Grijalva, however remained adamant. He pointed out that they were too few in numbers since so many had died from wounds sustained at Champotón, and they were also running short on supplies. The cassava bread, for example, on which expeditioners had come to rely on had become moldy. Grijalva also pointed out that Diego Velázquez had not granted them permission to colonize, which the other ship captains agreed was true. However, some pointed out that the governor had not expressly forbidden them to colonize. Nevertheless, Grijalva held firm, but he did agree to a compromise in late June.

Pedro de Alvarado could sail directly to Cuba and show Velázquez some of the gold and other items of value they had collected. Alvarado, although keen on adventure in Mexico, agreed to do that—most likely because he disliked the unenterprising leadership of Grijalva. Gold valued at between 16,000 and 20,000 pesos was loaded on the caravel as well as other items of little intrinsic value. Don Pedro likewise bore letters the other captains had written to their families. Grijalva in a missive to his uncle pointed out that the most successful trade items intended for the Indians had been glass beads, pins, needles, scissors, and combs. He might also have added small hand mirrors made of polished metal, which delighted Indians who had never seen their own faces.

While Alvarado's expedition sailed to Santiago, Cuba, the other expeditioners sailed north along the coast of Mexico to lands beyond those settled by Totonacs. Captains of the two naos and a brigantine found battling headwinds difficult and slow going. But somewhere north of the southern border of a province known as Pánuco, the mariners were astonished by a maritime attack on their ships by Indians traveling in large war canoes. Based on events that happened during and after the conquest of Mexico, these natives were undoubtedly Huastecs. They had acquired copper-headed axes, which they used to cut cables on Montejo's ship. Furthermore, the Huastec's boldness in attacking much larger ships from dugout canoes was such that the Spaniards had to resort to firing cannons and crossbows to drive them away. According to linguistic specialists, the Huastec language was related to the Mayan, but separation from Yucatecan speakers for many centuries had perhaps made that tongue as different from its parent language as Spanish is to Latin.

The Grijalva-led vessels continued to make little headway against the wind, and somewhere near modern-day Cabo Rojo off the east coast of Pánuco the captains reversed direction and began the long voyage back to Santiago. Their return route followed the coast of Yucatan in the opposite direction of their outward journey and then proceeded along the entire north coast of Cuba. It appears that Grijalva did not reach home port until around mid-November 1518.

This second expedition to Yucatan from Cuba has largely been unfairly downplayed by historians and by Cortés himself to further embellish his own accomplishments. Don Hernando dismissed it almost in its entirety by writing that its personnel had not seen a single town despite all the months it spent at sea, and that when the expedition returned it was "without having done anything at all." Quite the contrary was true. The 1518 expedition had extended Spanish knowledge of Yucatan from Champotón—the extent of the Hernández expedition—to Cabo Rojo. Along the way they were the first Europeans to visit lands of the Chontal Maya and to learn of a great and powerful kingdom ruled by Aztecs. The Grijalva mariners had established good relations with the Totonacs, which would later prove valuable to Cortés, and their commander was the first to see the merits of using double translators. Lastly, Spaniards at Santiago were excited by the nearly 20,000 gold pesos brought there by Alvarado. The prospect of even greater riches in the future made preparing for a third expedition in 1518–1519 a virtual certainty.

The conduct of Pedro de Alvarado on the Grijalva expedition was understandable, given his reluctance to accept any authority other than his own, but his actions were unfair to his commander. Don Pedro remained irritated that Grijalva had criticized him for leaving the fleet without permission and sailing up the Río Papaloapan. Worst of all, Alvarado thought the timidity of the expedition's leader in refusing to set up a colony in Mexico was unforgiveable—never mind that Grijalva was following orders. It would take a different captain to keep Alvarado even partially under control, and that person would be Hernando Cortés. Ironically, Cortés had never commanded men in battle until 1519, but he would not be found wanting in that capacity when circumstances placed him in that position.

There is no direct proof of when Cortés and Alvarado met in Santiago, but there is ample circumstantial evidence that it was no later than when don Pedro returned to Cuba in late summer 1518. Alvarado was the toast of the Cuban capital for several weeks, because of the gold he brought on the caravel *Santiago*, and Cortés was one of the richest men in Cuba, as well as a resident of the port city and its former chief notary. In any event, the two men had much in common, and they soon became close friends. Both were from Extremadura; both were about the same age; both had important family connections in Spain; and both were cardsharps who won consistently by using marked decks of cards. Don Pedro's younger brother, don Jorge, was also a gambler who could read the backs of cards. Again, the three conquistadors would collude during the conquest of Mexico to cheat their own men-at-arms out of what little gold they had obtained. After all, as they may have reasoned, important captains would no doubt lose face if beaten at cards by lowly men-at-arms.

In late summer and into early fall, there was no indication that Hernando Cortés would lead the third expedition from Santiago to Yucatan and beyond, but don Hernando was an early co-investor in it along with Governor Diego Velázquez. At the same time, other mariners who returned to Santiago on the caravel captained by Alvarado informed Velázquez that don Pedro had been insubordinate to his nephew Grijalva by sailing away from the fleet without permission. The likelihood of Alvarado being allowed as a ship captain of the third expedition was remote. Furthermore, he had vowed never to serve again under the command of another, but that would change in the conquest of Mexico.

In early fall 1518, Pedro de Alvarado left Santiago with his three younger brothers and moved more than halfway down the south coast of Cuba where they sought other employment, but not before don Pedro apparently had a parting conversation with Cortés. Alvarado believed any further expeditions should plan to colonize inland from San Juan de Ulúa. The Aztecs had been invariably friendly; and they had mentioned a great empire that lay beyond snow-capped Mount Orizaba, the highest peak in Mexico and third highest in the Northern Hemisphere of America at about 18,500 feet. As it turned out, the third expedition would take a different route than that followed by the first two. It would take a direct route to Yucatan along the south coast of Cuba, and in doing so pass by the town where the Alvarado brothers had relocated. Don Pedro, the "Spanish Achilles," would join the 1519 expedition and pursue his own role in the conquest of Mexico. He would have a role in so many battles and conquests beyond that he would earn the title "the Ubiquitous Conquistador."

CHAPTER 5

The Cortés Expedition to Yucatan and Mexico

The third expedition that sailed from Cuba in late 1518 was complex in origin, disputed in sponsorship, and led to an irreparable rupture in friendship between Diego Velázquez and Hernando Cortés. Regardless of what the Hieronymite friars at Santo Domingo might authorize, Velázquez was determined to send out nothing more than a holding expedition while he waited for appointment as *adelantado* of Yucatan. Even so, this undertaking would be larger than the previous ones and more expensive. Accordingly, don Diego needed a partner, and Hernando Cortés was one of the richest men in Cuba. Although the governor initially had no intention of making don Hernando the expedition's commander, his money was welcome.

Velázquez first tried to recruit another nephew as expedition commander, but that individual turned down the offer when asked to invest three-thousand ducats. His second preference was Vasco Porcallo, but ironically—given his final choice—don Vasco was viewed as uncontrollable. On the advice of his accountant who knew men with money, Velázquez chose the magistrate of Santiago who had been his protégé for more than ten years—Hernando Cortés. A letter sent to don Hernando, at that time prospecting for gold on one of his estates, asked him to return to Santiago and speak to the governor, which he did. Two weeks later Cortés accepted a commission to explore the "islands" of Yucatan and San Juan de Ulúa with the title of "captain general of the expedition." Velázquez wanted his appointee to engage in modest trading while serving God and occupying land he intended to govern and become rich. Cortés was also enjoined to prevent blasphemy, card playing, and consorting with native women among his men. One might well ponder: was Velázquez over the ten years he had been associated with Cortés so obtuse and blind that he did not recognize his captain general was a cardsharp? Most likely, however, his restriction on card playing was intended to prohibit gambling.

By this time, Cortés had become friends with Pedro de Alvarado, and it seems don Pedro had informed him that while sailing with Grijalva he had heard rumors of a land distant from San Juan de Ulúa that was ruled by a great and powerful native chieftain. However, at the time preparations began for the third expedition, the Alvarado brothers had moved westward from Santiago along the south coast of Cuba. Cortés, then co-investor in the third expedition, began looking for men and ships, and he busied himself buying provisions. To recruit men, the captain general hired *pregoneros*, town criers, who made announcements following Mass on Sundays. Their messages promised riches beyond belief for would-be conquistadors who joined the new expedition, and all were reminded that the previous one had yielded almost twenty-thousand gold pesos.

As mentioned in the Introduction, there is a misconception that conquistador captains were members of the Spanish army, and the men-at-arms they commanded were soldiers. In fact, even lower-ranked conquistadors were entrepreneurs. They had to buy their own clothing and weaponry, and only captains were wealthy enough to own a horse. Cortés, while wealthy by most standards, lacked liquidity. He borrowed, with his encomienda and vassals as security, twelve-thousand gold pesos, an amount somewhat more than invested by Governor Velázquez. Because don Hernando was a respected and well-known magistrate in Santiago, he helped men he recruited obtain credit from city merchants. In all, Cortés assisted in arming about 350 men in the ranks, and he followed by purchasing three ships and five horses in Santiago.

Cortés was also intent on recruiting Pedro de Alvarado. Don Pedro's share of the nearly twenty-thousand gold pesos had permitted him to buy his own ship and horse. He was experienced, having accompanied Grijalva along the coast of Mexico from Yucatan to San Juan de Ulúa, during which he had seen evidence of human sacrifice and asked what lay beyond a perpetually snow-capped peak that was visible at times from San Juan.

As Cortés continued preparations for the expedition, Velázquez sent his steward Diego de Ordaz dockside "with orders to keep his eyes open and see that no plots were hatched in the fleet, for he was always distrustful of Cortés." However, don Hernando also had friends who brought him reports on what the governor was saying to his associates. Then, what Cortés had feared most, happened. Velázquez decided to end their partnership. Instead of dismissing Cortés in person, the governor sent his confidant, Luis de Medina, with papers to notify don Hernando of his dismissal as captain general of the expedition. While traveling to Santiago from the governor's hacienda outside the capital, Medina was suspiciously stabbed to death and the assailant threw his body into a ravine. A close associate of don Hernando came upon the scene, lifted the governor's papers from Medina's corpse, and delivered them to his friend. That prompted Cortés to hasten preparations for getting underway with the fleet, and to that end he purchased three more ships.

Still lacking from Cortés's provisions was fresh meat. He ordered one of his friends to go to Santiago's only butcher shop and buy all its recently slaughtered animals, as well as live pigs and cattle in holding pens. Fernando Alonso, the slaughterhouse owner, refused to sell what don Hernando wanted, so Cortés sent a squadron of armed men and took everything without payment. When an outraged Alonso protested the seizure, Cortés signed a note promising full recompense at some point in time. Attempting to soothe hard feelings, don Hernando removed a gold thistle emblem and chain from his neck and gave it to the aggrieved *matadero,* who left in anguish wondering what Velázquez would do to him, and what people in Santiago would do without meat. Unknown to Cortés, Alonso immediately carried his complaint to the governor, and at that time Velázquez came in person to confront Cortés—perhaps thinking he could convince his longtime friend not to sail on his own.

Cortés was well prepared for the confrontation, and he met don Diego in a boat flanked by musketeers and crossbowmen. Velázquez apparently said words to this effect: "Is this any way to treat a friend?" Cortés is alleged to have replied that he hoped Velázquez would forgive him, but he had thought about what he had invested in the expedition and could not be dissuaded. Don Hernando then returned to his flagship. It and the other five vessels crowded with 350 men lifted anchor and got underway in the evening of November 18, 1518, leaving the governor dockside in a fury. As Cortés left Santiago or perhaps soon thereafter, Velázquez labeled him a renegade conquistador who had defied a Crown-appointed governor. Ordinarily, that was a capital offense in an absolutist framework of government, especially given Bishop Juan de Fonseca's antipathy for all conquistadors. Furthermore, at that time, Fonseca was essentially in complete charge of the Spanish government throughout the nearly two-year absence of King Charles I from Spain.

Before following Cortés and his fleet, it is important to note just how thorough the captain general had been in recruiting and equipping this third expedition, which was to establish a colony. Perhaps most important in the long run, don Hernando recruited a shipwright and boat builder from Seville named Martín López. It said that López's contemporary Michelangelo could look at a huge block of marble and see a sculpture within; in similar manner, López could look at a tree and see part of a ship to be fashioned from within it. This extraordinarily talented man is the subject of a book-length study on the crucial role he would assume in the conquest of Mexico, and he is listed as the subject of a second book in the bibliography at the end of this chapter.

Cortés used iron ingots for ballast in his vessels, as well as placing onboard all metal he could find in Santiago such as nails and worn-out horseshoes. He next recruited a blacksmith along with his forge. The smithy would later shape innumerable crossbow quarrels, or bolts, and sharpen the tools of carpenters and boat builders. Among other recruits was Julián, the lone Maya interpreter in Santiago. He had learned some Spanish over two years' time, and he spoke fluent Yucatecan Maya. Onboard also went as many kegs of gunpowder as Cortés could buy in Santiago, as well as small falconet brass cannons and medium-sized Lombards. From his own estate, Cortés provided hundreds of pounds of salted pork and bacon. However, in his haste to leave Santiago, he had not been able to acquire enough cassava bread, but the busy capital general had found time to purchase several decks of playing cards intended for marking.

Cortés plotted a different course than had been followed by the two previous expeditions—this time along the south coast of Cuba, which was on a direct path to the island of Cozumel. The south Cuban coast was more settled and richer than the north, and along the way was where Pedro de Alvarado and his three brothers had relocated, as well as many of the captains who would later serve under don Hernando in the conquest. Cortés reached his first port at Macaca, and there an old associate named Francisco Dávila sold him a thousand rations of cassava bread from his properties. On this stop, the future Conqueror also dispatched one of his ships to Jamaica to buy eight-hundred slabs of cured bacon and two-thousand additional rations of bread.

At Trinidad, the next port-of-call, problems arose. Velázquez had sent riders on horseback racing along the south coast carrying letters he had drafted. Those missives forbade any Spaniards in Cuba from assisting Cortés. To further complicate matters, Francisco Verdugo, the magistrate of Trinidad, was married to Velázquez's sister. But as the garrulous old conquistador Bernal Díaz wrote, Cortés could be very persuasive with "honey-coated" words. After a time, Verdugo became friendly, sold don Hernando three more horses and provided fodder for them and the other mounts aboard the expedition. In addition, the magistrate informed Cortés that a ship had recently left Trinidad with supplies for Panama, then known as Darién.

Cortés sent Diego de Ordaz on a fast brigantine to overtake the supply ship loaded with a windfall of provisions that included several tons of cassava bread and fifteen-hundred pounds of bacon and salted chickens. The supply ship's captain not only complied in giving up his cargo, but also accompanied Ordaz back to Trinidad with his vessel containing a mare and its colt; and there, he also joined the expedition with his ship. Cortés defended his actions by insisting that Ordaz was not disloyal to the King, instead the incident was an example of nothing more than one Spaniard helping another. Furthermore, the supply-ship captain had been given an opportunity to gain wealth by agreeing to join a planned colony in Mexico.

While at Trinidad, Pedro de Alvarado and his three brothers, Jorge, Gonzalo, and Gómez joined the expedition. Alvarado also added his ship, which he would captain, as well as his charger. Although specific accounts are lacking on the day-to-day relationship between Cortés and the Alvarado brothers, they were likely fun times for don Hernando who had no brothers. The Alvarado siblings were a lively bunch led by oldest brother don Pedro. They liked to have fun, probably engaged in japery as brothers are inclined to do, and two of the Alvarado brothers—Pedro and Jorge—were also accomplished cardsharps.

In addition to recruiting the Alvarado brothers, Cortés added other men who would become important in the conquest of Mexico—some more so than others. They included Alonso de Ávila, Juan de Escalante, and most important Cristóbal de Olid. The last would become one of the major captains in the conquest. He later betrayed Cortés, and like others who did so paid a high price for his disloyalty. At another port, some eighteen leagues distant from Trinidad, Cortés added Alonso Hernández de Puertocarrero, Gonzalo de Sandoval, and Rodrigo Rangel, a native of don Hernando's hometown of Medellín. Sandoval, who was only about twenty-one years of age, would be most important in the conquest of Mexico and beyond, and he would later become the favorite captain of men in the ranks. As an interesting sidelight, don Gonzalo loved chess. Somehow, during all the marching and fighting that lay ahead, he managed to keep a chess board and full set of pieces; and chess would become a favorite form of entertainment with conquistador captains during their idle hours.

The last port-of-call on the south coast of Cuba was Old Havana. Knowing this, Cortés sent Alvarado ahead on horseback to prepare for their arrival there while he sailed later with his flagship, *Santa María de Concepción*, and the rest of the fleet. During the night, the flagship became separated from the other vessels and ran aground. This was a serious matter, given that there was no way to alert the other vessels of the ship's distress. To save the flagship, Cortés took immediate steps. He was close enough to shore to transfer cargo by boats and store it safely, and he was lucky that wind and waves did not destroy his stricken ship. When at last it refloated, don Hernando moved the ship into deeper water and dropped anchor. There followed the exhausting work of reloading cargo into boats and transferring it back where it belonged. In all, *Santa María de Concepción* was seven days later than the other ships in arriving at Old Havana.

Cortés reported that there was great rejoicing and much relief with his arrival as captain general of the expedition. However, Bernal Díaz commented that for a week they had played the game of "who shall be Captain until Cortés comes?"

Nonetheless, three brigantines were made ready to sail eastward on a rescue mission when at last the flagship appeared on the horizon. That, according to Díaz, brought an abrupt end to the game of "Who shall be Captain?"

While at Old Havana, the Cortés expedition attained its full complement of eleven ships, about six-hundred men that included technicians, men-at-arms, and sailors, as well as sixteen horses. With his usual thoroughness, Bernal Díaz described all the mounts and commented on their characteristics such as "not much good" or "a grand galloper." He labelled Cortés's charger a "vicious dark chestnut stallion." The captain general's warhorse would bite or kick anyone other than him who came near it. To the relief and satisfaction of everyone other than don Hernando, the stallion would die shortly after the expedition reached San Juan de Ulúa.

Among other personnel added, none was more important than a friar of the Order of Merced named Bartolomé de Olmedo. Cortés chose fray Bartolomé as chaplain of the expedition, and he accompanied don Hernando throughout the conquest of Mexico. No other person was as significant as he in counseling Cortés to become more moderate in his view of paganism than the Merced friar. The Conqueror nevertheless frequently chose to ignore fray Olmedo's advice—to his disadvantage. Whatever else may be said about Hernando Cortés, he was a devout Catholic with a fierce hatred of paganism.

At Old Havana, Cortés took additional actions to establish his authority over everyone on the expedition. He added a steward and secretary to his household and fray Olmedo became his confessor. Don Hernando also warned independent-minded fellow conquistadors that orders he gave were to be obeyed without exception. Since Velázquez had previously declared him a renegade conquistador under sentence of death, there was no possibility of the expedition returning to Cuba.

When the fleet got underway from the last port in Cuba, Cortés ordered his pilots to set a course for the island of Cozumel where all ships would rendezvous. This was important should a vessel become separated in the night—something that no doubt brought recent memories to don Hernando. Cozumel also lay on the direct path to Yucatan, and the Conqueror had received information from Grijalva that two shipwrecked Spaniards were thought to be living among pagans on the island. If possible, they had to be rescued and returned to life among Christians. [**Figure 7**]

Alvarado's ship was the first to reach Cozumel, and don Pedro immediately went ashore. The Mayas, just as they had done when Grijalva had approached a year before, wisely fled to the interior. That provided Alvarado an opportunity to seize a flock of abandoned turkeys. When Cortés arrived later, he reprimanded don Pedro and remarked that his conduct was no way to pacify a country. Alvarado nonetheless defended his actions because he had only taken what had been left behind. The incident soon passed, but it served to remind Alvarado and others that Cortés was captain general of the expedition.

As relations improved with the Mayas on Cozumel, Cortés ordered Julián to ask several chieftains if they had knowledge of any men like himself living on the island. They agreed there were two who were held as slaves by fellow caciques about two days' journey to the interior. Don Hernando was delighted by the news, and he ordered two Mayas to carry letters he wrote to the Spanish captives. The natives agreed to do so but suggested that ransom be sent to the men's owners to facilitate their release. So along with the letters, Cortés sent all manner of beads. Both Spaniards were informed that a brigantine would anchor off the coast of Cape Catoche, a distance up the coast, and remain there for eight days to pick them up should they be able to obtain their freedom.

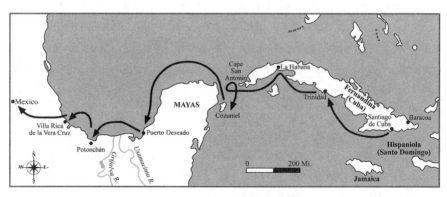

Figure 7. Journey of Hernando Cortés (1518–1519).
Adapted from Thomas, *Conquest*, 160–161.

Cortés's letters were received by the two shipwrecked Spaniards who been on Cozumel for eight years. In that time, Gerónimo de Aguilar, a priest who had taken vows in a minor order, had long hoped to return to the company of his countrymen. He begged his Indian master to accept the gifts and release him from bondage and eventually won his freedom, whereupon Aguilar set out for the coast in hope of rescue. The second Spaniard, Gonzalo Guerrero, reacted quite differently. He had chosen to live with a Maya woman and fathered three children by her. However, in the manner of natives on Cozumel, his face was covered with tattoos and his ears had been pierced. Having adopted the appearances of a native, Guerrero knew he would never again be welcomed in Spanish society. He nonetheless asked to receive the gifts sent by Cortés, and the messenger allowed him to do that. Meanwhile, when Aguilar finally reached the coast near Cape Catoche, the brigantine sent to pick him up had left on the eighth day, and the freed man had arrived on the ninth. Much saddened, Aguilar had no choice but to return to his former master and again live there.

Cortés, however, unleashed his anger on Diego de Ordaz. Why had he not waited longer at the cape? Why had he not brought back any word of the two Spaniards living as slaves among pagans in the interior of Cozumel? It was terrible thing to leave fellow Christians in bondage, but the expedition had been delayed long enough. The eleven ships weighed anchor and got underway for Yucatan, but what occurred next would be later be interpreted as a miracle sent by God, and it would lend new hope of rescue for Gerónimo de Aguilar.

Just hours after the fleet embarked in fair weather in early March 1519, at 10 o'clock that morning there were loud shouts coming from one of the brigantines. Soon after it fired a cannon so that all on the other vessels might hear it. The ship's captain Juan de Escalante shouted that his vessel had sprung a leak and was sinking. As it turned out, almost all the expedition's cassava bread was on that brigantine. Cortés ordered the ships back to Cozumel for careening the brigantine and transferring the supply of bread onto several other vessels. That took days, and in that time span Aguilar somehow learned that Spaniards had returned to the island. He made haste back to Cape Catoche, only to again find no ship waiting for him. But Indians told him the men he sought were only a short distance away to the south. The former castaway hired canoeists with a few glass beads he had kept, and they rowed him to the fleet. When Aguilar arrived there and recognized fellow Spaniards, he began weeping and thanked God. Acquiring a translator who understood Spanish and could speak Yucatecan Maya was a fortuitous stroke of luck for Cortés, for Aguilar was far more skilled as a translator than was Julián. Perhaps of interest, for eight years Aguilar had not spoken or heard his birth tongue, and thereafter his speech remained halting.

As Aguilar became more at ease with fellow Spaniards, he explained that he and Guerrero were among some six others who had survived shipwreck in 1511. They had launched a ship's boat and reached shore on Cozumel only to find themselves among Mayas who practiced human sacrifice and cannibalism. The Indians placed the men in a cage where they were to be fattened and eaten. All of them except Aguilar and Guerrero had suffered that fate. They escaped the others' fate when claimed as slaves by two chieftains. Aguilar further horrified his new shipmates with additional stories of human sacrifice he had witnessed, which served to strengthen their sense of Christian mission.

The fleet left Cozumel in mid-March and sailed north to the Isla de Mujeres where they stopped to take on water and salt. The expedition progressed by rounding Cape Catoche and following along the same route previously taken by Córdoba and Grijalva. Again, however, one of the ships became separated at night. The remaining vessels continued to look for it by having one of the brigantines sail close to shore, but their search was unsuccessful. However, when the expeditioners entered what Grijalva had named *Puerto Deseado*, or "desired port," they found the missing vessel commanded by Alonso de Escobar.

Remembering that Grijalva had reported the abundance of rabbits inland from the port, the Spaniards hunted rabbits with crossbows to provide fresh meat for at least some of the six-hundred men. While pursuing rabbits farther into the interior, they miraculously found the female greyhound that had been left behind the previous year. It was still catching rabbits but happy to be reunited with Spaniards. The greyhound joined perhaps a dozen very different canines onboard the fleet. Those were dogs of war, huge mastiffs closely resembling Russian wolfhounds. In battles that lay ahead with Mayas and later Aztecs, the canines trained to kill Indians would create mass confusion, terror, and death. Bartolomé de las Casas, again the great defender of the Indians and accomplished historian of the Indies, wrote that a mastiff could kill an Indian every minute.

On leaving the desired port, Cortés led the fleet to the mouth of the Río Usumacinta and arrived there around March 20. Shortly thereafter the mariners sailed on to the newly named Río Grijalva, formerly known as the Río Tabasco. This was another stream with a large volume of flow that entered the sea as freshet, which allowed Spaniards on the vessels to top off their water kegs. Later, the fleet sailed up the river for about a mile and a half and anchored near a Maya city named Potonchán, an important commercial center.

Indians in canoes approached the ships and asked those onboard what they wanted. Cortés replied through Aguilar they needed food and would pay for it. The Indians replied that the Spaniards should assemble the next day at a square in the city where they would receive food, and the Spaniards agreed to do that. During the night, however both Indians and mariners took steps to deceive— the Mayas sent their women out of the city while preparing for battle, and the Spaniards brought ashore additional men from the ships who were armed with crossbows and muskets. When morning came, the Mayas provided only enough turkeys and maize for about ten people. They did give the Spaniards a mask of gold but told them to leave immediately. Cortés refused, and a standoff ensued for two days during which the Indians provided a few more turkeys and ears of corn. On the third day, the Mayas stopped bringing food and warned the Spaniards to return to their ships and leave, or they would all die.

Cortés through Aguilar replied that his intentions were peaceful and that he only wanted to trade for goods and food. Apparently out of patience with the Spaniards, the Indians replied with angry shouts and loud rattling of their weapons, at which point don Hernando began planning to lead men in battle for the first time. He returned to the anchored ships and launched boats containing light cannons, crossbows, and muskets. Some Spaniards who had sailed with Grijalva remembered a pathway that led to the rear of the city, and during the night Cortés sent one-hundred men armed with swords, lances, and muskets along it under the command of Alonso de Ávila. Don Alonso's orders were to wait until he heard the firing of cannons and then attack from Potonchán while Cortés as captain general would lead armed men ashore from the ships.

The next morning, dozens of armed Mayas appeared onshore. Again, Cortés through Aguilar pleaded with the Indians to accept the Spaniards as friends. The Mayas replied by unlimbering a shower of arrows that delayed landings from ship's boats. Cortés ordered cannons fired, which alerted his men in the city to attack, while he led an assault by jumping ashore with sword in hand. Men in the fog of combat can act strangely. The shore was wet from rain, and mud sucked off one of don Hernando's shoes. Footwear was perhaps the most difficult item of apparel to replace on the expedition. Cortés, in mortal danger, fought off Indian attackers with one hand while searching for his shoe with the other. He was relieved when one of his men plucked the missing shoe from the mud and handed it to him. His bravery nonetheless impressed the men in ranks. It would be on display throughout the many battles that lay ahead, and Cortés never asked fellow conquistadors to do anything he would not do twice. Without the discipline that comes from training in army units and chain-of-command orders, conquistador captain generals had to earn respect almost every day.

Spaniards won this first battle at Potonchán by attacking the Mayas from both front and back, but the Indians were far from cowed or defeated. The victors retired to their ships for the night, but the riverbank near the city supported dense mangroves that partially disguised the movements of natives. By morning, hundreds of armed Chontal Mayas awaited further attacks from the ships. Aware of this danger, Cortés ordered all sixteen horses unloaded from the ships and managed to get them on shore. It took an entire day to do that, and it required a second day of exercising the horses to get strength back in their legs so that they could be ridden. Once accomplished, it set the stage for the first major battle in the conquest of Mexico, which was probably fought on March 22, 1519.

Confident in their superior numbers, the Chontal Mayas began to leave the mangrove-lined shore and congregate outside the city on an open plain that contained a field of Indian corn. Cortés decided to try once more to arrange peace talks with the Indians by sending Julián to negotiate with them, but no one could find the translator. He had come ashore during the night and left every article of his clothing hanging on a bush before fleeing naked as the day he was born. It was a stunning comment made by the Maya translator on how much he had come to appreciate life among Spaniards and their "superior" Christian culture in the two years he had experienced it. Cortés expressed concern that Julián knew too much about Spaniards to allow his escape. After the ensuing battle had ended, he would send outriders on his trail to apprehend or kill him, but they failed to find Julián who knew Spaniards well enough to never stop running until he had put a great distance between himself and his former companions.

The Mayas had the same weapons as those later used by the Aztecs. They included fire-hardened wooden lances propelled with great force by *atlatls*, spear throwers that had the effect of extending the arm and therefore leverage. They also used bows to fire short arrows that Bernal Díaz called "darts." The Indians' most deadly weapon, however, was a two-handed wooden sword flared like a fraternity paddle, called a *macuahuitl* in Nahuatl. Along its edges were embedded obsidian chips that cut like razors. Another weapon the Spaniards hated was a slingshot that propelled rocks about the size of walnuts with so much speed the incoming projectiles could not be seen before striking flesh and bones. The slingshot design consisted of two woven cotton cords each about two and a half feet long. One of the cords had a loop at its end that went around the thumb and served as an anchor, the other was open ended. Both lower ends were attached to a pouch of deerskin that held a rock. The slingshot was charged by whirling it around one's head until it attained great speed, followed by releasing upper ends of the cords. The slingshot projectiles were often not deadly, but they caused painful welts on legs and broken bones on hands and fingers.

Prior to the battle, Spaniards set up about one dozen cannons spaced along one side of the plain where more than one-thousand armed Mayas had congregated. Behind the cannons were an almost equal number of mastiffs restrained by leashes. Close behind them were horses ridden by Spaniards with ten-to twelve-foot lances armed with steel points. Spaniards began the battle with a barrage from their cannons, firing scraps of metal and startling the Indians with the loud boom of ordnance. There followed mastiffs charging the field, causing confusion, terror, and death. Then came horses with riders protected by armor. Last were perhaps three-hundred men-at-arms bearing swords and shields because in hand-to-hand fighting, muskets and crossbows took too long to load and fire. In perhaps a little more than one hour of fighting, an estimated 850 Mayas lay dead. The Spaniards suffered some wounds but had only two fatalities.

One footman received an arrow through the vision slot in his helmet, which killed him instantly; a second bled to death from a neck wound. However, on display had been the awesome superiority of European technology, horses, and mastiffs against Indian defenses. The Spaniards suffered more wounds than might otherwise have occurred because thousands of locusts from the cornfield took flight during the battle, and the insects obscured incoming arrows fired by the Mayas that otherwise men might have seen and avoided.

The battle at Potonchán need not have been fought, and to explain why it took place will place most of the blame on Cortés and his men. Conquistadors in many respects were crusaders who found it intolerable that pagans also engaged in human sacrifice and cannibalism. The Chontal Mayas, on the other hand, were proud people who felt no obligation to give food to unwelcome strangers who practiced a religion as alien to them as theirs was to Spaniards. In the future, the Mayas would be far more difficult to defeat than were the Aztecs. The former lacked the Mexica's enormous population, but their decentralized government and the remoteness of Yucatan from Central Mexico made campaigning there significantly more difficult.

After the battle, Maya caciques approached Cortés and asked if they could bury their dead rather than leave them exposed to scavengers—a request readily granted by the captain general. Once burial was finished, the chieftains agreed to talk about conditions for ending hostilities, and during that interval Gerónimo de Aguilar had important information to share with Cortés. He had overheard some Mayas remark that they believed the cannons, which they called *Tepustles* (their word for unfamiliar iron), had acted on their own rather than being fired by Spaniards.

So, as talks began, Cortés set up one of the Lombards and loaded it with extra powder but no ball. Through Aguilar he told the caciques that he would ask the "Great *Tepustle*" to speak if it discerned that the Maya chieftains were sincere in wanting an end to fighting. The cannon had a long fuse, and a Spaniard hidden in a bush ignited it with a flint striker. When the cannon fired, the caciques fell back in terror but soon made a generous offer of gifts in the hope of securing peace. Cortés, however, had one more trick up his sleeve.

One of the mares in estrus was brought to where conversations were taking place. Downwind was tied a stallion that picked up the scent of the mare, and it went into a frenzy of pawing dirt and straining at its tether. Cortés through Aguilar told the Maya chieftains that the stallion doubted their sincerity in wanting peace and was angry with them. But he would speak to the horse and assure it that it was mistaken. Meanwhile, one of his men moved the mare off to the side, and the stallion immediately calmed.

These anecdotes illustrate Cortés as a shrewd and cunning negotiator who had no qualms about exploiting the Indians' unfamiliarity with European animals and technology. The gifts the Indians offered in response would significantly tip the scales in favor of Cortés and Spaniards in the conquest of Mexico. The caciques brought forth twenty young women and presented them to don Hernando and his captains on the condition that they would return to their ships and go away. The men accepted the women and brought them on board the ships. Within a day, the horses had been reloaded, and the eleven ships sailed down the Río Grijalva. Unknown to Cortés was a young woman in the group named Marina, a baptismal name given by fray Bartolomé de Olmedo. She spoke both Nahuatl and Chontal Maya, which would make her a great asset in the campaign that lay ahead. Much more about her unfolds in this chapter and those that follow.

For five days the fleet sailed in good weather toward the goal of reaching San Juan de Ulúa. Cortés was pleased that men who had sailed with Grijalva and knew the coast mentioned familiar landmarks, such as the Río Coatzalcoalcos, the Sierra of San Martín, and where they first had first seen a clear view of snowcapped Mount Orizaba. As they neared San Juan, mariners pointed to the Isla de Sacrificios where they had first encountered evidence of human sacrifice. The entire fleet dropped anchor near the shore where the present-day city of Veracruz is located on Holy Thursday, March 27, 1519.

Prior to going ashore, Cortés notified all ship captains that everyone on their vessels had to be aware of his orders. No one under pain of severe punishment could demand anything whatsoever from a native, nor could they accept a gift without his approval. While he was still issuing orders, a canoe filled with Indians approached his flagship. Their language was completely unintelligible, and don

Hernando ordered that Gerónimo de Aguilar who had sailed with Alonso Hernández Puertocarrero be brought by boat to his ship. But Aguilar was also ignorant of the Indians' tongue. He, however, mentioned that the mistress of don Alonso—one of the twenty native women awarded by caciques at Potonchán knew a language other than Maya.

Cortés ordered the woman brought to his flagship. When she arrived by boat and began chatting with Indians in the canoe as easily as one might speak to a neighbor, Cortés had her brought aboard his flagship. Through Aguilar, don Hernando learned that the woman's baptismal name was Marina, and that the Indians in the boat wished to come aboard his flagship and welcome him and his men to their land. Don Hernando then accepted the Indians' request. Perhaps Cortés knew Grijalva had used double translators on his voyage; in any event, thus began a system of double translation, from Aztec Nahuatl to Maya between Marina and Aguilar and from Maya to Spanish between Aguilar and Cortés. The same conversation link worked in reverse from the expedition's captain general to the Aztecs, as would later happen throughout the conquest.

By way of luck—or as the Spaniards claimed, through divine intervention —the 1519 expedition had had to return to Cozumel shortly after departing because a vessel containing almost of the cassava bread was sinking. That permitted a second opportunity to recruit the translator Aguilar. He and Marina provided Cortés with his team of double translators. As a bonus to Cortés, Marina became his mistress, his confidant, and his companion over the next five years, and they seldom spent a day or night apart. Marina would also give birth to a son by Cortés after the conquest; the mestizo Martín was named after don Hernando's father. Marina herself would become highly respected by Spaniards, who soon gave her the honorific title of Doña Marina. She would become without question the most important woman in the conquest of Mexico, a fact made possible by the tragic experiences of her early life.

She began life with the name Malinali in a small village about twenty-five miles from Coatzacoalcos, which was located near the border of lands occupied by Chontal Mayas. The child's father had been a lord, *tlatoani*, of a region called Painala. He died young, leaving Malinali with her mother who later married another lord. The couple gave birth to a son who took precedence over Malinali, but only if she were removed from the line of succession. The mother decided to sell her daughter when she was eight or nine years old to merchants who took her into Chontal Maya territory, where she became a cacique's house slave. To hide the betrayal of a child, Malinali's mother and her stepfather claimed their daughter had died. They acquired the body of a young slave girl who had died at about the same age as Malinali, placed it in a wooden casket, and buried it while likely feigning their loss. So, for all intents and purposes, Malinali no longer existed.

Malinali, however, remembered her birth tongue and during the twelve years she lived at Potonchán had learned to speak fluent Chontal as well as understand the Yucatecan dialect. Her odyssey brought a remarkable woman to San Juan de Ulúa and into the company of Cortés on Easter Thursday, 1519. During her five-year association with don Hernando, she received another name, Malinche, after the goddess of grass. Because of her close association with Cortés, he at times was likewise was called Malinche. Doña Marina, whose name reminded Spaniards of the sea, demonstrated further linguistic ability by becoming adept as speaking Castilian. At some point in the future, Cortés would dispense with Aguilar and speak directly to her. But she remained the only person on the expedition who could understand Nahuatl, and that gave her unique importance throughout the conquest.

Prior to going ashore at San Juan de Ulúa, Cortés appointed two captains to subordinate positions. Pedro de Alvarado became second in command and captain of the horse guard. Don Pedro would lead the cavalry contingent in future battles, and in the meantime, Cortés appointed round-the-clock guards for the horses throughout the conquest. Francisco de Mesa, who had served in the Spanish army and campaigned in Italy, was made captain of ordnance. At every campsite, Mesa positioned the cannons, the most valuable of which were breech-loading Lombards capable of rapid fire.

Welcomed by two dozen friendly Aztecs who had approached the ships in a canoe, some three-hundred Spaniards came ashore. Most of the rank-and-file men had to sleep on the beach without cover. By contrast, their Aztec hosts assembled huts roofed with fresh-cut fronds to accommodate the captains. Rank had its privileges. Even so, it soon become clear that the narrow beach backed closely by sand dunes was an unacceptable base from which to undertake colonization of the land. Nevertheless, the expeditioners would remain where they landed for several weeks.

The next day was Good Friday, and Cortés ordered some footmen to help carpenters set up an altar for Mass. Others were sent inland to cut wood for campfires. In the afternoon of Good Friday, a large contingent of Indians approached from the north. They spoke a language Marina could not understand. Pointing to themselves, they asked to be called Totonacs. The Indians bore gifts of beans, meat, fish, maize cakes, fowl, and cotton cloth. Don Hernando responded by giving two shirts and two red berets to the chiefs. As evening approached, the Totonacs returned to the north.

On Easter Saturday, an emissary of Moctezuma with a large train of servants approached the Spaniards. They came with enough food for the entire expedition to last several days, as well as a few jewels. Cortés forbade any Spaniard from accepting even a nugget of gold, which no doubt caused grumbling among his men. He did set up a table to supervise officially sanctioned trade, with Aguilar and Marina serving as translators. Trade items offered by the Spaniards included glass beads, hand mirrors, pins, scissors, and needles. In exchange, the Aztecs offered small gold objects.

On Easter Sunday, Moctezuma's steward named Tendile (also spelled Teudile) arrived from the nearby town of Cuetlaxtlan, where he served as governor, to greet Cortés. He came accompanied by many aides decked out in feathers, sandals, and embroidered cloaks. They, likewise, brought gifts of food. Through dual interpreters, Tendile said his great lord Moctezuma had heard of the Spaniards' victory at Potonchán and that he wished to honor them as powerful warriors. Also present was a second gathering of Totonacs who mingled freely with the Mexica, and they also brought gifts. Marina asked one of the high Aztec chieftains about the Totonac language, and according to Bernal Díaz, he haughtily replied that it was a barbarian tongue. That, however, was far from the last example of Aztec arrogance.

In recounting exchanges between Tendile and Cortés, as well as to avoid confusion in names used here and elsewhere, it is important to note that Moctezuma's subjects called themselves *Mexica*, which meant "people of Mexico."

The term "Aztecs"—a term commonly used by outsiders, the use of which has persisted until the present day—referred to the last of seven Nahuatl-speaking tribes who had migrated from a region called Aztlan. "Aztecs" therefore means "people of Aztlan." Aztlan is not a specific place identifiable on any map, but it was a region located some two-hundred miles northwest of present-day Mexico City from which the Mexica first emigrated around the year 1100.

Next, Tendile honored Cortés by performing a ritual that momentarily puzzled don Hernando. He wet a finger in his mouth, touched ground, and "ate dirt." Marina hastened to send a message through Aguilar to Cortés. He had just received the highest compliment a Mexica lord could offer a stranger. It was extremely important that he respond in like manner, which Cortés did. There followed an amazing outpouring of Mexica-inspired welcoming of strangers to their land. Tendile ordered his men to build several hundred huts for the visitors, each with frond-covered roofs to shed rainwater. Two-thousand servants then came forward and placed themselves at Cortés's disposal. Don Hernando correctly assumed that the throng contained spies for Moctezuma, and he became more suspicious when Aztec agents expressed the desire that all Spaniards sleep on the beach instead of on their own ships out of reach.

Since it was Easter Sunday, Cortés ordered his carpenters to erect a large wooden cross, and before it knelt hundreds of Spaniards. That greatly interested Tendile, who asked Marina why such powerful and extraordinary men would demonstrate reverence for two crossed sticks? She, having lived among Spaniards less than a month, was probably equally perplexed. Nonetheless, when Mass ended, Tendile, Cortés, and some of his captains sat down to a meal provided by the Aztecs. Through interpreters, don Hernando lied by stating his King Carlos I had heard of Moctezuma and that he had sent him as an emissary to meet the great native ruler. Tendile replied that Moctezuma was no less great a monarch, and he added that he would consult with his lord regarding Cortés's desire to meet with him. But first Tendile wished to present even more lavish gifts on orders that came from Moctezuma.

The Mexica high steward ordered a large chest brought forward. In it were gold objects and beautifully made cotton cloths. Servants then came bearing more food that included cooked turkey, baked fish, and a variety of fruits. Cortés in return gave out more glass beads, an inlaid armchair, some pearls, and a crimson cape with a gold metal on it. The metal bore an image of St. George slaying a dragon. Tendile accepted the gifts without enthusiasm on behalf of Moctezuma. Bartolomé de las Casas would later comment that Tendile regarded the value of Cortés's gifts as comparable to that of excrement. Recognizing that the high Mexica steward was not impressed with his gifts, Cortés added that he hoped the great Moctezuma would sit in the armchair. To which, Tendile remained silent.

Cortés then employed different tactics to impress Moctezuma's steward. He marched men in military formation to drum and fife. His captain of ordnance Francisco de Mesa fired several salvoes from the Lombard cannons loaded with extra powder but no ball. At first, the noise of their discharge caused Tendile and his high chieftains to fall to the ground in terror. They soon regained their composure and were thrilled at the display of horsemanship that followed. As the tide withdrew it created more space along the beach. That permitted Alvarado as captain of horse guard to arrange chargers in twos and gallop them in formation with small brass bells that adorned their bridles.

As Tendile prepared to depart and report on the Spaniards to Moctezuma, Cortés asked him a fateful question. Did his king have much gold? One can imagine don Hernando's excitement when the high steward replied that yes, he did have much gold. Tendile had one final request. Could the artists he had brought with him sketch on cotton cloth impressions of the strangers so that Moctezuma might know them better? Cortés agreed. Bernal Díaz who seemingly described everything, wrote about what followed. The artists brilliantly sketched the body and face of Cortés and his captains, the horses, the cannon and cannon balls, the ships, the sails, and even two greyhounds that roamed the beach. While observing this, Tendile noticed the helmet of a man in the ranks. It was half gilt but elsewhere somewhat rusty, and he asked Cortés if he could take the helmet and show it to Moctezuma. He said it resembled the headgear of their war god Huitzilopochtli, a powerful deity in the Mexica pantheon. Cortés ordered the man-at-arms to give up the requested item. On receiving it, Tendile stated that when he came back with word on whether Moctezuma would meet with Cortés, he would return the helmet filled with gold. Following that promise,

Tendile placed a secondary steward in charge of several dozen Mexica women who had orders to make maize cakes every day for the strangers. With those matters concluded, Tendile gathered his entourage of caciques and burden bearers and set out for the Mexica's capital named Tenochtitlan.

CHAPTER 6

Aztecs: From Migrants to Masters of Mexico

Tendile reached Tenochtitlan after about seven days' travel. There he shared with Moctezuma and his advisers impressions of the strangers who had come ashore. Along with his oral report were sketches on cloth made by a talented artist who had arrived with him. For the first time, the Aztec emperor saw drawings of ships, previously described as "floating houses," horses, as "giant tame deer," and muskets, as "sticks that belched fire and sounded like thunder." Moctezuma "received the new information . . . with alarm." One source claimed the emperor almost died of fright; another wrote that he was filled "with dread, as if swooning." No one could talk to him—at almost every moment he sighed—and for the first time his soothsayers and closest advisers saw him weep.

Historians long contended that Moctezuma's despair was because he believed the Spaniards were gods, and that this belief played a significant role in determining the outcome of the conquest of Mexico. More recent scholarship has brought that interpretation into question. Not surprisingly, on initial encounters natives did not know what to make of these strange men with their ships, horses, and weapons. However, prolonged contact planted doubt among Indians regarding the divinity of the newcomers. For example, on Cozumel the Mayas seized one of the survivors of the 1511 shipwreck. Thinking him likely immortal, they held his head under water until he drowned but were not sure he was dead until his body began to smell on the second day. On the other hand, the

Aztecs later used the word *Teules* (gods) when referring to Cortés and his men. As a test of their possible divinity, the Aztecs at one point offered don Hernando a cup of blood from a recently sacrificed slave to see if he would drink it. His obvious revulsion did not fit their concept of a god. Also, over time the obvious mortality of Spaniards and their horses again caused the Indians to reassess their first impressions of Spaniards as possibly being white gods.

Spaniards, nevertheless, had other advantages, such as their superior technology and a number of deadly diseases, most notably smallpox, which had spread from Africa to Europe by way of the slave trade. Those external influences along with problems within the Aztec Empire itself figured prominently in determining the outcome of the Spanish conquest. That said, one cannot entirely discount reports of Moctezuma's lingering doubts that Cortés might be the deified Toltec ruler Quetzalcoatl, who had gone into exile but was prophesied to return from the east to reclaim his kingdom. Otherwise, why would the Aztecs have offered Cortés a cup of blood? This uncertainty likely influenced the Emperor's decision-making, and it caused him to vacillate by sending gifts to the coast instead of ordering his warriors to drive the newcomers into the sea or at least back to their ships. Others at Moctezuma's court, especially the Emperor's brother Cuitlahuac, saw the Spaniards as the threat they posed to the Mexica, but the emperor held ultimate authority. Finally, it is important to note that in Cortés's substantial writings, there is not an instance in which he claimed to be a white god to impress the Indians. In any event, in view of his militant commitment to Christianity, he likely would have viewed such an assertion—even if used temporarily to gain an advantage—as sacrilege.

Returning to the Aztec's remarkable rise to power from humble origins, one might assume that they have had little reason to fear six-hundred Spaniards. However, a brief look at their history will serve to provide a better understanding of why they failed to defeat the Spaniards who were so few in numbers. The beginning of an epic migration that eventually made the Aztecs lords and masters of much of Central Mexico started to the west and north of the present-day town and archeological site known as Tula, Hidalgo, located about forty-five miles north of Mexico City. The centuries-long goal of these migrants, the last of whom were the Aztecs, was to move south toward the Central Valley. That geographic feature, however, is not a true valley; in fact, it is an oval basin surrounded by mountains on three sides and high terrain to the north. The landform is roughly seventy miles in length from north to south and forty miles in width from east to west.

When the Aztecs arrived, the basin contained three large lakes at slightly differing elevations and varying degrees of salinity. Lake Texcoco lay in the center and received water from Lake Xaltocan in the north and Lake Xochimilco to the south. As the ultimate destination of all drainage, Lake Texcoco had higher saline-content water from dissolved minerals than its tributaries. For example, Xochimilco was about nine feet higher, and it had the freshest water due to numerous springs that fed its southern shore.

By the middle of the twelfth century, desirable living conditions in the southern end of the basin had prompted the founding of urban centers, including Azcapotzalco, Culhuacan, Chalco, Tacuba, Texcoco, and Xochimilco. These city states had differing degrees of power and influence over the basin, and over time they had claimed almost all arable land along the lakes' shores. That meant latecomers from the north increasingly had no desirable places to settle. Such was the situation that eventually confronted the Aztecs, who began their migration from Aztlan in the year 1111 as the seventh and last tribe to leave. Their initial advantage rested solely on the fact they spoke the same Nahuatl language as the older residents of the basin. They also possessed something far less obvious—an indomitable force of will, by which they transformed themselves in just more than three centuries into the supreme masters of Mexico. [**Figure 8**]

Mythic origins of the Aztecs began on an island called Aztlan in Lake Mezcaltitlan. In their journey to Tula, they divided into seven clans and carried an image of Huitzilopochtli (meaning Hummingbird from the Left or South) concealed within an ark made of reeds. The avatar of this powerful god was so sacred and revered that no one dared look at it, much less touch it. When the migrants reached more favorable locales, they stopped for as long as twenty years, during which they constructed ball courts and temples to house their idol. They also planted such crops as beans, maize, amaranth, and chiles.

On other occasions, the wayfarers moved on before crops reached maturity when commanded to do so by their idol, even at the expense of abandoning elders

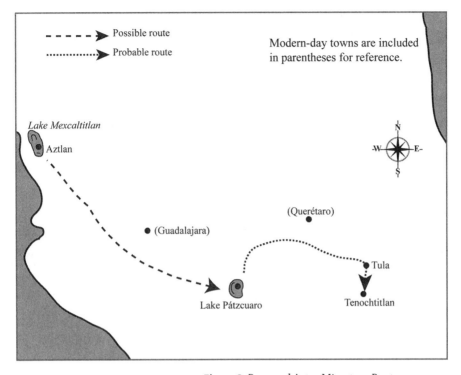

Figure 8. Proposed Aztec Migratory Route.

who could not keep pace. Often going hungry, thirsty, and almost naked, their spirits were lifted by the promise of better days ahead. Those prospects were reinforced in dreams that Huitzilopochtli sent to his priests who shared them with lesser folk. The Mexica, as their god's chosen people, would someday become kings, lords, and rulers of countless vassals. In that bright future, they would enjoy great riches and fine clothing. In the meantime, however, they would have to suffer by practicing agriculture supplemented by hunting and eating deer, rabbits, birds, and snakes.

Since the Aztecs had a priesthood, and used the ritual calendar of pre-Spanish Mexico with its fifty-two-year cycle, practiced agriculture, and spoke Nahuatl, they were never as far from civilized life as the nomadic Chichimecas in the north who dressed in skins and sought shelter in caves. Accordingly, the Aztecs "definitely come within the pale of Middle American civilization, though possibly situated at the farthest extreme of its cultural spectrum."

It took about fifty years for the Aztecs to reach Tula, at one time the main city of the powerful and sophisticated Toltec people. In later years, however, the city had fallen into full decline. At that time, its main inhabitants were unimpressive bands of Otomi and more primitive Chichimecas. The Aztecs stopped at Tula long enough get a sense of it as a once-great center of Toltec culture and they made a few minor improvements around the city. As a result of this they cultivated an imaginary bond with the Toltecs and later presented themselves as heirs to their culture. Equally important, a new personification of Huitzilopochtli sprang forth. The Mexica's avatar of the god Huitzilopochtli was of virgin birth from Coatlicue, the monstrous double snake-headed woman with a belt of severed hands and hearts and a skirt of writhing rattlesnakes that stands inside Mexico City's Museum of Anthropology and History. According to legend, she conceived Huitzilopochtli when she was cleaning a temple and lost a feather duster that wound up in her womb. Henceforth, Huitzilopochtli morphed into a warrior god, and under his influence the Aztecs became increasingly combative. As "masters of violence" they developed an inclination to wage perpetual warfare, and over time came to love the clash of arms so much that the prospect of death became almost meaningless. Later, prior to their quest for dominance in the Central Valley, the Aztecs' willingness to bear arms as mercenary allies would stand them in good stead.

Having enjoyed years of repose at Tula, the Aztecs received a severe tongue lashing from Huitzilopochtli, their divine guardian and tutelary numen, or supernatural presence. How dare they enjoy peace and comfort, thereby forsaking their martial mission? They must leave Tula and depart on the next leg of their journey to greatness. Through his priests, Huitzilopochtli delivered a message. "I will serve as your guide; I will show you the way." Lake Texcoco would be their final stop. The exact year of their arrival is unknown, but it was likely around 1250.

From the moment of their arrival at the lakes, the older basin residents regarded the Aztecs as unwelcome squatters. The newcomers were expelled from one temporary settlement after another over several decades until they arrived at Chapultepec, the famed "Grasshopper Hill," around the end of the 1200s. Chapultepec, however, provided nothing more than another brief respite, because the more powerful people of Azcapotzalco claimed the site and forced them to move yet again. They next sought temporary refuge on the south shore of Lake Texcoco, which was claimed by Culhuacan. Desperate, the Aztecs, then only several hundred in numbers, begged the local king, Coxcotli, to assign them a permanent residence, and he agreed to do so. Their new locale was Tizapan, a barren and rocky region to the south of present-day Mexico City that was filled with poisonous vipers. Coxcotli viewed the Aztecs as undesirable neighbors and hoped they would starve on Tizapan or be killed by snakes, but quite the opposite happened. "Instead of dying from the bites of vipers, the Mexica killed them and transformed them into their sustenance."

The Aztecs, in addition to their penchant for waging war, were like their contemporaries in fourteenth-century Europe in another respect. They saw the advantage of making strategic marriages with the daughters of their more powerful and settled neighbors. With that goal in mind, the Mexica began to shed their image as semi-barbarian nomads and establish ties with the people of Culhuacan, who claimed descent from the ancient Toltecs. Thus, they lived and plotted for twenty-five years, during which they strengthened their ties with the Culhuas by serving as valued mercenaries in a war with Xochimilco.

About 1325, and at the behest of Huitzilopochtli's numen, the Aztecs nearly made a fatal mistake. They asked the king of Culhuacan to give them his virgin daughter so that they might pay her a "special honor" by making her a goddess. To the eternal regret of King Achitometl, he agreed. Unknown to him, the Mexica immediately sacrificed and flayed his daughter to honor Xipe Totec, a major deity worshipped by many native cultures in Mexico They then invited the Culhua monarch into a darkened temple filled with incense. When his eyes adjusted to the darkness and smoke had cleared, he saw a Mexica priest dancing in his daughter's skin.

Achitometl "howled for his warriors to avenge the deadly insult." They pursued the bewildered Aztecs who thought they had bestowed a great honor on the young virgin, and forced their men, women, and children into the waters of Lake Texcoco. The displaced Mexica eventually found refuge on one of several "squashy little islands" named Zoquitlan, which has been translated from Nahuatl as "Mudville." Because Zoquitlan was regarded as a "no man's island" that bordered territories claimed by Azcapotzalco, Texcoco, and Culhuacan, none of the three powerful city states asserted sovereignty over it. To do so might start a war over a seemingly worthless and swampy island. That would later prove a serious mistake, especially for Azcapotzalco. Tepanecs of that city were a sister culture of the Aztecs who also spoke Nahuatl.

Having thus obtained land of their own where they might reside undisturbed, the Aztecs saw the fulfillment of a prophecy made by Huitzilopochtli, reflected today on Mexico's flag and currency. The fierce war god told his followers they would know the end of their long migration from Aztlan had arrived when they observed an eagle with a snake in its beak while perched on a nopal cactus. They viewed that omen on Zoquitlan and knew they had found a permanent home. Soon after, the Mexica began construction in 1345 on what would become their great capital on the renamed island of México-Tenochtitlan.

Around 1372, the Aztecs decided to choose a leader with ties to an external dynasty that would lend greater prestige to their island home. Over time, their relations with Culhuacan had improved remarkably—there being of course ample room for betterment. Since the Culhuas were heirs of the Toltecs—whom the Aztecs wished to emulate—the selection of a Mexica nobleman married to a noblewoman of that city state as their ruler had much to recommend it. Thus, the Mexica nobleman Acamapichtli became the first Aztec monarch and, following his marriage to the Culhua princess Ilancueitl, began a dynasty. [**Figure 9**]

The young couple and the Mexica soon faced a crisis with the powerful Tepanecs of Azcapotzalco. Their king, Tezozomoc, made a questionable claim to México-Tenochtitlan, primarily because he had the strength to do so, and because he wished to squelch any increase in power for the Aztecs under their new king. The Tepanec leader demanded tribute obligations from the Aztecs in such excruciating detail it seemed impossible to meet them. For example, not only were the Mexica to supply ears of corn, beans, tomatoes, chiles, and wild amaranth, they also had to bring a heron and duck. Both fowl had to be sitting on eggs, and at the precise moment of their delivery have chicks starting to peck out of their shells. That, however, proved not a problem, because Huitzilopochtli's numen was equal to the task.

Aztec submission to the tribute demands of Tezozomoc continued during his long reign but no longer involved miraculously timed hatchlings, and payments were extended to Acamapichtl's successors, Huitzilihuital and Chimalpopoca. Despite their galling subservience to the Tepanecs, the Aztecs continued to build their capital with calculated slowness. They realized that if their city manifested too-rapid growth, it would alarm a more powerful enemy. In that event, they knew full well the outcome of an all-out attack by Tepanec warriors: certain defeat, destruction of their capital, and the enslavement of all surviving Mexica.

Early on, the Aztecs built small, elongated mounds of dirt in the shallows of Lake Texcoco, located inward from its southern shore, which as mentioned received fresh water from numerous springs. The Mexica used these *chinampas*, already known to older residents of the basin for agricultural purposes. Such human-created plots of land were enormously labor intensive, and the slow pace in which they were constructed failed at first to alert the watchful Tepanecs. *Chinampas* began with the cutting and weaving of mud-soaked reeds that poked through the surface of lake waters. The plants were woven together to form crude rafts of vegetation. Those were maneuvered into intended locations, secured in place by wooden stakes, and then covered with mud brought in by canoes or silt scooped up from the lake bottom. Green vegetables, ear corn, and amaranth seeds were sowed in rich, saturated soil elevated a few inches above lake level. This form of cropping required no irrigation, and barring floods—unfortunately, a recurring hazard in the basin—or drought that dried the lake, the people of México-Tenochtitlan had a dependable food supply, often from two harvests in a year. This was important because the Aztec capital would later support a very large population.

Chinampas, erroneously called "floating gardens" in present-day Xochimilco, were small fields of plants that lay nearby the expanding Mexica city. Sluggish canals separated these "islands," which permitted the tending and weeding of vegetation by Aztecs in poled canoes. The waters in Lake Texcoco were too saline to be potable, and their constant disturbance in tending crops made them too turbid for other domestic use. Consequently, freshwater from a few wells in the city had to be supplemented by transporting it in earthen jars by canoes from Chapultepec to the capital, where it was dispensed at the public market.

Any interruption of this supply of water would place the Aztecs in dire straits. Springs at Chapultepec poured forth thousands of gallons of water each day, but that source belonged to Tepanecs in Azcapotzalco. That circumstance alone does much to explain the Mexica's near-total subservience to their hated Tepanec masters. It was a stranglehold that had to be broken if the Aztecs were to achieve the greatness promised by Huitzilopochtli. The Aztecs were eventually given an opportunity to do that when aged Tezozomoc entered the last years of his rule as *tlatoani* of Azcapotzalco. The Tepanec king lost focus and became less demanding of tribute. His death, however, in 1426 "completely changed all this." The aged ruler's militant son Maxlatzin became the new king of Azcapotzalco, and he had long despised the Aztecs as crude barbarians who had begun under-paying tribute. To demonstrate his awesome power, Maxlatzin hired assassins who murdered the reigning Mexica emperor, Chimalpopoca, in his own city of Tenochtitlan. Stunned and frightened, the Mexica then elected their fourth emperor named Itzcoatl, the son of Acamapichtli. [*See* **Figure 9**]

Itzcoatl, *tlatoani* of Tenochtitlan, received conflicting advice from his most trusted advisers. Should he humble himself before the great Maxlatzin? Or were the Aztecs finally strong enough to wage a war with the Tepanecs, which would liberate them as tribute-paying vassals and in doing so obtain a dependable source of water for their city? As debate continued, Tlacaelel Cihuacoatl ("Snake Woman"), destined to become the most influential Mexica leader in the fifteenth century, entered the discussion. The nephew of Izcoatl, Tlacaelel was twenty-nine years of age and full of fight; he advised war with the Tepanecs and his words eventually carried the day. Finding a willing ally in the equally persecuted and tribute-paying people of Texcoco, the Aztecs launched the first of continuing wars with the Tepanecs in 1427. The date is important because it also marked the year the Mexica became an imperial power.

The battles that followed were fierce and bloody. Situated on the western shore of Lake Texcoco, Azcapotzalco sent invading Tepanec warriors wading through shallows toward Tenochtitlan. Aztec legend has described the ensuing battle as a clash between Huitzilopochtli's numen and Coltic, the Tepanec's humpbacked divine master of war. Others more recently have called the ensuing battle "an Aztec Armageddon." The Mexica fought as they had never fought before. Their dead and wounded sank into the muddy waters of Lake Texcoco, but in the end warriors of Huitzilopochtli forced Coltic and his minions to retreat.

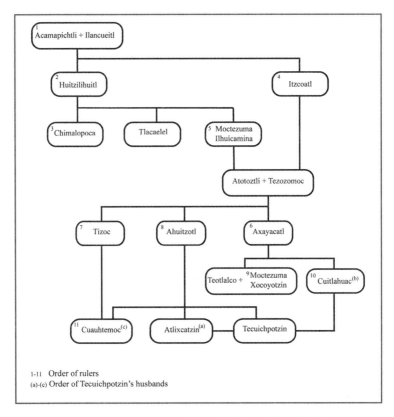

Figure 9. Rulers of Tenochtitlan.

The Mexica followed victory by launching an all-out siege of Azcapotzalco, one of the great urban centers of the basin, which Tezozomoc had made into an imperial city. For the next four months, the Aztecs and their Texcocan allies fought desperate battles with the Tepanecs. When the city fell, the allied forces led by Tlacaelel had triumphed. Emperor Izcoatl then took command, and he ordered his warriors "to devastate the city, burn the houses, and spare neither young nor old, men and women." However, adolescents and children were spared death but enslaved and put to hard labor, an early example of Indian-to-Indian slavery.

Tacuba (also called Tlacopan), which had remained neutral throughout this first phase of war with the Tepanecs, became the most important city on the western shore of Lake Texcoco. Tacuba, like Texcoco, became a valued ally of the Aztecs; and following the destruction of Azcapotzalco, the three city states of Tenochtitlan, Texcoco, and Tacuba formed a triple alliance in 1428 that would last just short of a century.

The new-formed Triple Alliance pursued a continuation of war with the Tepanecs, some of whom had fled their city before it fell. Under the leadership of Maxtlatzin, renewed conflict lasted for five years into the 1430s. In the end, the fate of Maxtlatzin remains uncertain. In one account, he escaped the final battle of the Tepanec wars; in another, he was clubbed in the head and his heart torn out. What is certain is the emergence of three Aztec leaders with important titles of office who directed the imperial Aztecs in the years that followed the Tepanec wars—one of them, Tlacaelel, Lord of the House of Darts, lived for five more decades. The other Mexica leaders with shorter lives were Itzcoatl, emperor of the Aztecs, and Moctezuma Ilhuicamina, general of the Aztecs' armies.

The end of the Tepanec wars resulted in the Aztecs controlling most of the shoreline of Lake Texcoco. The Mexica had gained access to the freshwater springs located on Chapultepec heights, and the end of war brought hundreds if not thousands of Tepanec slaves under Aztec control. This forced labor was put to work in linking the Aztec capital to surrounding shores by building elevated causeways. Their construction required moving by hand thousands of tons of rock and dirt, which served as fill. Corridors eventually connected Tenochtitlan with shorelines to the south, west, and north of the city. All elevated walkways had gaps in them spanned by removable wooden bridges. They permitted canoe traffic to circle the lakes, and bridge movability gave security to Tenochtitlan should it be attacked by outside land forces. However, given where Aztec imperial expansion was headed over the next ninety years, the prospect of a native power greater than that of the Triple Alliance was highly unlikely.

Peace by the early 1430s, in the aftermath of the five-year Tepanec war, permitted Tlacaelel to enact a series of reforms. The "Snake Woman" decided that Huitzilopochtli needed a great temple built in his honor. He had served the Mexica well in identifying where they should build their capital, and he was especially needed as they undertook expansion of their empire. Huitzilopochtli was probably the most important deity in the Aztec pantheon, although it later contained a collection of gods who would compete with him. The Hummingbird from the

Left, however, had morphed into varied personae—he was "a sorcerer, an omen of evil, a madman, a deceiver, a creator of war, a war-lord, [and] an instigator of war."

Almost half of Huitzilopochtli's descriptive names relate to war. With his guidance and under Tlacaelel's command of warriors, the Aztecs conquered the people of Xochimilco, Cuitlahuac, and Chalco, all located along and within Lake Xochimilco. Once completed, the Mexica seized and burned their illustrated manuscripts (codices), which contained their history. Tlacaelel next burned similar codices that even recorded the history of the Mexica. Their "new history" was reformulated in such manner as to deny the Mexica's seminomadic origins. Next came the fictitious assertion that the Aztecs had always been descendants of the Toltecs.

Tlacaelel's aims are perhaps apparent. Indians in the defeated city states would be easier to dominate if they had no proof of their origins; and, at same time, Tlacaelel wanted to elevate Huitzilopochtli and his mother, Coatlicue, to the status of creator deities of the Toltecs. Reimagined as deities of Tula, they were portrayed as the "wellspring of high culture, political organization, and refined arts." An impression was thus created of the Aztecs as a Mesoamerican "vision in time." That notion intensified throughout the remainder of the fifteenth century and reached its apex under Moctezuma Xocoyotzin (the Younger) in the early sixteenth century. Here, another observation needs mention. If history has no value, as some have claimed, why have totalitarian regimes insisted on changing it to cast themselves in a better light? Often at the same time, they have carried out the destruction of all sources that contradicted that contrived image.

Tlacaelel also relied on ancient Nahua beliefs to give still another important role to Huitzilopochtli. According to Aztec cosmogony, the world had gone through four cycles, each ending in cataclysm. The then-present era, or fifth cycle, was the new "Sun" of movement. It, too, was likely to end in calamity just as had the Suns of Earth, Wind, Fire, and Water. Huitzilopochtli was the Sun, and since the great orb had to travel across the sky each day, it must have energy that came from "the precious liquid" (blood) that keeps humans alive. Accordingly, if Huitzilopochtli received a continuing supply of blood from sacrificial offerings, the Mexica world in the "Fifth Sun" would never end. So how could the Mexica ensure enough blood to satisfy their god of war and the sun?

The obvious answer was to launch successful wars of conquest in central and southern Mexico. Young men in those locales would then be marched into Tenochtitlan and sacrificed atop the great pyramid. Above all, a dependable source of human hearts and blood had to be found. This necessity went hand-in-glove with Aztec imperialism. But another consideration is the Aztecs' belief that certain people's blood was not an appropriate offering to Huitzilopochtli. Quality folk and their blood had to come from certain city states containing Nahuatl-speaking victims, assuredly not from the barbaric Chichimecas in the north.

The first emperor in the new surge of Mexica imperialism was Izcoatl's successor and the first monarch to take the name Moctezuma. He relied on his brother and principal adviser Tlacaelel, who thought it important that the *tlatoani* have his house and court in order. Joining him were a host of appointees—agents, stewards, headwaiters, doormen, and pages. Also needed were treasury agents responsible for keeping track of tribute paid by subject people. Other bureaucrats included a multitude of religious ministers, in such profusion that there was one for every five commoners. In short, some of the trappings of a modern state were put in place. Tlacaelel also insisted on enlarging the great pyramid in Tenochtitlan to honor Huitzilopochtli and other Mexica deities. Moctezuma Ilhuicamina therefore undertook conquests of nearby dominions, and later those more distant. Sacrifices also increased commensurate with the expanding scale of the Great Temple (*Templo Mayor*).

The logistics of acquiring increased numbers of sacrificial victims and marching them into Tenochtitlan proved troublesome. Accordingly, the resurgence of flower wars (*xochiyaotl*) became commonplace after the death of Izcoatl in 1440. The *Guerra Florida* took place between the Aztecs and specified opponents, among whom were inhabitants of Tlaxcala, Huejotzingo, and Cholula. These engagements resembled a tournament in that they took place at arranged times and on specified grounds. Contrived combat between forces roughly equal in size was conducted on a "give-and-take" basis. In short, the Mexica recognized they would lose warriors, who would be sacrificed on the altars of their opponents, while they themselves would obtain an acceptable number of offerings. Rank and file combatants, however, were not told the purpose of the flower wars. In effect, they represented unknowing victims of perpetual Orwellian wars of religion.

Following the first ten years of Moctezuma Ilhuicamina's reign as emperor, a disaster of biblical proportions began in the first years of the 1450s. Four years of famine due to increased salinity of Lake Texcoco that stunted the growth of plants, presaged by a plague of locusts in 1446 and a devastating flood in 1449, prompted Moctezuma to seek the help of Nezahualcoyotl (Hungry Coyote), his old ally in Texcoco during the Tepanec wars. Under of the direction of the Tezcocan sage, workers constructed a bulwark against future inundations. A dike, which served to separate fresher water from Lake Xochimilco from the more saline water in Lake Texcoco stretched for 5.4 miles. Ironically, its completion was followed by drought and the crop-killing frosts that occasionally frequented México-Tenochtitlan's roughly mile-and-a-half elevation.

Once Nezahualcoyotl finished dike construction, he turned his attention to supplying potable water to Tenochtitlan. Under his direction, two parallel aqueducts of wood and stone ran three miles from Chapultepec's underground springs into the Aztec capital. Each aqueduct, elevated so as not to interfere with boat and canoe traffic on the lake, was about six feet wide. This arrangement permitted the use of one flume while the other was cleaned and repaired. For the first time, Tenochtitlan had an uninterrupted supply of that other precious liquid, fresh water.

During the great famine that spanned the years 1450–1454, Aztec conquests of outlying areas were largely placed on hold, while flower wars provided blood sacrifices to the gods. Those continued, but over the next fourteen years of Moctezuma Ilhuicamina's reign, Aztec conquests extended into the Gulf Coast north of San Juan de Ulúa, into the present-day states of Puebla and Tlaxcala, as well as into Oaxaca in the south. When this first Moctezuma died in 1468, the Aztecs had conquered areas previously controlled by Totonacs in the north and Mixtecs in the south.

Counting 1468, it was fifty-two years on the Aztec calendar before Spaniards would land at San Juan de Ulúa. A fifty-two-year span of time was the equivalent of a Mexica century, arrived at by meshing gears on two disks that rotated in sequence. One contained 365 teeth (the solar calendar); and the other, 260 notches (the ritual calendar). A selected day on the first coincided precisely with a specific day on the second only once in fifty-two years. This cycle (called a bundle of years) then repeated. Years of the solar calendar were divided into four groupings named Rabbit, Reed, Flint, and House, and each year was preceded by numbers one through thirteen. Accordingly, each of the fifty-two years had a designation like 3 Rabbit, or 12 House. In any event, 1519 may have coincided with 1 Reed on the Aztec calendar, believed by some soothsayers to be when Quetzalcoatl might return.

Following the death of Moctezuma Ilhuicamina, the title of *tlatoani* was perhaps offered to Tlacaelel. If so, he declined the honor, remarking that "after all, the previous kings did nothing without my opinion and counsel, on all matters, civil or criminal. . . . So, do not worry, because I will point out to you who shall be your king and lord." His choice as Emperor was Axayacatl, Itzcoatl's grandson. In 1469, the year of Axayacatl's accession, a son of the new king named Xocoyotzin was about two years of age.

Four years into Axayacatl's reign in 1473, violence erupted between Tenochtitlan and Tlatelolco. The latter was a large urban district located north of Tenochtitlan. The Tlatelolcos were also Mexica, as well as kinsmen of the Mexica, and they had traditionally been regarded as subjects of the rulers of Tenochtitlan. Trouble began in the Tlatelolco market. Sons of prominent men in Tenochtitlan began flirting and joking with daughters of Tlatelolco lords. The male youths asked the young virgins to accompany them at least partway toward their homes in Tenochtitlan. En route the maidens were set upon and violated. The young virgins' male relatives in Tlatelolco vowed revenge, and matters escalated into more heated exchanges over several days, followed by violence.

The initial clash of arms reaped lives on both sides, but the Tenochas had the upper hand in numbers and weaponry. Inspired by a fiery speech delivered by Tlacaelel, the Tenochas prepared an all-out invasion of Tlatelolco. The old warrior who had won so many battles urged on his men with these words: "the enemy lies right behind our houses. You will not have to climb mountains or go down cliffs." He added that victory would amount to little more than shooing flies off their bodies. The lords of Tlatelolco were equally militant and overconfident, declaring that Tenochtitlan "will become the dung and place of excrement for Tlatelolcos."

The decisive battle did no go well for the Tlatelolcos. As the fight with Tenochas turned against them, their warriors fled. The lords of Tlatelolco then resorted to desperate measures. They ordered their women to disrobe and offer themselves to Tenocha attackers. Some of the women slapped their stomachs in suggestive manner, others squirted milk from their breasts—all to no avail. They were cast aside, and the lords of Tlatelolco died fighting atop a pyramid dedicated to Huitzilopochtli. Thereafter, Tlatelolco was a large and important district essentially under the control of Tenochtitlan.

Perhaps thinking their forces invincible, Axayacatl and Tlacaelel next ventured an ill-advised invasion of the powerful Tarascan kingdom to the west and northwest of Tenochtitlan. The Tarascans (known today as Purépechas) were armed with copper weapons, and they convincingly defeated the Aztecs—their only loss in warfare with other native forces. That, however, turned out to be little more than a bump in the road of Mexica imperialism. Tlacaelel appears to have died in the late 1470s, although his death did not spell the end of Aztec expansion. In fact, it escalated along with human sacrifice, which after a brief hiatus would reach an unprecedented scale. After the death of Axayacatl in 1481, the Aztecs chose Tizoc as their king, but he was of a different mettle than his predecessors. The new emperor showed little taste for warfare, despite warnings from his advisors that Huitzilopochtli would be unhappy with him. It seems his court, worried by Tizoc's lack of interest in enlarging the Mexica Empire, hastened his death by placing something poisonous in his food. He died in 1486, still a young man.

What Tizoc lacked in martial spirit was more than compensated for by his successor. Ahuitzotl was the last of three brothers who succeeded Izcoatl. He ordered the largest expansion ever of the great pyramid in Tenochtitlan. While construction was underway, the new emperor launched conquests to obtain an acceptable number of sacrificial victims appropriate to celebrating completion of the Great Temple. Aztec warriors were sent to the "far corners of Mesoamerica" to conquer lands as distant as the Isthmus of Tehuantepec and Guatemala. There followed long marches for captives who would surrender their hearts and blood atop the great pyramid, which towered more than a hundred feet above its base.

Intended victims ascended steps to the apex of the pyramid where they were handed over to four Aztec priests. Each of them seized a limb and flopped the unfortunate on his back over a large convex stone, the *techcatl*. With pressure on the limbs, the taut belly of the victim was thrust upward. A fifth priest plunged a sharp flint knife just below the left rib cage, reached in, and ripped out the heart. It was held skyward to honor the war-and-sun god and then thrown into a receptacle and burned. "The body, spilling blood, was then flung off the stone and went tumbling and bumping down the step side [of the pyramid] onto a flat area near the base called . . . 'the blood mat.'" This ritual slaughter continued for four days. With machine-like efficiency, Aztec priests dispatched an undetermined number of victims—with estimates ranging into tens of thousands.

It should be noted that the Aztecs did not invent human sacrifice, even within Mesoamerican culture. What set them apart was the scale and "inflationary process" of their sacrificing of victims. If at one time ten sacrifices seemed an acceptable offering to satisfy a god, it was not long before that number reached a thousand. This in part may be explained by the Aztecs controlling such a densely populated empire. A corollary premise—that such horrific public sacrifices served to terrorize subject people into subservience—does not stand up well to analysis since other cultures in Mesoamerica did not treat their prisoners any better. Furthermore, the lords of outlying communities did not themselves have to face becoming "altar fodder" in Tenochtitlan.

A "highly contentious theory" that the Aztecs practiced human sacrifice and cannibalism because they lacked animal protein in their diet, has been advanced by anthropologist Marvin Harris. Since consumption of human flesh was an exclusive privilege of nobles, cannibalism hardly aided the dietary needs of commoners. Furthermore, only the arms and legs of sacrificial victims were consumed—a clear indication that flesh consumption involved more than using humans as "livestock." In short, Aztec human "sacrifice, inseparable from religion, involved the killing of *certain* people on *certain* occasions and was in no sense an act of mass gourmandism."

Perhaps the most plausible explanation for large-scale human sacrifice is offered by Nigel Davies. He and other scholars have questioned Huitzilopochtli's position in the Aztec pantheon—important without doubt; but preeminent, questionable. It is also important to note that Tlaloc, the rain god, had a separate altar from Huitzilopochtli's atop the Great Temple. Increasingly, Huitzilopochtli was challenged for divine supremacy by Tezcatlipoca and Quetzalcoatl. Those powerful deities and lesser-known ones in a "very crowded pantheon" attracted cults of followers. They soon developed "a mania for religious ceremony that knew no bounds, a process generated less by piety than a compulsive will to power." The elite cults of gods other than those worshipping Huitzilopochtli also demanded ritual and ceremony to differentiate themselves from other cultists, "which thus tended to become an obsession."

The late French historian Robert Ricard offered an interesting insight on problems that arose when multiple gods represented forces of nature that were observable in the daily lives of people. For example, the earthquake god could flatten a mountain protected by its respective god; or the god of fire could burn a forest that was allegedly protected by its own deity. Humans in a rational world are aware that they must die at some point and face enough fears without multiple gods seemingly being at odds with each other. The trend over time, as posited by Ricard, was for the number of gods to diminish as polytheism gave way to monotheism. In doing so, the eventual one supreme God is removed from responsibility for earthy occurrences by convincing the faithful that they can never know His will with certainty but nevertheless believe in His supreme and awesome power.

Aztec elites, like many who occupy privileged positions, placed value on such goods as jade and beautiful quetzal feathers. These became even more desirable and exotic if they came from distant lands. Accordingly, the military arm of the Mexica was the key to acquiring such status symbols; and as a bonus, warriors brought back sacrificial victims well beyond those acquired in the flower wars. In gratitude, sacrificial offerings began to honor an even greater number of gods. This expansion of human sacrifice served to anger increasing numbers of subject people, and in doing so sowed seeds of anger among the subject Indian nations. That enmity was observed and cultivated by Hernando Cortés, but it lay nearly a score of years in the future.

The eighth Aztec king, Ahuitzotl (1468–1502), died at a relatively young age, and several scholars have attributed his death to an accident that befell him in 1500. His signature engineering project was to supplement Tenochtitlan's source of fresh water by constructing a second aqueduct that linked Coyoacan to Tenochtitlan. A holding-dam in Coyoacan burst and released such a torrent of water that hundreds drowned in the capital. Panicked by fear of drowning, Ahuitzotl failed to duck beneath a low stone lintel as he fled his palace. He lingered for two years before dying of concussed brain injuries. However, usually reliable fray Diego Durán offered perhaps a more plausible explanation for the emperor's death. The Dominican chronicler wrote that Ahuitzotl died of a malady contracted during his last military campaign: "it was a strange and terrible illness [,] and the doctors could not understand it. . . . With the disease he withered up, began to lose his vigor, and before he died was reduced to skin and bones."

The ninth Mexica emperor was about thirty-four years of age in 1502 and took the name Moctezuma Xocoyotzin (the Younger) to distinguish him from his great grandfather Moctezuma Ilhuicamina. In his first years as *tlatoani*, the new Mexica king engaged in almost constant warfare, during which he led Mexica armies in person. He extended Aztec banners into the then-furthest regions of the Gulf of Mexico and as far south as Nicaragua and Honduras. These expeditions, which were generally successful, expanded the limits of Mexica control more widely than at any previous time.

Later in his reign, Moctezuma became more profoundly religious, given to meditation, hampered by indecision, and inclined to believe nothing happened by chance. He increasingly placed stock in omens and often relied on soothsayers. There was also a legend, perhaps given some credence by the new emperor, that the rightful ruler of the Toltecs was Quetzalcoatl who would return from the east in the year 1 Reed, which again may have coincided with the year 1519. Be that as it may, Moctezuma also relied on his brother Cuitlahuac and his nephew Cuauhtemoc, both of whom regarded "Cortés and his band of conquistadors as a group of criminals."

Moctezuma also began to shed pretensions of modesty and took steps to put his stamp on internal affairs. He dismissed the bureaucrats who had served Ahuitzotl and replaced them with officials of his choosing. He did so because those appointed by his uncle "were of low rank or children of commoners." Those officials were regarded as unworthy to serve a high-ranking emperor like himself. The new appointees were sons of the highest nobility in Tenochtitlan, Texcoco, and Tacuba, and all were products of the elite center of learning (*calmecac*). Such nobles were further educated in the precepts of their new mentor, Moctezuma Xocoyotzin; and such mid-level nobility became known as *pipiltin*.

Near the mid-point in his reign, Moctezuma demonstrated an astonishing arrogance and viciousness. His non-titled Mexica subjects had to address him while lying prone. Fray Diego Durán, the Dominican priest and renowned scholar of post-conquest Mexico, asked a contemporary of Moctezuma to describe what the emperor looked like. He replied, "Father, I shall not lie to you about things I do not know. I never saw his face." The informant explained that he dared not lay eyes on the emperor because "he would have been killed in the same way others who looked on him were slain." A few rare instances came to define Moctezuma's extreme cruelty. The Mexica had some of the most brilliant artists in Mesoamerica, and the emperor would occasionally commission one of them to do a painting. If he thought the work exceptional, he would order the artist blinded so that he could not duplicate his genius in the service of someone else.

It seems Moctezuma had not entered formal matrimony prior to becoming the ninth *tlatoani* of the Mexica in 1502. Soon thereafter, he married Ecatepec princess Teotlalco, who became his principal wife. Aztec emperors had unlimited choices in concubines and secondary wives, but a special ceremony determined a marriage that produced legitimate offspring—meaning by Mexica standards an heir of a *tlatoani* worthy of succeeding him. That unique marriage, called "the tying and untying of a blanket," was so named because it took place just prior to consummation. Following that, the couple remained secluded for three days during which only a serving woman was admitted to their presence. Moctezuma's children from this marital rite included three sons and a daughter. The sons all suffered varying misfortune and were dead by 1520. One was declared insane and soon died; another, rendered paraplegic by a disastrous fall, did not live long after the accident; and the third, Chimalpopoca, would be accidentally killed by Mexica while attempting to rescue him from the hands of conquistadors. A daughter born around 1509, and named Tecuichpotzin (little royal maiden), was later viewed by Spaniards as Moctezuma's only legitimate heir. Other children of Moctezuma, born to secondary wives, became important in the 1520s and some of their descendants held privileged status for centuries beyond that decade.

During Moctezuma's eighteen-year reign as emperor, Tenochtitlan continued to increase in size and population. Three narrow causeways linked the city to surrounding shorelines—again to the north, west, and south. The southern elevated walkway was longest at just more than six miles in length and served to link the capital with Ixtapalapa. In the final mile from Tenochtitlan, that causeway doubled in width and presented a grand entrance to the city. The major buildings of the capital were constructed of stone, and palaces of former Emperors were large enough to accommodate several hundred people. All buildings, large and small, had flat roofs. The highest structure in Tenochtitlan was the often expanded Great Temple. For public amenities, Tenochtitlan had a zoo that featured exotic animals and birds from as far away as Central America. An enormous Tlatelolco market with all manner of food and necessities for life in the city would later impress Spaniards. The Mexica economy operated almost totally through a barter system. The only monetary units were much-prized cacao beans that were used to round out inequities in the perceived value of exchanged items.

Estimates of the population of Tenochtitlan in 1519 have ranged from one-hundred-thousand upward, and it seems likely that Tenochtitlan was one of the larger cities in the world at that time. In early April on the Aztec calendar, Moctezuma met there with his advisers to decide what to do about several hundred Spaniards who had arrived in eleven ships. After their decision, Tendile would return to San Juan de Ulúa and deliver it, along with a large amount of treasure, to Hernando Cortés and his captains.

CHAPTER 7

Cortés and the March Toward Tenochtitlan

A mong those Moctezuma questioned on how best to deal with strangers on the coast was his steward Tendile, the only one in the group who had seen the newcomers. He was also the emperor's governor of Cuetlaxtlan, a town located a short distance inland from San Juan de Ulúa. In responding to the emperor, Tendile said that he did not think the strangers were gods. He had seen them sweat, urinate, and defecate like ordinary men. His comments supported what Moctezuma had heard from Mayas after the battle of Potonchán. Two conquistadors had been killed there, so they were not immortal. That assessment of the Spaniards was echoed by the emperor's brother, Cuitlahuac, who counseled attacking the unwelcome visitors, killing all of them if possible, or at a minimum driving them back to the "floating houses" that had brought them to a shore claimed by the Mexica.

Moctezuma nonetheless demurred and suggested that if he sent lavish gifts to these strange and powerful men, they would be satisfied and go away. His failure to comprehend the Spaniards' unquenchable thirst for gold is understandable. The Mexica admired gold for its beauty and malleable qualities, but they did not equate the metal with wealth. The emperor was also perplexed by Cortés's insistence that he had come in peace as emissary of a great king who wanted only to send greetings to him as another powerful monarch in a distant land. If what the great captain said about himself and his men were true about their purpose in coming to Mexico, it would be cowardly to attack men who had come as ambassadors.

Again, Moctezuma had become more intensely religious during the latter part of his reign, and he worried that the strangers might have been sent by the gods Quetzalcoatl and Texcatlipoca. If so, those deities' emissaries must be honored with lavish gifts. He ordered woven baskets presented to the newcomers that contained such items as jewels set in gold, beautiful quetzal feathers, obsidian, turquoise, and golden images of ducks, jaguars, deer, and monkeys. Other gifts included cloaks, shields, masks, earrings, breastplates, and diadems. The Emperor followed by giving orders to one of his emissaries with the formidable name of Teoctlamacazqui: "Go, do not delay. Make reverence to our lord." When the official met Cortés on the coast, he asked if any Spaniards had an unusual appearance and might possibly look like a god (*Teule*) of the Mexica. Don Hernando asked Pedro de Alvarado with his unusual reddish blond hair to join them. The high Mexica official was pleased and called don Pedro Tonatiuh, "child of the sun" in Nahuatl—a nickname he retained throughout the conquest.

The Mexica emissary created excitement with the lavish gifts his burden bearers presented to Cortés. Among them was the helmet which Tendile had previously acquired from one of don Hernando's men-at-arms. The returned headgear contained gold dust and nuggets valued at several hundred gold pesos. It led the Spaniards to speculate that somewhere in the interior of this new land the Mexica operated gold mines, but it was a vain hope. Indians in Mexico did not work pit mines, nor did they pan for gold. All such metal in the possession of Aztecs had come from trade or been found as nuggets lying on the ground or along stream beds.

In the entourage of the emperor's emissary was an Indian who looked remarkably like Cortés. From the sketch of don Hernando made on cloth by a Mexica artist and presented to Moctezuma, he had ordered his attendants to find someone who looked like the strangers' great captain. Bernal Díaz wrote that the Indian's likeness to don Hernando was so remarkable that it prompted the men-in-ranks to make japes about "their Cortés," and "our Cortés." It was welcome fun for Spaniards stuck on a narrow beach. If one can sympathize with conquistadors, they had been assailed by sand fleas and mosquitoes that made their lives miserable both day and night. Particularly annoying were offshore winds that picked up sand that contaminated food, adding to the conquistadors' discomfort.

After accepting the lavish gifts sent by Moctezuma, Cortés attempted a stratagem. He appeared unimpressed and threatened to put the Mexica diplomat and his associates in fetters for bringing gifts of so little value. Don Hernando had been told the Aztec emperor had great wealth, and his apparent willingness to shower gifts on strangers probably reflected a weak ruler he could exploit to his advantage. Accordingly, Cortés feigned anger and ordered the Mexica governor and retinue to return to Tenochtitlan and report his dissatisfaction. Gifts offered in the future must be far more lavish as deserved by men who were emissaries of a great king in a distant land.

Nonetheless, the gifts accepted by Cortés would cause trouble in the ranks of Spaniards that would continue throughout the conquest of Mexico. Difficulties arose among dissidents who believed the expedition's captain general had usurped treasure that rightfully belonged to Diego Velázquez, because by then he had probably been appointed *adelantado* of Yucatan. The malcontents included don Diego's kinsman, Juan Velázquez de León; Cortés's former majordomo Diego de Ordaz; Francisco de Montejo, future conquistador of Yucatan; and Juan de Escudero, the one-time constable of Baracoa. The last had been Cortés's enemy since 1514 when he had insulted and cursed don Hernando while marching him off to jail. It was foolish for Escudero to have joined any undertaking led by Cortés, and he would soon pay a terrible price for his error in judgment.

Fray Diego Durán stated in his writings that Moctezuma had given an unequivocal order to his representative: Determine if Cortés might possibly be Quetzalcoatl, and he had failed to do that. Whether the emperor punished his appointee for non-compliance is not known. What is certain is that Tendile would serve again as Moctezuma's agent in future dealings with the Spaniards.

Meanwhile, Moctezuma had to decide what to do about Cortés's demands for greater amounts of treasure and his insistence on a meeting to deliver greetings from his king across the "great waters." Since the formation of the Triple Alliance in 1428, Aztec emperors had been obliged to consult with the kings of Texcoco and Tacuba on important matters. They were members of Moctezuma's supreme council, as was the deputy emperor, high priests, and the emperor's brother, Cuitlahuac. The last was a pragmatist. When permitted to speak, he said: "My advice is not to allow into your house someone who will put you out of it." Cacama, the king of Texcoco, offered a different recommendation: If, as he claims, this supreme captain of the strangers is an emissary of a great monarch, the Mexica emperor had a solemn obligation to receive him as an ambassador. However, should that captain be dishonest, Moctezuma had brave caciques and warriors who would defend him.

Those present at the meeting appear to have accepted the recommendation of Cuitlahuac. The Mexica should do everything possible to prevent the strangers from entering Tenochtitlan. If that meant offering even more lavish gifts to keep them on the coast, it was a price worth paying. It should also be made clear that the emperor would not travel to the coast to confer with the strangers' great captain. To ensure compliance with these directives, the greatest magicians of Mexico should be assembled and ordered to use "all their knowledge and power, to impede and frighten off the [unwelcome strangers] in order that they should not dare to come to Mexico." Last, it was imperative that Tendile determine with absolute certainly whether the visitors on the coast were gods returning from the east who had prior claim to Tula.

On or about May 1, Tendile reappeared on the coast and sought out Cortés. As newly appointed emissary of Moctezuma, he brought colored cottons, feather work, gold and silver jewels; and most important two large gold and silver-covered wooden disks. The gold object was approximately six and half feet in diameter and about two inches thick, and it weighed about thirty-five pounds, while the silver disk was somewhat smaller and weighed perhaps twenty-four pounds. The first represented the sun; the second, the moon. Both were exceptionally beautiful. The depiction of the sun had an engraved image of a king seated on a throne at its center, while the moon's disk had a similar positioning of a queen.

Tendile also invited Cortés and his captains to sit with him at a meal of cooked turkey, eggs, and tortillas. To the nauseating disgust of the Spaniards, all food items had been sprinkled with the blood of recently sacrificed slaves. The Europeans' revulsion and refusal to even taste the food was presumably all the proof Tendile needed to report to Moctezuma that they were certainly not gods, or even emissaries of any deities known to the Mexica.

Tendile, then gave Moctezuma's reply to Cortés's request that they meet. It was not possible, the emperor said, for several reasons. If, however, there was anything in Mexico that the great captain wished to acquire and send his king, he had only to ask for it. The emperor also sent word that the hoped Cortés's monarch would send him more of his "usual, good, strange, and never-before-seen men." However, a meeting between the Spanish captain and the Mexica emperor was not even discussable. Furthermore, Moctezuma could not come to the coast because he had duties to perform in the Mexica's ceremony of flowers in May.

Cortés responded by sending gifts in appreciation of those he had received. They included clothing, a glass cup, and three shirts of Holland cloth. Again, don Hernando repeated that it was essential that he meet Moctezuma, or his king would be unhappy with him. Tendile said he would deliver the message to his emperor but offered no hope that it would change the course of events. As he left for Tenochtitlan, Tendile's departing message was that the Spaniards should move inland from the coast's sand fleas and mosquitoes. Cortés, recognizing that it would be easier for the Aztecs to surround them if they moved away from the shore and their ships, did not comment.

Tendile later returned for his third and final visit to the coast. Again, he brought gifts of cotton goods, feather work, and four beautiful pieces of jade. This time the Mexica governor told Cortés he had to leave Mexico since it would be impossible for him to meet with Moctezuma. Don Hernando replied that he intended to stay until he had done so. His response irritated Tendile who left and took approximately two-thousand Mexica with him. Among them were women who had made maize cakes daily and cooked food for the strangers. It was a serious loss because provisions on the anchored ships were nearly exhausted.

Cortés believed a clash of arms was about to begin, but that did not happen. He sent Alvarado with a hundred men-at-arms into the interior to look for maize. About nine miles inland, they found an abandoned village with a temple that contained additional evidence of human sacrifice—blood and flint knives. In two similarly abandoned villages they found ample amounts of maize. Meanwhile, it had become increasingly obvious to don Hernando that the beach at San Juan was not an acceptable base on which to remain. Accordingly, he dispatched two ships up the coast to look for a more suitable location. The vessels, however, encountered head winds that forced their captains to turn about and return to San Juan.

Some six-hundred men had spent more than a month on a beach opposite the island, and resentment of conditions there grew along with other complaints. Cortés was advantaged by having the company of Doa Marina, Pedro de Alvarado, and his three brothers. Others were not only irritated by idleness and lack of friends but also resented Cortés's storing aboard his flagship all gifts presented by the Aztecs. Furthermore, despite strict orders from their commander captain that prohibited individuals trading European trifles one on one with Indians in exchange for a bit of gold, it had nonetheless taken place. To unhappy dissidents, it seemed Cortés had turned a blind eye on his favorite men-at-arms who engaged in this forbidden trade, while confiscating a bit of treasure from those whom he regarded less favorably. In addition, many unhappy conquistadors wanted to go home to Cuba where they had family. For Cortés, returning to Cuba where Diego Velázquez had placed a price on his head would never be an option in Mexico.

Unexpectedly, shortly after Tendile had ordered Cortés to leave Mexico, five Totonacs approached from the north. All were chieftains, and neither Marina nor Aguilar could understand their language. Marina in Nahuatl asked if any of them were translators who dealt with Aztec tribute collectors in their towns. Two of the caciques understood her. With language removed as barrier, Cortés asked through his interpreters if there was dissatisfaction in Totonac towns where its inhabitants were subjects of the Aztecs. His question brought forth a torrent of complaints from the caciques. Aztec agents of Moctezuma demanded tribute in food and goods, as well as young men and women every eighty days. The men were used as sacrificial offerings to Mexica gods, while the women were sometimes violated but always enslaved. Furthermore, other nearby subject people would welcome any opportunity for an alliance against the hated Aztecs—information that was not lost on Cortés.

To the further delight of don Hernando, the Totonacs asked if he and his men would like to live near their town of Cempoala, located about twenty miles to the north. Within two or three days, every Spaniard had vacated the beach and harbor at San Juan. All eleven ships were able to sail north and drop anchors at a much smaller but secure harbor. Most of the men sailed on the vessels that also carried the sixteen horses. That number, however, did not include Cortés's chestnut stallion. According to Bernal Díaz, the sudden death of the stallion that bit or kicked all who came near it except for Cortés was cause for celebration among men in the ranks. However, the number of horses was still sixteen, because one of the mares had foaled. About one-hundred Spaniards chose to walk up the beach to Cempoala under the command of Jorge de Alvarado.

A detailed modern map of Mexico will identify the location but not name of Villa Rica de la Veracruz, the first town in Mexico founded by Spaniards. It was north of Cempoala by about ten miles and often called simply Veracruz from 1519 until the later years of the 1590s when the present-day city of Veracruz was founded at San Juan de Ulúa. After the conquest of Mexico, Hernando Cortés built the first private residence and Catholic church in Mexico at the renamed present-day town of La Antigua, whose name refers to its status as old or former Veracruz.

As mentioned, dissident elements among the six-hundred Spaniards had become increasingly vocal. Led by Juan Velázquez de León, kinsman of the governor of Cuba, there arose strong minority sentiment that the Cortés expedition was not authorized to colonize Mexico. Neither it nor anyone else had approval to do that from the Hieronymite friars on Española, and founding the first colony in Mexico should be the prerogative of Diego Velázquez. To counter such arguments, Cortés arranged to have his loyal captains ask him to create a town and organize its governance. Such a suggestion was also consistent with the right of the king's subjects to speak their mind on such issues.

This subterfuge allowed Cortés to say he was only acting in accordance with long-established Spanish practices. While the Conqueror engaged in laying out a town around a central plaza, partisans of Diego Velázquez approached him and said they no longer wished to remain under his command. The delegation also demanded a ship that would permit them to sail to Cuba. Cortés had his secretary record the names of those who wished to disavow his leadership, and he emphatically denied their request for a ship. To have allowed men to return to Cuba would have resulted in their disclosing his location in Mexico, as well as reporting on the sumptuous treasures he had received. Among those abruptly turned away was Juan Escudero.

When the new town was laid out, Cortés appointed men he knew to be trust-worthy. Francisco de Montejo had made his peace with Cortés and received appointment as *alcalde*, head of the town's council and chief magistrate; as captain of expeditions, Pedro de Alvarado; and as chief constable, Alonso de Ávila. Cortés would later acknowledge that he had failed to see the leadership qualities of young Gonzalo de Sandoval, but that would soon change. Don Gonzalo, perhaps because of his youth and honesty, became popular with men in the ranks. He would soon become Cortés's ears, reporting to him on what was being said by low-ranked conquistadors. Sandoval often did not divulge the men's names, and he would later refuse to join card games organized by Cortés and the Alvarado brothers with the intent of cheating fellow conquistadors. Nonetheless, when it came to his treatment of Indians, Sandoval would be just as harsh as Alvarado or Cortés.

In establishing a new Spanish municipality, it was commonplace to assign lots (*solares*) to individuals. There followed appointments of council members (*regidores*), and Cortés made certain all appointees were stalwart allies. This created intense and outspoken opposition from Juan Velázquez de León, Diego de Ordaz, and Juan Escudero. They, in turn, sought support from similarly minded men, whereupon Cortés had several of them placed in irons and imprisoned on one of the anchored vessels. Matters worsened when Gonzalo de Sandoval learned that Juan Escudero had planned to kill a captain, commandeer his ship, and return to Cuba with news of where Cortés had landed.

The captain general, supported by Alvarado and Sandoval, decided to make an example of the ringleaders. The plotters had recruited several sailors and a pilot named Diego Cermeño, capable of navigating a ship to Cuba. They were tried by members of the new municipal council, or *cabildo*. Escudero and Cermeño were condemned to hang, and the sentencing of Escudero especially pleased Cortés. After the executions, Escudero remained on the gibbet for a year. His corpse left to crows served as an indelible reminder of the cost of betraying the main captain of the expedition. As always, don Hernando would never be a good man to have as an enemy. Cortés next confronted Diego de Ordaz and Juan Velázquez de León. They could join the bodies of Escudero and Cermeño, or they could pledge unwavering loyalty to him. They chose obedience, and in the conquest of Mexico both became among Cortés's most dedicated and valued captains.

Cortés next demonstrated an audacity that surprised even his closest friends. He ordered the captains of eight of the eleven ships anchored off Villa Rica to sail their vessels on to the beach and disable them. His instructions were clear: anything salvageable from the broken vessels including such items as iron ingots, planking, canvas, rope, cables, and grommets had to be stored for possible use in Mexico. In the second half of the sixteenth century, an apocryphal account gained currency that Cortés burned all eight vessels. That made no sense but still appears as a possibility in a Goggle search. As suggested by historian Sir Hugh Thomas, that error probably began when someone long ago misread longhand Spanish. The word broken (*quebrado*) was likely read as burned (*quemado*). Lest there be any doubt about Cortés's intent in beaching eight ships, in his second letter to the Emperor Charles V, he wrote of an incident that occurred "eight or ten days after having broken up the ships on the coast." The Conqueror's strategy in disabling vessels is probably obvious, but in his own words: "[the expeditioners] then had nothing to rely on, apart from their own hands, and the assurance that they could conquer and win the land or die in the attempt."

Of the remaining seaworthy ships, one nao and two caravels, Cortés chose the larger vessel, equipped it with the best sailors and pilot, and sent it to Spain around mid-July 1519 under the dual command of Alonso Hernández de Puertocarrero and Francisco de Montejo. Aboard were about fifty sailors and an important letter drafted by the cabildo members of Villa Rica and addressed to King Charles I, as well as almost all the treasure—other than the gold and silver disks—to be received as gifts from Moctezuma. The cabildo letter is counted as Cortés's first of five sent to King Charles I of Spain, later Emperor Charles V, although don Hernando did not write it. Nonetheless, it is doubtful that Cortés would have allowed councilmen he had appointed to write any-thing even remotely critical of him. However, Cortés may well have also sent *his* first letter along with the cabildo missive. If so, it has never been found. Circumstantial evidence suggests the existence of a separate letter because Cortés was always insistent on defending himself in his own hand. The Conqueror later drafted his first letter (although counted as his second), but problems arose in delivering any correspondence to King Charles, because in May 1520 he left Spain at the port of La Coruña in the extreme northwest of Spain to be crowned Holy Roman Emperor. For the next year and a half, Charles moved across Western Europe from his first landing in Flanders, to Worms where he confronted Martin Luther, to his later arrival in Vienna, prior to his eventual return to Spain in 1522 as Holy Roman Emperor. Letters sent to him in this time frame at times failed to reach him. For example, the Cabildo Letter of 1519 was not found in the Imperial Archives of Vienna until the second half of the nineteenth century.

At the time of the July sailing from Villa Rica to Spain, Hernández Puertocarrero's short-time mistress Doña Marina was taken from him, so also was his fine gelding named Altivo that was claimed by Cortés to replace his "vicious" stallion. Great captains enjoyed great privileges. Still, the Conqueror had many things to attend to before his planned march to Tenochtitlan, which destruction of his fleet had made essential. Among those problems was the shortage of food at Villa Rica, located about a day's march from the Totonac town of Cempoala, located inland from the coast.

Cortés sent Alvarado, as captain of expeditions, into the interior with one-hundred men in ranks, as well as fifteen crossbowmen and six musketeers. What don Pedro discovered was unexpected. Every town he entered was deserted, and the former inhabitants had taken the last scrap of food with them, with one exception. In their haste to depart, they had failed to take the arms and legs of recently sacrificed men in a temple. In other places, only the trunks of bodies remained. But the Totonacs in one town had also left behind turkeys. To the irritation of footmen, because there were no burden bearers, some of them had to carry the birds with legs bound and wings flapping against their legs for several miles back to Villa Rica de la Veracruz.

Soon afterward, twelve Indians appeared there and invited Spaniards to visit their great cacique at Cempoala. Cortés thought it prudent to accept the invitation but proceeded with caution. He sent scouts on horseback ahead of the main column, which was armed with small cannons, swords, muskets, and crossbows. The Spaniards were about three miles from Cempoala when stopped by Totonac chieftains who greeted them in the name of their great cacique. The emissaries bore fragrant roses and displayed every sign of friendship. Through interpreters, don Hernando learned that their king was so fat he could not welcome him and his men outside the town.

Still wary, Cortés sent Alvarado and eight horsemen into Cempoala to assess its defenses, while he organized protection for the stalled column. The scouts returned with glowing accounts of the town. It was by far the largest they had seen in Mexico, built around a central plaza with small courtyards extending off each side. The smaller squares were flanked by numerous rooms. The outriders also reported having been greeted by throngs of friendly men, women, and children. Cortés then moved his command into the city, where he was welcomed by an enormously obese cacique. He was so fat he could not walk and instead rode atop a litter supported by four stout Indian nobles. From that time onward, Cortés and his men called the chieftain of Cempoala the "Fat Cacique."

The Totonac King invited the Spaniards to spend the night in apartment-like quarters, which they agreed to do but served notice that in the morning they would return to their ships. On the following morning, the Fat Cacique unexpectedly placed more than four-hundred Indians at the Spaniards' disposal. Some were skilled load bearers, called *tamemes*. They could carry up to fifty pounds for around fifteen miles without stopping to rest. The men-at-arms were no doubt delighted that they did not have to bear anything back to Villa Rica. Even men in the ranks thought it beneath their standing to have to carry a single item other than weapons.

Cortés and his men took leave of the Fat Cacique and began the march back to the coast. At the end of the first day, they slept in a deserted village near the fortified town of Quiahuitzlan. On the following morning, they marched to the settlement and were much impressed that it stood amidst great rocks and lofty cliffs. Bernal Díaz observed that had the town's residents chosen to oppose them, it would have been difficult to capture Quiahuitzlan. Instead, they entered halfway into the fortified town before they saw a single Indian. He greeted the Spaniards and led him to a large plaza that contained a sacrificial temple atop a small pyramid. Within the town's square were fifteen Indians all dressed in good mantles. One held a brazier emitting incense, and he fumigated Cortés and several captains standing next to him. The Indians' spokesman then asked the Spaniards to rest and bade them welcome.

Cortés responded by giving the men some green beads and other trifles from Spain. The Indians countered by having their women appear bearing cooked turkey and maize cakes. The Spaniards had barely sat down to eat when a messenger from Cempoala arrived with news that the Fat Cacique was on his way to the town atop a litter borne by Totonac nobles. When the cacique arrived, he joined with the town's head chieftain in complaining of the many abuses Moctezuma had visited on them. Every year the natives in some thirty settlements, having been defeated in battle by the Mexica and thereby made their subjects, had to give up their young daughters. They were ravished by Aztecs and later made slaves. Their handsome young men, because the Mexica's gods demanded only the best hearts, were sacrificed in Tenochtitlan.

Cortés through his interpreters attempted to console the Totonac leaders by saying that he would protect them and do all he could to help since he had been sent by an even greater king to redress such injuries and punish evildoers. The chieftains, however, were in no way consoled, and they pointed out quite reasonably that the Spaniards had no idea of the great number of warriors possessed by the Aztecs. Again, Cortés attempted to allay their fears, and again he failed. As the conversation continued, runners from Cempoala arrived to inform the Fat Cacique that five Mexica tribute gatherers had just arrived there. The chieftain was so distressed that he broke into tears.

Cortés told the Totonac headman that he and his men would return to Cempoala and help confront the Aztec tax collectors. When Cortés and his command arrived, they occupied the town's huge plaza with its pyramid and sacrificial altar. Meanwhile, the five Mexica had been housed in a room decked with flowers, provided with food, and served ground cacao and water sweetened with honey—a beverage so special that only Indian nobility were permitted to drink it. The five Aztec tribute assessors and collectors had scolded the Totonacs at Cempoala for harboring Spaniards without the permission of Moctezuma. As punishment for their misdeeds, an unscheduled allotment of young men would be marched off to Tenochtitlan and sacrificed.

The tribute collectors soon emerged from their quarters and walked past Cortés and his men without the slightest acknowledgment of their existence. They were dressed in fine cotton mantles and deerskin sandals but carried only a crooked staff as a symbol of their untouchable authority, while accompanied by servants who shooed flies from their bodies with whisks. Other servants swept the ground in front of them to remove troublesome pebbles that might cause discomfort under the soles of their deerskin sandals. To the Spaniards, the five Mexica probably seemed the embodiment of arrogance on parade.

Cortés's response again demonstrated his ability to dissemble. He ordered several Totonac caciques to seize the five Mexica, place them in fetters, and guard them in an apartment. The chieftains were horrified and at first refused his order because it was unheard of brazenness to even touch an Aztec tribute collector. They protested that Moctezuma when informed of such an outrage would send his warriors to kill or enslave everyone in Cempoala, and then flatten the town. Cortés insisted that he would not only protect the Totonacs in Cempoala, but also in their other towns; and they would never again have to pay tribute to the hated Aztecs. Finally, the caciques laid hands on the Mexica tax gatherers and even flogged one of them who refused to accept restraints. In carrying out don Hernando's orders, the Totonacs feared that no ordinary human beings would dare to defy the great Moctezuma and his agents. They therefore concluded the Spaniards had to be gods.

The Totonac caciques asked Cortés's permission to sacrifice the five Mexica prisoners, so that they could not return to Tenochtitlan and report their mistreatment. The Conqueror rejected their request because he had something far more devious in mind. First, he had likely secured by extension an alliance with Totonacs in some thirty towns out of fear of Moctezuma's wrath. He then told Aguilar and Marina to inform the Mexica captives that he had saved their lives by not allowing the Totonacs to sacrifice them. To further "protect" the five Aztec prisoners, Cortés removed the Indian guards and replaced them with his own men-at-arms.

The Conqueror told his guards to determine which two of the five prisoners seemed most intelligent and to bring them unnoticed by Totonacs to his headquarters at midnight. When the selected Mexica arrived, Cortés had his interpreters ask them who had ordered their arrest, as though he knew nothing about it. When they said the Totonacs were responsible, don Hernando feigned anger. How dare they treat emissaries of the great Moctezuma so unjustly? He removed their fetters and told them to go at once to Tenochtitlan and tell their emperor that he had saved their lives when the Totonacs had insisted on sacrificing them.

The two tribute collectors expressed gratitude for their freedom but reasonably said that to get to the Mexica capital they would have to travel by many Totonac towns where their lives would again be in danger. Cortés agreed because their dying did not suit his overall goal, which was to send mixed signals to the Aztec emperor. Accordingly, he had his captains escort the two men to the coast, where they were rowed in a boat beyond Totonac-controlled lands and released. That same night, he had fetters removed from the remaining three Aztecs and arranged for their transfer to the coast as well. There they were placed aboard one of the beached ships and placed in irons for a short time. Later, they were rowed to safety and released while carrying messages of good will to Moctezuma.

The final act in Cortés's duplicity played out the following morning. He appeared angry in reporting to the Fat Cacique that his guards had gone to sleep and allowed the Aztecs to escape. The men would be punished, but regrettably the five tax collectors would soon report their mistreatment by the Totonacs. At that juncture, a continued alliance of Spaniards and Totonacs throughout the conquest was assured. In the short run, the Indians regarded the Spaniards as *Teules*, and they helped them build houses for the roughly one-hundred Spaniards who would remain at Villa Rica. More important, the Totonacs also assisted in building a fort to secure the harbor as a base of operations for the Spaniards' entry into Mexica-controlled lands.

The Fat Cacique was so impressed with the godlike Spaniards that he offered to bestow his daughter, or possibly niece, as a bride to Cortés. The Conqueror thanked him but explained that he had a wife, but the Totonac chieftain would not take no for an answer. When the young woman was brought forth, she was well on her way to matching the corpulence of her father, or possibly uncle. Several men in the ranks could not resist audible snickers. Afterward, Cortés presented the burly woman as mistress to the loudest of those who found humor in his awkward situation.

The Conqueror had more serious matters on his mind. He summoned the Fat Cacique and his leading sub-chiefs into his presence, and he informed them that since he had promised to protect them from Moctezuma and his many thousands of warriors, they must clean their temples of blood and gore and never again perform human sacrifice. Some of the younger hotheaded Totonacs protested that they could not in safety fail to honor their gods, to which Cortés replied that his king was more powerful than Moctezuma. Furthermore, the Spaniards were determined to convert all Indians in Mexico to their Catholic faith. To that end, the Totonacs must erect a large cross in their plaza and pay homage to it daily. Bartolomé de Olmedo, the Mercedarian friar who was Cortés's confessor and spiritual adviser in the conquest, cautioned don Hernando not to expect the Totonacs to understand Christian veneration of the cross without proper instruction, but the Conqueror remained adamant.

As Cortés prepared his expedition to march inland, he summoned the Fat Cacique and told him he needed two-hundred burden bearers to transport the artillery and other heavy items. The head chieftain readily agreed but also honored don Hernando's second request to supply fifty of his best warriors. In all, the Conqueror had around 350 Spaniards in his force plus 250 Totonacs. Sailors from the eight beached ships had been added as men-at-arms, or they were assigned to defend the settlement and fort at Villa Rica. Left in charge of all base operations at Villa Rica was Captain Juan de Escalante, one of Cortés's more capable officers.

The combined expeditioners along with fifteen horses left Cempoala on August 16, 1519. They had marched only one day before being overtaken by a Totonac runner who bore bad news. Four ships had appeared off the harbor at Villa Rica but refused to enter it. Instead, the vessels continued down the coast for about nine miles where their captains dropped anchors near the mouth of a small river. Those Spaniards, who had been sent by Francisco de Garay in Jamaica, were the first of two challenges that would face the Conqueror in his determination to be the sole conquistador and colonizer of New Spain.

Francisco de Garay had long experience in the Indies. Having sailed on Columbus's second voyage in 1493, he was one of only a few Spaniards who had struck it rich on Española. Don Francisco was the most successful owner of swine herds in Spanish America, and he often bragged that he used five-thousand Indians to care for his myriad hogs. The governor sold salted pork and bacon to virtually everyone on Española and to expeditions leaving the island for Spain. He also owned mining property along with an encomienda, and he had become rich by claiming the largest gold nugget found on the Caribbean islands.

Don Francisco then traveled to Spain as a wealthy man and negotiated with the Crown for concessions in the Indies. He was successful in being named co-governor along with Juan de Esquivel of largely unsettled Jamaica, where Garay had again become a swine-raising entrepreneur without peer. More important to the conquest and settlement of Mexico, Garay was also granted a royal license to explore and colonize what would soon be called "Florida," which encompassed the entire northern Gulf Coast from the peninsula of Florida to a river on the coast of Mexico called the Río de las Palmas. That stream today is known as the Río Soto la Marina, and it enters the Gulf near the port of La Pesca about ninety miles north of the Río Pánuco.

With permission obtained from the Hieronymite Friars at Santo Domingo, Garay organized an expedition of four ships and 270 men and placed it under the command of Alonso Álvarez de Pineda. The flotilla left Jamaica and sailed north to the east coast of Florida and attempted to proceed along it, but headwinds forced it to turn about. The ships then sailed along the west coast of Florida, followed by traversing the Gulf Coast to a short distance beyond the harbor at Villa Rica. Someone on the Pineda expedition, perhaps one its pilots, drew a sketch map of the Gulf Coast from Florida proper to include Grijalva's previous explorations to Yucatan and Mexico. This map was the first to depict an enormous expanse of coastal North America. Only two rivers are identified on the 1519 sketch map—the Río Pánuco and the Mississippi. The latter was named the Río del Espíritu Santo because it was discovered on the feast day of the Holy Spirit (June 2 in 1519). The Pineda expedition attained its farthest extent when it encountered Cortés's men at Villa Rica, and it then proceeded shortly beyond the town in mid-August. Among its important accomplishments were the definitive recognition of

Florida as a peninsula—not an island as long perceived—and it mapped the last unexplored region of the Gulf Coast.

When Cortés learned of this unwelcome competition, he left Alvarado and Sandoval in command and set off immediately for the coast. Accompanying him were four horsemen and fifty of the most capable men-at-arms. They arrived at Villa Rica after nightfall but immediately turned south without stopping to rest. As they approached the anchored ships, Cortés and his men encountered three Spaniards who had come ashore. They informed don Hernando that they were part of an expedition sent by Garay to establish his colony in Mexico, and the purpose of their captain was to meet with Cortés and determine a boundary between his claims and those of their sponsor.

Cortés stripped the three men of their clothing and dressed an equal number of his men in their garb. When the full contingent reached its destination, it was just prior to dawn. The Conqueror hid about a dozen men in some trees, while the three imposters sent signals to the ships to send a boat to retrieve them. When twelve men in craft approached the beach, four of them jumped out to speak to their presumed shipmates, while the others stayed offshore. Those who landed were soon overpowered by Cortés's men emerging from the trees. Others remaining in the boat escaped by returning to the ships that were already lifting anchors.

Alonso Álvarez de Pineda as captain of the small flotilla returned to the north and entered the Río Pánuco but with seven fewer men that when he had arrived off Villa Rica. The captain, himself, however remains a mysterious man who continues to intrigue historians. Despite his importance at this juncture in 1519 —a notoriety that soon increased—this ship captain continues to elude the best efforts of researchers in discovering anything whatsoever about him. Furthermore, we know his name only because Bernal Díaz recorded it. But it is a certainty that Álvarez de Pineda and his mariners remained on the Río Pánuco, inland from present-day Tampico, for forty days while staying abroad the four vessels before returning to Jamaica in fall 1519.

Cortés marched back to Villa Rica and spoke briefly with Juan de Escalante. The Conqueror warned him to be vigilant of any intrusion from the north that might be made by partisans of Garay. Don Hernando then returned to

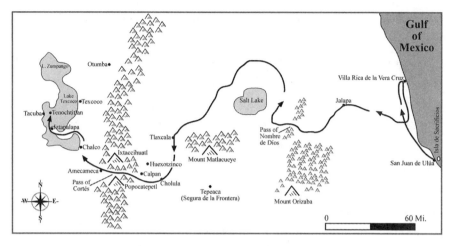

Figure 10. Cortés's Route from San Juan de Ulúa to Tenochtitlan. Adapted from Thomas, *Conquest*, 228-229.

his expedition, encamped a day's march beyond Cempoala. Still ahead for the inland march of 650 Spaniards and Totonacs lay a difficult trek of some two hundred miles to Tenochtitlan. Indian allies had to carry everything including brass cannons, kegs of gunpowder, and supplies over difficult terrain. The heavier medium-sized Lombard cannons were transported on two-wheeled carts pulled by Totonacs. [**Figure 10**]

Without doubt, ascent to mountain passes of around ten-thousand feet in elevation would not have been possible without the Totonac burden bearers doing the heavy lifting. As mentioned, Spaniards in sixteenth-century Mexico were loath to carry items, which they regarded as demeaning tasks befitting peasants, not those claiming status as hidalgos, the lowest rung on the nobility ladder. Added to the difficulty of the impending march was the men's lack of physical conditioning and appropriate clothing for any altitude significantly above sea level; and even Tenochtitlan, their ultimate destination, lay at an elevation of 7,200 feet. Difficulties with altitude and weather aside, the battles lay ahead with the three-part Indian kingdom collectively known as Tlaxcala, which in its unified whole comprised almost the entirety of the present-day Mexican state of Tlaxcala.

The first objective of the Cortés expedition was to negotiate the rise in terrain from Cempoala to Jalapa, which is at 4,600 feet. They next viewed the Cofre de Perote, which stands at 14,000 feet but is greatly exceeded in elevation by the nearby and perpetually snow-capped volcanic peak Orizaba, at approximately 18,500 feet high. The Aztecs revered the latter and as mentioned called it "Mountain of the Star." After descending from mountains and peaks, the Spanish expeditioners and their Totonac allies experienced near freezing temperatures as they trudged by salt lakes, marshes, and inhospitable expanses of sand and volcanic ash that lay on the western slope of the Cofre. Bernal Díaz described the extreme discomfort of cold nights in thin clothing. In what might well be called the badlands of Mexico, there was no drinkable surface water or edible vegetation. Hunger and thirst were rampant for Spaniards and Totonacs alike. There was also a problem finding forage for the fifteen horses—the recently foaled colt having been left at Villa Rica. Having survived difficult terrain, the expeditioners still had to traverse increasing elevations of seven to eight-thousand feet to reach the plains of Puebla and Tlaxcala that lay ahead.

In the ensuing ascent, the trekkers encountered lands belonging to a town named Xocotlan. It was allied with the Mexica, so the Spaniards approached the *cabecera* (head town) with caution. They asked a secondary chieftain for food, which he gave little of and even that with ill will, according to Bernal Díaz. Cortés asked the town's great cacique, called Olintecle, about Moctezuma and what he knew of Tenochtitlan. The chieftain replied that his Lord Moctezuma's strength lay in thousands of warriors. They were posted on the frontiers of his kingdom and neighboring provinces. As for Tenochtitlan, it was built on an island joined to shorelines on three sides by elevated causeways. The walkways had openings through which water could flow from one lake system to another. Wooden bridges spanned the gaps, and they could be removed should the city be attacked from land. Within the city itself, all houses and buildings had flat roofs loaded with stones that could serve as breastworks if needed. Getting from one part of Tenochtitlan to another required either bridges or canoes to cross its canals. When asked about the wealth of Tenochtitlan, the chieftain replied that it had great stores of gold, silver, and *chalchihuites* (turquoise).

The more Spaniards heard from Olintecle, the more determined they became to continue their advance to the Mexica's capital city, and why not? Their ships had been disabled, and again their captain general could not in safety return to Cuba. When the Spaniards indicated their intent to continue their approach to Tenochtitlan, the head chieftain of Xocotlan expressed amazement at their daring. Cortés replied that he served an even greater king in Spain, and as his representative he was determined to end the practice of human sacrifice in Mexico, while bringing knowledge of his God to all Indians. To that end, he ordered his carpenters to erect a cross in the town's plaza.

For the first time on his path of Catholic inflexibility, Cortés yielded to the objections of fray Bartolomé de Olmedo. The friar warned don Hernando that Indians of the town had not received instruction in the Catholic faith. And he added: "It seems to me, sir, that the time has not yet come to leave crosses in the charge of these people for they are somewhat shameless and without fear, and as they are vassals of Montezuma [sic] they may burn the crosses or do some other evil things, and what you had said to them is enough until they know something more of our holy religion." As Bernal Díaz commented, the matter came to an impasse and no cross was erected. Nevertheless, the garrulous conquistador wrote that the plaza of Xocotlan had piles of thigh bones and an enormous wooden rack with pegs that contained in his estimation one-hundred-thousand skulls, and he repeated the number for emphasis.

The Cortés expedition left the town that had initially given it reluctant succor, but that attitude changed near the end of their stay. The Totonac caciques remarked on how the Spaniards were so powerful that they had defeated the Chontal Mayas in battle at Potonchán. Such men must be treated like gods, and it would be foolish to not shower them with gifts of food and clothing. Bernal Díaz commented that the leather shoes worn by the Spaniards had fallen apart. That forced them to use what he called "hempen" footwear, probably sandals made of rope. Those and other amenities were parting gifts bestowed on the Spaniards as they left the people of Xocotlan.

The road that the Spaniards chose to follow led to the province of Tlaxcala, which was nearby. That choice, however, was against the advice of Xocotlan's chieftains who urged a different route that would have taken them to Cholula.

The Totonac warriors in Cortés's forces advised him not to trust the people of Cholula because they had recently become allies of Moctezuma. It was better, they counseled, to deal with the Tlaxcalans, since they were enemies of the Aztecs. Nevertheless, Cortés selected two Totonac headmen and sent them ahead of his column into Tlaxcalan lands with the message that he and his men had come in peace and on behalf of their king, Charles I. That, however, would soon not bode well for the emissaries' state of mind.

CHAPTER 8

War in Tlaxcala and Spaniards Enter Tenochtitlan

The Cortés expedition, outfitted with provisions and probably footwear that they had acquired at Xocotlan, marched southwest toward the border of Tlaxcala, which it crossed on August 31. The following day, having not heard back from the two Totonac emissaries sent ahead with the proposal of friendship, the full complement of Spaniards and Totonacs advanced toward lands claimed by Tlaxcalans. They soon came upon the messengers who had been taken prisoner and threatened with having their hearts torn out. The men were so terrified by their ordeal that they could barely speak. They did manage to relay a message from the Tlaxcalans who had mocked their description of the Spaniards: "Now we are going to kill those whom you call *Teules* and eat their flesh. Then we shall see whether they are as brave as you proclaim. And we shall eat your flesh too."

Such haughty words, according to Bernal Díaz, gave the Spaniards cause for "serious thought" but soon served to strengthen their resolve to march on after they had commended themselves to God. The Totonacs assured don Hernando that the Tlaxcalans would meet them and resist any entry into their lands. They were right, but first the Spaniards had to get through a fortress built of stones and mortar. Even with pickaxes, the Spaniards had difficulty demolishing the obstruction that barred them from entering the road ahead. Cortés asked the Totonac warriors why Tlaxcalans would build such a fortification, and they told him all entries into their lands were defended by such structures, because they and the Mexica had been enemies for many years. Such barriers were necessary, said the Cempoalans, to help impede the great number of warriors possessed by Moctezuma, who sent forth his legions every year following autumn harvests to wage war with the Tlaxcalans and other Nahua enemies.

The column of Spaniards and their Totonac allies had not advanced far beyond the leveled fortress when their scouts reported that thirty Tlaxcalans were observing their movements. Cortés ordered his scouts to follow the spies and try to capture one without harming him for interrogation, and he sent five horsemen to assist them in case they encountered an ambush. When the Tlaxcalan spies saw the horses move forward, they beckoned them onward and into battle. The engagement ended in a standoff, and far from allowing the Spaniards to capture one of the Tlaxcalans for questioning it resulted instead in the wounding of two or three horses.

Cortés then ordered a full-scale attack, and in the ensuing battle his men killed five Indians. Shortly thereafter, an estimated three-thousand Tlaxcalans who had been lying in ambush launched a counteroffensive. The Indians showered arrows on the horsemen while engaging the footmen with lethal two-handed swords, their blades studded with obsidian chips. The Conqueror responded by firing cannons, muskets, and crossbows. The Indian combatants slowly retreated but kept their ranks in good order. In the engagement, the Tlaxcalans wounded five Spaniards, one fatally; but they also left behind seventeen of their dead.

This first fighting took place on level ground that greatly advantaged the fifteen mounted conquistadors, who took Indian lives with their swords and steel-tipped lances. The ten-to-twelve-foot lances were particularly deadly, and Spanish horsemen used them to attack the eyes and lower bodies of Indians, while avoiding their chests where lances might be more difficult to extract from ribs. While campaigning in Mexico, the Spaniards had no vegetable oil to dress their wounds and those of the horses to prevent infections, so they used the fat of dead Indians as salve. That practice, according to Bernal Díaz, was employed again and again throughout the conquest. The Tlaxcalans, like many Indians in the Indies, bred small dogs for food; and the conquistadors dined on several of them after this battle.

On the following day as the Spaniards and Totonacs marched on, they encountered Tlaxcalan forces and their Otomi allies occupying both sides of the road with an estimated six-thousand warriors. The Indians needed no prompt and attacked the expeditioners uttering war cries accompanied by the din of conch trumpets. They fired arrows from bows and hurled what Bernal Díaz called "darts," fire-hardened wooden projectiles launched with great force by atlatls. Other Indians armed with slingshots let loose a barrage of stones that sped so fast Spaniards could not see incoming rocks that caused painful welts and bruises. The fighting was deadly, and in the engagement dozens of Indians died from point-blank fire, unlimbered by Spanish cannons, muskets, and crossbows. Cortés asked the royal notary Diego de Godoy to take notes affirming that the loss of Indian lives was not the responsibility of his conquistadors who had come in peace. That defense was specious because Spaniards were on the offensive. However, niceties of Spanish legality had been met by reading the Requirement and invoking the principles of just war, employed earlier in campaigns on the Caribbean islands.

During a lull in the fighting, Cortés sent three prisoners, probably Otomi warriors who had been captured in the previous engagement, forward as peace emissaries. This strategy backfired and only served to increase the fury of the Indians, who then attacked with even greater resolve and forced the Spaniards to retreat momentarily. The Conqueror rallied his men-at-arms by invoking a battle cry made famous during the long wars of the Reconquest: *"Santiago y cierra España!"* The words invoked the name of their warrior saint and roughly meant: "close in Spain!" With new intensity the Spaniards pressed forward and again killed many Tlaxcalans, including three of their captains.

The Indians feigned defeat and retreated toward some ravines and broken ground that hampered the use of Spanish horses. This was planned strategy used by the Tlaxcalans, for lying in ambush were more than forty-thousand warriors under the command of their great captain Xicotencatl. He ordered his best fighters to cut through the ranks of the Spaniards and capture or kill a horse—as it turned out one ridden by Pedro de Morón, who was an excellent caballero. The attackers were so determined that they wrenched the lance from Morón, badly wounded him, and cut off the head of his horse with one stroke of a two-handed broadsword called a *macuahuitl*, its blade edges studded with knapped obsidian. The Spaniards were momentarily stunned but rallied, and with determined efforts by ten conquistadors, all of whom were wounded, barely managed to rescue Morón. He, however, was so seriously injured that he died the following day. Remarkably, the Tlaxcalans had meanwhile seized the dead horse and its severed head as trophies, taking both away from the battle. Spaniards nevertheless claimed victory in the engagement because they had killed many more Indians than they had lost men-at-arms.

Never in their years in the Indies had Spaniards encountered any adversary comparable to the Tlaxcalans in terms of strength in numbers or ferocity in battle. Meanwhile, according to Bernal Díaz, the Indians cut the horse into pieces, distributed its parts, and paraded the charger's head throughout their towns to prove that the great tame deer ridden by Spaniards could be killed. As for the Spanish conquistadors, the battle offered only a taste of what lay ahead. Tens of thousands of well-armed Indian warriors still stood between them and the conquest of Mexico. Again, Bernal Díaz placed things in perspective: "Horsemen, musketeers, crossbowmen, swordsmen, and those who used lance and shield, one and all, we fought like men to save our lives and do our duty, for we were certainly in the greatest danger in which we had ever found ourselves."

The initial battle with the Otomi and Tlaxcalan warriors was fought on September 2, following which Cortés withdrew his forces to an abandoned town to take stock of the situation. Two horses had been killed; fifteen of his men wounded; and five of the remaining chargers were injured. Towns near the Spanish encampment had been vacated so quickly that the Indians left behind turkeys that satisfied the appetites of Spaniards. The Conqueror then addressed his men with words of encouragement and a warning: They had to resume the offensive, or their Indian opponents would see inactivity as a sign of weakness, and even badly wounded conquistadors would have to fight as best they could. Cortés believed the best evidence of their determination to gain passage through Tlaxcala en route to Tenochtitlan was to send riders ahead to scout, so he prepared eight of his best horsemen and an equal number of healthy horses. He meanwhile posted guards around his camp throughout the night. The Spaniards and their Totonac allies held fifteen Tlaxcalan captives, two of whom were chiefs.

Had don Hernando decided to assess his overall situation at that time, he assuredly would have found it less than ideal. About fifty of the original six-hundred who left Santiago de Cuba had sailed to Spain with Puertocarrero and Montejo. They, however, were primarily sailors. Additional sailors from the eight beached ships were mostly used to build houses at Villa Rica and man the fortress there. In all, one-hundred and fifty men had remained on the coast under the command of Juan de Escalante. Since the battle with the Mayas at Potonchán, forty-five of Cortés's five-hundred men-at-arms had been killed, died of wounds, or succumbed to illnesses. The Conqueror still had around two-hundred burden bearers and forty Totonac warriors, but he had lost two of the fifteen horses. Five more chargers were so seriously wounded they could not be ridden for days. That left eight horses, which don Hernando soon dispatched with scouts.

Before moving onward, Cortés addressed his men on battle strategy. He spoke first to his horsemen on the importance of using their lances, again as Bernal Díaz had so indelicately put it, to strike Indians in their eyes or lower bodies. Two cavaliers had had lances wrested from their hands, because the weapons had become lodged in the chests of Indians. That mistake had contributed to caballero Pedro de Morón's fatal injuries. The Conqueror then turned to his swordsmen. They *had* to remain disciplined and in formation. If they were right handed, their left would be protected by the right hand of a conquistador on that side of them. Obviously, don Hernando did not know this when he spoke, but two massive battles lay ahead with the Tlaxcalans—one of them being an almost unheard of night engagement—during which disciplined swordsmen did not "carry the day," but they certainly "carried the night."

Cortés next tried his hand at diplomacy. He released the two cacique prisoners. The translators Aguilar and Doña Marina spoke kindly to them and gave them beads. Don Hernando also gave them a communication intended for their high chieftain, assuring him that Spaniards did not wish any more harm to befall Tlaxcalans, but he and his men had to pass through their country on their way to Tenochtitlan to speak to Moctezuma.

The message reached Xicotencatl at his camp, which was about two leagues' distance from where the expeditioners had camped. The Tlaxcalan general replied that the Spaniards should go where his father Xicotencatl the elder lived, a place regarded as the main city or capital of the three-kingdom Tlaxcalan confederation. There, they and their Indians allies would find the peace they sought by dying on sacrificial altars honoring Tlaxcalan gods whom they had offended by entering their lands. The Tlaxcalan people would also feel peaceful toward the strangers after becoming thoroughly satiated by consuming their flesh and drinking their blood. That was the message Xicotencatl gave the two Indians chieftains, which they delivered on returning to the Spanish encampment. On receiving it, as Bernal Díaz wrote, Cortés viewed the Tlaxcalan high cacique's reply as "haughty."

There followed a battle between Cortés's command and a Tlaxcalan army on a scale not previously experienced in the Indies. One conquistador described Indian warriors assembled on a plain that stretched before him as "large enough to eclipse the sun." Spaniards, however, were notorious for inflating what might be called biblical estimates of Indian foes. For example, they regularly described a lot of Indians as ten-thousand strong, while using forty-thousand to denote extremely large numbers of the same warriors. That made Spanish victories appear more impressive, and after all they were estimates. But there is no doubt the Tlaxcalans put the best army they could muster on the field for this second battle.

The din of combat in this engagement was so great Cortés's orders could not be heard by his captains and men-at-arms. However, in his letters to Charles I, don Hernando was always reluctant to admit adversity encountered by his forces, even as he exaggerated the numbers and strength of opponents. Nonetheless, Bernal Díaz described this massive battle as "dangerous and perilous." The chronicler added, "we were in considerable confusion," followed by commenting that he and fellow conquistadors faced a hail of stones from Indian slings, danger from their fire-hardened wooden javelins, and even greater peril from their obsidian-bladed swords. Nonetheless, the chronicler admitted Spanish success in the second battle of the Tlaxcalan War only came from "the simple use of steel swords."

There were other factors that help explain how so few Spaniards could hold their position even when outnumbered by Indians in perhaps a fifty-to-one ratio. Tlaxcalans and their Otomi allies, who had played such a prominent role in the first battle of the Tlaxcalan War, preferred to take captives whom they might later sacrifice to their gods rather than dispatch their foes immediately. Second, the Indians lined up their forces somewhat like a marching band. They sent the first file forward until it faltered; then they sent rank two forward, then three, and so forth. This meant that of the warriors who could potentially have thronged the battlefield with their numbers, only a limited number were engaged in fighting Spaniards at any given time. Third, and in the end most important, the Tlaxcalan nation consisted of a three-kingdom confederation that easily united to fight the hated Aztecs almost every year. But what about these newcomers to their land with their awesome weapons and horses used in fighting? Might not an alliance with them prove beneficial in weakening or destroying the power of Moctezuma's massive numbers of warriors? Predictably, differences of opinion regarding how to deal with the Spaniards arose between Xicotencatl and his deputy, who were both jealous of each other. When Cortés learned of this discord, he was delighted, for the wily captain general was a master of deceitful diplomacy. Nevertheless, a third battle in the Tlaxcalan War remained, one that would prove decisive in this first attempt by a Western European nation to conquer an empire in the Americas.

The Tlaxcalans summoned their priests, and they insisted that the Spaniards were men and not gods. After all, they ate turkeys, dogs, bread, and fruit. Their guns, while deadly, did not produce lightning, nor were their dogs in fact dragons. The two Totonac ambassadors had nonetheless insisted that the conquistadors were *Teules*. Somehow errors in translations between Totonacs and Tlaxcalans led the latter to believe the visitors' powers waned after dark. That led the younger Xicontencatl to prepare a night attack. He first sent fifty trusted men as alleged peace emissaries to the Spanish camp with orders to study them and learn their weaknesses. Included with the men were "four miserable old women" with the recommendation that the visitors eat them if hungry.

Cortés was not impressed, and he noticed that the Tlaxcalan entourage was more interested in observing his forces than seeking peace. In his words, the Indians behaved in a "spying manner and want of frankness." The conqueror ordered his men-at-arms to seize one of the Indians and interrogate him. Under questioning, and perhaps by use of torture to loosen his tongue, the man admitted that he and his companions were spies and that Xicotencatl intended to attack the Spaniards that night. The Conqueror's ensuing actions are not for the faint-of-heart reader. He cut off the hands of some of the fifty emissaries, the thumbs of others, and ears and noses of many of the remaining ones. Their severed body parts were placed on cords and tied around necks of the maimed. Along with the victims sent back to Xicotencatl went this message: "it is unworthy of brave soldiers and upright citizens to stoop to such odious stratagems . . . we are ready to receive you in battle at any hour . . . by day or by night."

Always aggressive, Cortés organized his forces and attacked the Tlaxcalans before darkness had completely fallen. Spaniards unlimbered their cannons, muskets, and crossbows. Eight cavaliers armed with shorter lances that were less likely to be wrested from their hands tore through outliers of massed Indians with orders to again aim their thrusts at the eyes or lower bodies of the Indians. This third battle of the Tlaxcalan War was a devastating rout of the Indians, and it eventually forced them to flee through cornfields back to their city.

Although the Spaniards' victory should have been cause for immediate celebration, circumstances would not permit it. The Spaniards returned to their camp and remained there for several days. Among rank and file and even some of the captains the mood was not mutinous but rather one of consternation. Since leaving Cuba, fifty-five in all had died—ten in Yucatan and forty-five in Mexico. Cortés did not dispute those numbers in a letter to King Charles I. The men were tired and many of them wounded. They asked don Hernando how they could possibly defeat the Aztecs who had innumerable warriors when they as conquistadors had difficulty confronting much lesser-numbered Tlaxcalans. They also complained of having left friends, families, and houses, and for what? Among the most vocal was Alonso de Grado, previously a staunch supporter of the conquistadors' goals.

Claiming that the Tlaxcalan War was already won, Cortés spoke successfully against a prevailing mood of despair. He pointed out that if they returned to Villa Rica without going to Tenochtitlan, their Totonac allies would turn against them. It was better, argued the Conqueror, to die in a good cause than to live in dishonor, and he concluded with these words: "So, gentlemen, if one way is bad, the other is worse." But it was obvious that if the war with Tlaxcala was not finished, trouble lay ahead. It was therefore Cortés' good fortune to soon learn that the war had indeed concluded. In the words of historical anthropologist and prolific author Ross Hassig, "peace had come none too soon."

Cortés's followers were in trouble. They comprised around 330 men-at-arms, many of whom were wounded, but that number also included such non-combatants as blacksmiths, carpenters, and a shipwright without peer named Martín López. Only thirteen horses remained, and five of those were so badly wounded they could not be ridden for days. The Spaniards also commanded fewer than 250 Indian allies. No matter loomed so large as securing an alliance with the Tlaxcalans and their warriors, and Cortés took steps to ensure that it happened.

The Conqueror and his fellow conquistadors entered Tlaxcala's main city on September 18, 1519, and they were warmly received by its leaders. Their assigned quarters consisted of "very pretty houses and palaces" near the main temple. Food was brought forth for Spaniards, as well as for their Totonac allies, and even the Spanish mastiffs and horses were given their share of cooked turkey and maize, respectively. Such welcome circumstances offered the Spaniards twenty days' repose. Their stay was important in many ways, and it started with rest, followed by the realization they had won the third battle with few losses. The conquistadors also appreciated the Tlaxcalans' balm of friendship, which lessened their homesickness and longing for Cuba.

As days passed, Spaniards marveled at the Tlaxcalan's principal city with its clean streets and market where Indian women shopped every day. Also available to the newcomers was an opportunity to barter glass beads and other trifles for trousers and shirts. The most important thing to emerge from Cortés's stay at Tlaxcala was his ability to forge a lasting alliance that would extend throughout the conquest. Unknown to him, it was an accord that would last for decades. Crucial to initial success was the Conqueror's friendship with two aged leaders of the Tlaxcalan confederation, Maxixcatzin and the elder Xicotencatl. Many in Tlaxcala revered these elder statesmen, but the younger Xicotencatl was not one of them. He did not share his father's enthusiasm for the foreigners, probably because he had been beaten in the night battle. Friction would remain between Cortés and the young military leader of Tlaxcala, perhaps because there was not room in Mexico for two such similar egos. However, don Hernando through force of personality, just as he had inspired most of his men-at-arms and captains, managed to gain the respect of two Tlaxcalan elders. In doing so, as historian Sir Hugh Thomas has observed, Cortés had demonstrated remarkable skills as a "consummate politician."

But there was another side to Cortés: that of an inflexible Catholic crusader who believed he could convert Indians to Christianity and end human sacrifice by fiat. He was tempted to try that approach again with the Tlaxcalans, having won an alliance that was crucial to his success in the conquest of Mexico. It took the combined efforts of fray Bartolomé de Olmedo, Juan Velázquez de León, and Pedro de Alvarado to dissuade him. Perhaps advice from the Mercedarian priest proved most persuasive. He told Cortés not to press the issue because "I would not like you to make Christians by force. Wait till they gradually feel the weight of our admonitions."

Throughout his stay at the Tlaxcalan's main city, Cortés had maintained a base at their original campsite where he at times received even Moctezuma's ambassadors. The Conqueror treated those men with courtesy since he still hoped to enter Tenochtitlan without fighting. Again, he demonstrated adroit if not duplicitous cunning by listening as the Mexica representatives insisted that the Tlaxcalans were wicked, thieving, and treacherous. The Nahua diplomats were nonetheless amazed that so few Spaniards had managed victories over foes the Mexica had thus far not been able to defeat. A still uncertain Moctezuma ordered his Nahua ambassadors to determine without fail whether the Spaniards were gods. Accordingly, the emissaries served food sprinkled with fresh blood from a sacrificed slave to Cortés himself who happened then to be in camp conferring with some of his captains. The Conqueror angrily rejected the offering, and he told the Nahua ministers that he was not a god but rather a man of flesh and blood. He had come in peace only to deliver greetings to Moctezuma from his king across the great waters.

As the Mexica ambassadors left to report to Moctezuma, they urged the Spaniards, then only about halfway to Tenochtitlan, to come immediately to their great city by way of Cholula, whose people had recently become their powerful allies. At Cholula, the Mexica said, the Spaniards would be welcome and safe, but the vile and traitorous Tlaxcalans would not be allowed to enter that city. Soon after, Cortés, with the support of his captains, decided to continue their march to the Aztec capital by way of Cholula instead of by Huexotzinco, which was recommended by the Tlaxcalans. In making that decision, don Hernando counted on pleasing the Aztecs while at the same time demonstrating to his new-found allies in Tlaxcala that he could protect them from their Cholulan enemies.

Tlaxcala's main city lay twenty-five miles from Cholula. On October 12, Cortés and his command left the comfort of the previous twenty days, during which they had been plied with food, given opportunities to trade for new clothing, and received in friendship. They were accompanied by thousands of Tlaxcalans. The wise old chieftains they were leaving behind gave them stark advice: You are going to meet Mexica in battle, and when you do be sure to kill everyone you can, "leaving no one alive; neither the young, lest they bear arms again; nor the old, lest they give good advice."

The Spaniards and their Indian allies covered about half the distance to Cholula before camping overnight. During travel the next day, they were met by several Cholulan leaders supported by a large escort bearing maize and turkeys as gifts. The caciques through interpreters told the Conqueror not to believe the lies he was likely told by the Tlaxcalans about their intentions. Cortés on cue gave a speech on the evils of human sacrifice and the benefits of worshipping the Christian God, which fell on deaf ears. One of the Cholulan lords replied that they could scarcely be expected to abandon their gods on the very day strangers entered their lands. Thereafter, according to the chronicler Andrés de Tapia, food became increasingly scarce every day, and when the Spaniards asked for fodder for their horses, they received nothing but water.

Cholula was an ancient city inhabited for at least a thousand years. It was noted for honoring and advancing the cult of Quetzalcoatl, the feathered serpent, and for having the largest pyramid by volume in the world. Its base covered an estimated 500,000 square feet, and it was taller than the *Templo Mayor* in Tenochtitlan. Spaniards, while admiring the great pyramid, were admitted to the inner part of Cholula and quartered in apartments around its plaza, but their Indians allies had to camp outside the city. The Cholulans, however, made it obvious over the next three days that the strangers were not welcome by giving them less and less food, and then nothing but water on the fourth.

Having been snubbed, Cortés consulted his captains on the best course to follow. Some wanted to return to Tlaxcala and from there take the road to

Tenochtitlan that passed through Huexotzinco, as recommended by the Tlaxcalans. Still other voices, probably those of Pedro de Alvarado, Cristóbal de Olid, and Gonzalo de Sandoval favored a preemptive strike on the Cholulans. Had the Tlaxcalan leaders been consulted, they no doubt would have favored that third option as well. Ominously, on the third night, the Cholulans vacated most of the city. On the following morning, Cortés supplied an armed guard for Doña Marina and sent her into the streets to learn what she could about what was happening. The only person she could find was an elderly blind woman who had been regarded as not important enough to have been moved to safety, but there was nothing wrong with the old woman's mind.

After speaking kind words in Nahuatl and gaining the woman's confidence, Marina asked her why the town was deserted. She allegedly replied that on the morrow the Cholulan warriors, aided by ten-thousand armed Mexica who were encamped beyond the city and beside the road to Tenochtitlan, planned to descend on "the bearded ones" and kill all of them. When Marina returned with this information, Cortés summoned the high chieftain of Cholula and asked why food and water had been cut off. The cacique apologized and assured the Conqueror that about two-thousand unarmed Cholulans would fill the town plaza the following morning to show good faith, and that the Spaniards would be given food and drink at that time.

Cortés suspected an ambush, and he asked fray Bartolomé Olmedo to bless him and the other Spaniards. The Conqueror then assigned Pedro de Alvarado, Cristóbal de Olid, Alonso de Ávila, and Juan Velázquez de León to apartments located near the corners of the town's square. They and all men-at-arms were armed with swords. The following morning, Cholulans filled the plaza. Cortés had the Requirement read to their headmen and afterward notarized by Diego de Godoy. Through Aguilar and Marina, don Hernando confronted the head cacique and asked why he planned to attack his men when they had come in peace. The chieftain denied that he had any such intentions. Why then, asked the Conqueror, were ten-thousand Mexica camped outside the town on the road to Tenochtitlan? The cacique replied that he knew nothing of nearby Aztec warriors.

At that point, Cortés ordered one of his musketeers to fire a shot that killed the Cholulan cacique. The discharged firearm was an agreed-upon signal for some 150 men-at-arms accompanied by a few Tlaxcalan chiefs to emerge from apartments on all sides of the plaza with drawn swords and begin killing the unarmed Indians. In perhaps a little more than an hour, every Cholulan lay dead or dying. Nothing in the multiple experiences of Hernando Cortés has tarnished his reputation quite like the wanton slaughter he unleashed in Cholula. It was one thing for him to kill Indians in battle, quite another to arrange the murder of defenseless men. Cortés, when later called upon by a magistrate to defend his actions, insisted that Doña Marina had not lied about what she had learned in talking to the old woman, and so he had ordered the attack to protect himself and his men but only after a reading of the Requirement. He also claimed that on the following march to Tenochtitlan he and his command saw ample evidence of where thousands of Mexica had camped outside the city. Nonetheless, the massacre at Cholula stands as the blackest mark on Cortés's role as captain general in the conquest of Mexico—a charge his apologists and defenders have been unable to remove. That said, evidence suggests that a plot orchestrated by Moctezuma and his advisers had been planned with the goal of killing the foreigners in Cholula and ending their advance on Tenochtitlan.

Cortés remained in Cholula for about two weeks. During that time, he ordered his Indian allies to clear and clean the plaza. He next ordered carpenters to erect a large cross in the town square, and at that time he could not be dissuaded by fray Bartolomé or his captains. He also soon received Moctezuma's ambassadors sent to Cholula who appeared "half dead with fear." Cortés told the Mexica representatives he believed Moctezuma had attempted to kill him and his men, even though he had come to Mexico with peaceful intentions. Consequently, the Conqueror declared, he would soon enter the Aztecs' land and do all the harm he could to his then-proven enemy.

Cortés, after honoring the Totonacs's request to return to their homes, organized his fellow conquistadors as well as about two-thousand Tlaxcalans and set out for Tenochtitlan, which was fifty miles from Cholula. Both cities are approximately 7,200 feet in elevation, but ahead for those on the march lay the mountain pass between the famous peaks, Popocatepetl and Iztaccihuatl. As they approached the volcano Popocatepetl, it was in an active phase. Diego de

Ordaz and Francisco de Montano asked permission to climb the peak, and don Hernando agreed to the delay. There is speculation the climbers hoped to find sulfur, a vital ingredient in gunpowder that was running low for the muskets and cannons. One of the remaining components of the explosive ingredients needed in gunpowder was carbon, which might have come from campfire ashes, but 75 percent of the third necessary ingredient was saltpeter, or potassium nitrate, and it was unavailable anywhere in Mexico.

From the top of the sierra, the southern end of the Valley of Mexico came into view. Just ten-miles away were blue lakes, with indications that a huge city loomed beyond them at about twice that distance. The apparent enormity of the Mexica metropolis caused mixtures of exhilaration and apprehension to course through some captains and many of the rank-and-file men. The more faint-of-heart wanted to return to Tlaxcala, but Cortés would not hear of it. The important city of Chalco beckoned straight ahead, situated at the extreme southeast shore of the lake system. [**Figure 11**]

Throughout the march from Cholula, Moctezuma's ambassadors urged Cortés and his men to stop their advance on Tenochtitlan by offering gifts of gold, cloth, and turquoise. The Indian agents further pledged annual tribute in riches to the Spaniards' king, provided his men did not enter the Aztec capital. Cortés treated the Mexica envoys with courtesy but said he must meet with Moctezuma to deliver his king's greeting to him. If he did not accomplish that goal, his monarch would be unhappy with him and continue appointing other commanders until his intentions were fulfilled. That being the case, the Conqueror replied that he was determined to enter Tenochtitlan.

When Moctezuma received Cortés's reply, he sent his nephew Cacama, Lord of Texcoco, with the promise of even more lavish gifts, provided the Spaniards would halt their advance on Tenochtitlan. Cacama stated that Moctezuma himself would have delivered the same message he bore, but the emperor was ill and could not personally attend the matter. In the meantime, if he could not stop the advancing foreigners, then fine apartments constructed of stone would be available for them at Chalco. The city was located about ten miles from Ixtapalapa where the southern causeway began. Upon reaching the apartments, Spaniards

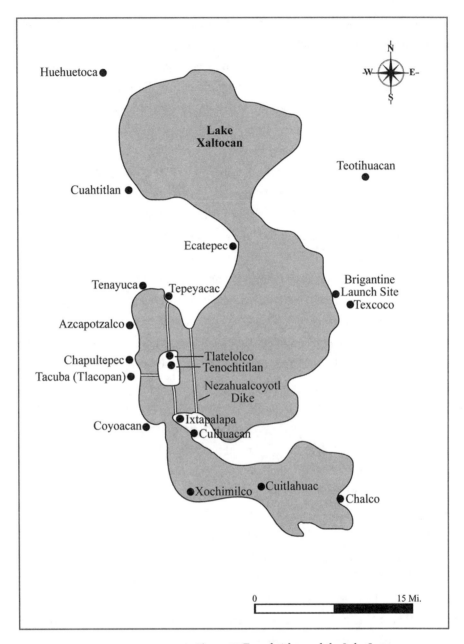

Figure 11. Tenochtitlan and the Lake System.

commented that the walls of their quarters were clean and covered with brilliant white stucco. That prompted some conquistadors to offer a rare compliment that they had never seen finer masonry in Spain.

The next day, Cortés and his followers skirted the eastern projection of Lake Xochimilco and began a march of about ten miles westward toward Ixtapalapa. About five miles into their trek, for the first time the great Aztec capital came into full view. When the column reached the entry of the southern walkway into Tenochtitlan, the sight brought forth astonished comments. In the words of Bernal Díaz: "When we saw . . . that straight and level causeway going towards Mexico, we were amazed and said that it was like the enchantments they tell of in the legend of Amadis, on account of the great towers and cues [pyramids] and buildings rising from the water, and all built of masonry. And some of our soldiers even asked whether the things we saw were not a dream . . . I do know how to describe it, seeing things as we did that had never before been heard of or seen before, nor even dreamed about."

Moctezuma, as was typical of him, still tried to prevent the Spaniards from entering Tenochtitlan but chose half measures. He ordered the western and northern causeways blocked with huge, spiny maguey plants at their entrances in such manner that it was impossible to get around them. The emperor left the longest elevated walkway at Ixtapalapa free of obstructions. It was over six miles in length and flanked by water. Mexica warriors in huge canoes carved from hollowed tree trunks, each capable of carrying one-hundred armed men, could attack unwelcome visitors throughout its length. That became unnecessary when the Mexica Emperor, despite advice to the contrary from some members of his private council, decided to invite the foreigners into Tenochtitlan; and he himself would meet and welcome them at the outskirts of the city.

Cortés spent hours with his captains on the night prior to entering the Ixtapalapa causeway with the goal of making the best possible impression of his conquistadors and Tlaxcalan allies. The Conqueror estimated the width of the southern portion of the raised walkway at about six yards, and he believed it could accommodate four horses aligned side-by-side. Next came footmen numbering about 310 Spaniards and 2,000 Tlaxcalans. The European contingent received orders to polish their swords and shields during the night, while the

Indian chieftains were to dress and paint themselves as though preparing for a great celebration. There was little the Conqueror could do to improve the appearance of the burden bearers, so they were placed last in formation and ordered to pull the Lombard cannons mounted on two-wheeled carts. Behind them were the greyhounds and mastiffs—all panting, whining, and sniffing unfamiliar surroundings. At first, Cortés decided to walk while leading the rear assemblage.

Cortés's choice for the four caballeros heading the advance on Tenochtitlan were likely Alvarado, Olid, Ordaz, and Velázquez de León—all dressed in armor. Positioned after his best horsemen was Cristóbal de Corral, mounted and bearing the standard of Castile and León. Sandoval and the rest of the mounted cavaliers apparently fell in behind Corral. That formation remained in place for about four miles. At that juncture, the final league of the causeway broadened to around twelve yards, whereupon Cortés moved four more horses and their riders forward. And at that time, don Hernando moved to the front of the column and led it on his gelding Altivo, followed immediately by the standard bearer.

On the final stretch of causeway, the Conqueror ordered the footmen to brandish their swords, crank their crossbows, and display their muskets. Indian allies near the rear of the column began whistling, shouting, and ululating. Aztecs in canoes were fascinated, having never seen such a spectacle. They paddled their watercraft along both sides of the walkway to get a better look at the entire procession. As the Spaniards approached the city proper a quiet settled over everyone, including the Indians, which was broken only by the snorting of horses. Ahead rose great palaces, innumerable flat-roofed houses, and an enormous pyramid with a temple atop it. Tenochtitlan then had an estimated population of nearly two-hundred-thousand inhabitants, perhaps second in population only to Naples and Constantinople.

At the edge of the great city, an Aztec delegation advanced to receive the newcomers. Moctezuma appeared on a litter under a canopy of beautiful quetzal feathers and rich cloth bordered in gold and silver. The emperor at an appropriate time descended from the litter and, surrounded by his personal retinue, walked toward the Conqueror. All were barefooted except for the emperor, who wore sandals. Ahead of Moctezuma, servants swept the ground with feather whisks. Cortés, already dismounted, approached. When the two men were only a few feet apart, the Aztec emperor wet a finger in his mouth, touched ground, and ate dirt as a sign of respect. Cortés immediately responded in like manner. However, as the Conqueror tried to embrace Moctezuma, he was stopped by the emperor's bodyguard, because no one dared touch the royal body. As recorded by the renowned scholar fray Bernardino de Sahagún, Cortés said: "Art thou not he? Art thou Moctezuma?" And the emperor replied: "Yes, I am he."

Cortés, along with his command and Tlaxcalan allies entered Tenochtitlan on November 8, 1519. After formalities of the encounter between the two parties had ended, Moctezuma ordered his aides to escort don Hernando and his 330 Spanish captains and men-at-arms to quarters set aside for them in the Aztec capital. They could hardly have asked for better accommodations, since they were housed in the huge palace formerly occupied by Moctezuma's father, the sixth Mexica emperor Axayacatl. Those amenities, however, were not extended to the Tlaxcalans. One can imagine Moctezuma saying that such vile and hated enemies of the Mexica would not be allowed to sleep under the same roof as his father had. On that point the emperor was likely adamant: the Tlaxcalans had to leave the city. They retreated down the southern causeway and camped near the town of Ixtapalapa. The removal of two-thousand Indian allies to a location some seven miles from where the Spaniards were housed in Tenochtitlan would seem to have made the Castilians more vulnerable to attacks, but that did not become a matter of concern. Events in far off Spain would determine whether Hernando Cortés would hang for defying a royal governor in Cuba or succeed without portfolio in the conquest of Mexico.

CHAPTER 9

Spaniards in Tenochtitlan and the Narváez Expedition

In July 1519, Hernando Cortés sent Alonso Hernández de Puertocarrero, Francisco de Montejo, and about fifty sailors to Spain. Loaded on the nao were almost all the gold, silver, gems, and other precious items collected in Yucatan and Mexico—exceptions being the large disks of gold and silver representing the sun and moon that were special gifts from Moctezuma. Normally, the Crown was due only one-fifth (the *quinto*) of such items. Cortés, however, was on shaky legal ground, having repudiated Governor Diego Velázquez in Cuba and later been denounced as a renegade conquistador by him. The almost complete consignment of treasure by the Conqueror, intended to win favor with the king, had caused grumbling from rank and file conquistadors as well as from some of the captains. Where was their share, since they were freelance adventurers hoping to get rich? Nonetheless, don Hernando as commander-captain of the expedition overrode their objections.

When Puertocarrero and Montejo arrived at Seville in the fall, treasury officials impounded the treasure on directives from Juan de Fonseca—pending orders from Charles I. The bishop, no friend of Cortés, was instead favorable to Diego Velázquez who had been recently appointed *adelantado* of Yucatan. At that time, the king had many things on his mind. Perhaps foremost, the awkward teenager had become increasingly unpopular since his arrival in Spain in 1516 following the death of his grandfather, Ferdinand the Catholic. The son of the psychologically unstable Queen Juana, Charles had grown up in Flanders; and he allegedly spoke not one word of Castilian on his arrival in Spain. In his retinue were rapacious Flemish and Burgundian advisers who intended to get rich at the expense of Spaniards. Those officials alienated the older, more conservative Castilian nobility, and in the early months of 1520 Spain drifted into an internal conflict known as the Revolt of the Comuneros—so named because the movement was primarily associated with the larger cities in Spain.

The ensuing turmoil caused King Charles I to travel often, especially after he learned that his other grandfather, the Hapsburg Maximilian I, had also died. That death meant the King of Spain would soon be crowned Holy Roman Emperor Charles V. Meanwhile, Cortés's representatives, having been rebuffed and insulted in Seville where even their personal possessions were impounded, set out across Spain hoping to gain an audience with Charles I. They often arrived just days after he had departed from a given locale, so they kept moving along paths taken by the king. In transit, they were joined by Martín Cortés, don Hernando's father, who would remain at court as advocate for his son. The trio finally overtook Charles at La Coruña on the far northwest coast of Spain in May 1520, just days before he and his advisers sailed for Flanders.

When granted an audience, Puertocarrero was articulate. He was related to important families in Spain, probably more closely than any of Cortés's captains. He described to King Charles what don Hernando had accomplished in Yucatan and Mexico, and he enumerated the articles of treasure intended for his Majesty that had been impounded in Seville. The king was favorably impressed and ordered release of the treasure with consignment to Crown coffers, as well as restoring the personal effects of Puertocarrero and Montejo. That was an initial and important victory for Cortés.

By the time Charles I sailed from Spain on May 20, 1520, fighting had begun, and he left the country in turmoil. He did not return to Castile until early 1522, then as recently crowned Charles V, to discover the Revolt of the Comuneros had ended favorably for him and his reign. The brief civil conflict is beyond the scope of this study, except to remark that many of the older nobility in Spain rallied in support for Charles as civil unrest progressed toward demands for social change, a trend supported by the lower classes—a not uncommon occurrence in history. Among those families who gained increasing favor with Charles V were surnames like Mendoza, Monroy, Velasco, and Guzmán.

While those events transpired in Europe, Cortés and his 350 fellow conquistadors settled into the palace of Moctezuma's father. At that same time, Francisco de Garay in Jamaica decided to send a colonizing expedition to Indian settlements along the Río Pánuco where Alonso Álvarez de Pineda and his men had previously anchored for about forty days. During that time, they remained aboard their ships as bases of operation before returning to Jamaica. Once there, Garay almost immediately sent Pineda and his mariners back to sea, and they sailed directly to the Río Pánuco rather than repeating the prior approach along the Gulf Coast west of what they had called Florida. The suddenness of Pineda's return suggests he was not adequately provisioned to colonize Pánuco. Instead, he had been sent by Garay to establish his claim to the province before Cortés might attempt the same from nearby Villa Rica de Veracruz. On the follow-up expedition, the governor of Jamaica had ordered Pineda to set up a colony along both banks of the Río Pánuco.

Garay, realizing that his fledgling colony had to be supported externally, sent supply ships on a regular basis until settlement had become more secure. Diego de Camargo, who had served under Garay in Jamaica since 1518, commanded the first of those efforts. He sailed to the Río Pánuco in early 1520 with three caravels, 150 sailors and men-at-arms, seven horses, and materials needed for the construction of a fort.

Several months after Camargo arrived, the Huastecs rebelled against Spanish occupation of their lands. It is perhaps remembered that these Indians had fought a naval battle with Juan de Grijalva in 1518. That engagement pitted Indians in war canoes armed with copper-headed hatchets against Spanish cannons and caravels. Even so, the Huastecs had managed to cut the cables on one of Grijalva's vessels. The Huastec revolt in summer 1520 killed forty Spaniards—including Pineda— and all the horses, and then destroyed the beginnings of Garay's colony. Camargo managed to save two caravels out of a total of six or seven, but both vessels had scant provisions. The ships with sixty men aboard fled downriver, pursued to the mouth of the Río Pánuco and beyond, harassed throughout by armed Huastecs firing arrows from canoes.

When the Indians broke off their pursuit, Camargo took stock of his situation. He was wounded and in charge of sixty men with almost no food. Some of the survivors chose being placed ashore in hopes of foraging their way to Villa Rica, but they were hunted and killed by Huastecs. Camargo and others aboard ships suffered a terrible fate. Normally, sailing two-hundred miles should not have been a problem for the caravels, but those were far from ordinary times. Both ships had been damaged in the fighting, and their crews were weak and exhausted in trying to perform the most routine matters on sailing vessels. One of the caravels leaked so badly it had to be beached. Those aboard joined the remaining vessel, but it sank at anchorage off Villa Rica. Among those who came ashore was Camargo, who died of wounds and near starvation. Others followed their captain in death with stomachs distended and discolored from having eaten little or no food for two weeks. Always observant Bernal Díaz called those unfor-tunates "the green bellies."

Garay, unaware that his colony had been destroyed, sent at least two more supply ships. His long-time business partner Miguel Díaz de Aux commanded the first, while an obscure captain referred to only as "Ramírez el Viejo" commanded the second. Both followed similar courses by first sailing to the Río Pánuco, but upon finding no colony there continued down the coast where the crews defected and joined the ranks of Cortés's men at Villa Rica. More important, both ships carried several kegs of much-needed gunpowder and a few horses, prompting Bernal Díaz to comment again that the total effort and expense of Francisco de Garay had redounded to the good fortune of Cortés—not to Garay himself in Jamaica.

Back at Tenochtitlan in late 1519, Cortés and his command would remain unaware of events in Pánuco, as well as news of the arrival of ships and men from there, until several months later. In the meantime, the Spaniards were treated well by Moctezuma and housed in the palace of his father Axayacatl. Bernal Díaz described the emperor as a man about forty years of age. He was thin in stature and had a scant black beard. His skin was "the natural color and in the shade of an Indian," while his countenance was pleasant. In accompanying Cortés and his men to their quarters, Moctezuma rode on a litter supported by four Mexica. He was the only man wearing sandals, while his retinue of more than two-hundred was barefooted. Díaz also stated that the emperor was very clean, because he bathed every afternoon.

Once his guests were housed, Moctezuma visited the Spaniards almost every day and asked whether they needed anything more to eat or drink. The Mexica also provided grass and water for the horses. On a later visit as the emperor exchanged pleasantries with Cortés, Bernal Díaz recorded an incident that showed profound disrespect for Moctezuma. As a rank-and-file conquistador left the palace to relieve himself, he broke wind as he passed the imperious Moctezuma. The emperor's guard quaked in fear, as though they had somehow permitted this deadly insult and would receive punishment for it. Cortés apologized and had the lout flogged, but there was nothing the Conqueror could do to make amends to the offended emperor.

A few less stressful days passed, and Cortés then asked Moctezuma if he might visit his city and admire its wonders—in truth to please the emperor and for don Hernando to assess the city's strength. The emperor agreed, but only if he and his retinue led the way, because he thought the strangers might unwittingly do or say something that would offend the gods. Cortés consulted his captains, and they feared a possible ambush to kill their captain general, since the emperor went about with more than two-hundred bodyguards, priests, and soothsayers. The captains thought it best to leave Alvarado with fifty armed men at the palace, while Cortés would be accompanied by more than two-hundred conquistadors, as well as all the horses, to ensure his safety.

The resulting assemblage of Spaniards and Aztecs that numbered about four-hundred men and thirteen horses soon arrived at the great plaza in Tenochtitlan and approached the base of the enormous Templo Mayor. Moctezuma stepped from the litter and supported by priests ascended the steps of the pyramid. At its top he burned incense to honor the war god, Huitzilopochtli, and the rain deity, Tlaloc. Before the Spaniards had ascended a single step, Moctezuma sent down six priests and two chieftains who attempted to assist the Conqueror's climb. Cortés would not allow them to touch him as he mounted the great cue on his own, but at the same time ordered his steward, Diego de Ordáz, to count every step, which numbered one-hundred and fourteen.

At the top of the pyramid was a platform where human sacrifices took place. On it was a large convex stone where victims were splayed before their hearts were torn out. Likewise, near the platform was a large brazier used to immolate hearts in honor of Huitzilopochtli and Tlaloc and a large snake-skin drum beaten during sacrifices. Moctezuma soon took Cortés's hand and pointed out the lake system. He also directed the Conqueror's attention to an unparalleled view of Tenochtitllan's estimated forty-thousand houses and several great palaces. Among the Spanish contingent atop the Templo Mayor was the master shipwright and boat builder named Martín López. In Castilian, Cortés told the carpenter to look for the best place from which to escape the city by water should that become necessary.

When both Spaniards and Mexica were again at the base of the Templo Mayor, Moctezuma told Cortés through Doña Marina and Aguilar that he wished to show them Tenochtitlan's aviary, zoo, and market. At the first stop, Bernal Díaz wrote that there too many birds to even mention them in full. They included great and small eagles, other birds-of-prey, and water birds, and the especially rare and resplendently plumed quetzal from Central American regions. The zoo had two kinds of carnivorous cats, probably cougars and ocelots. The smaller caged animals were wolves and foxes. But nothing topped the great market in Tlatelolco that left the dozens of Spaniards in awe.

On display in the marketplace was every kind of merchandise imaginable— from gold and silver objects to Indian slaves, both men and women. Varieties of cloth were spun from either cotton or henequen. Poultry and meat items included live turkeys, quail, and small hairless and voiceless dogs raised for food. Women offered tortillas, cooked items, and a variety of fruits. Apparel on display included shirts, trousers, and sandals. Finally, one could even purchase lumber, cradles, and benches. All exchanges involved barter. For example, Indians traded woven cotton blankets of varying sizes, honey from beehives, and some came with feather quills that contained small amounts of gold dust. The only items approximating currency were cacao beans, which were used to round out perceived inequities in the value of exchanged items. The great Tlatelolco market also expanded into several nearby streets.

But wonders had their limits. Spaniards hesitated to look in dark corners and corridors. Therein might lie baskets of arms and legs. Near the Great Pyramid stood graphic evidence of human sacrifice on a scale almost unimaginable. A great billboard-like structure called a *tzompantli* that displayed an estimated one-hundred-thousand skulls mounted on wooden pegs. Word-talented Bernal Díaz wrote that the vacant eye sockets stared at him like "infernal dice." Trouble started when Moctezuma offered at the conclusion of his guided tour to permit Cortés and a few captains to enter the Mexica's most sacred temple, which contained statue-like representations of two important gods.

One of the objects was a representation of Huitzilopochtli. All Aztecs gods had multiple identities and powers. Huitzilopochtli was the principal god of war but also represented the sun. As mentioned earlier, the Mexica believed the great orb needed the precious liquid of human blood to give it strength to travel across the sky each day. The image of the god Tezcatlipoca was carved from shiny black stone that extended from about halfway up its head to its feet. Revered as "god of the smoking mirror," a reference to the Aztecs' highly prized obsidian, the deity represented both good and evil. Tezcatlipoca was god of the underworld, and in May the feast of Toxcatl was primarily held to honor that deity—but more on that later.

On leaving the temple, Diego de Ordaz asked Moctezuma through Aguilar and Doña Marina how a ruler as great and powerful as he could believe the two deities were benevolent rather than idols who more closely resembled the devil. The emperor and his priests were instantly outraged. Moctezuma allegedly said to Cortés: "Malinche, [you] are a guest in my city and welcome to stay as long as you wish. But had I known that one of your captains would say such defaming things about our gods, I would not have agreed to bring you and your men into their revered presence. Huitzilopochtli and Tezcatlipoca have never forsaken us. Instead, each year they bring health to us, good harvests, and victory in warfare." As amends for such a terrible affront, the emperor stated that he must beg forgiveness from the gods and would do so by ordering increased human sacrifices. Perhaps Cortés caught a meaningful glance from fray Bartolomé de Olmedo and did not pursue the subject but remarked in cheerful manner: "It is time for your Excellency and for us to return." The matter ended but not without don Hernando resolving to end human sacrifice and find a place in which to offer Mass for himself and his men.

Although Moctezuma had denied Cortés's request to erect a cross in a temple alongside Mexica gods, the emperor did allow the Spaniards to set up an altar in a vacant building near their palace residence. Carpenters erected a cross, and priests offered daily Mass. But Moctezuma's concession did not ease the Conqueror's concerns, given the Spaniards' numbering only three-hundred and fifty in a city with a population of perhaps just fewer than two-hundred-thousand. To address this potentially dangerous circumstance, Cortés arranged a meeting with his captains.

Their discussions were far-reaching. Some captains recommended withdrawing at night from Tenochtitlan and not stopping until they reached Villa Rica. That approach was dismissed as cowardly, since it risked alienating the Totonacs whom the Spaniards had pledged to protect and upon whom they depended at their newly founded town of Villa Rica. Worse, it would likely result in ending the hard-won alliance with the Tlaxcalans. If, on the other hand, they retreated, but only to Tlaxcala, what then? Eventually, Cortés and his most trusted captains, including Alvarado, Olid, Sandoval, and Ordaz, decided on a high-stakes gamble. The Spaniards would seize Moctezuma and place him under house arrest in their palace residence. But for what offense, since the emperor has always treated them with the utmost respect and kindness?

At this same time, bad news arrived from Tlaxcalans camped beyond the southern causeway. They bore a letter from Villa Rica carried by a Totonac runner that was addressed to Cortés. Within the missive were details of an Aztec attack on a town called Nautla with important consequences. As a reminder, while sojourning among the Totonac people in 1518 Juan de Grijalva had ventured about fifty miles up the coast from San Juan de Ulúa and named a town "Almería" (Nautla to the Totonacs and as it is known in present-day Mexico.) The settlement by either name was on the northern fringe of Totonac-controlled lands. A Mexica governor and tax collector named Qualpopoca had visited Nautla-Almería and demanded the usual eighty-day tribute. The Indians refused to pay because

Cortés had freed them of obligations to the Aztecs. Moctezuma's agent threatened reprisals, and the town's caciques appealed to Juan de Escalante, whom Cortés had left in charge at Villa Rica.

Escalante was one of Cortés's most able and respected captains, and in the manner of his commander general gathered a few Spaniards and Totonac allies and marched to defend the town. A battle ensued, and Escalante's Indian allies soon deserted and took to their heels. Left undermanned, Escalante attempted a somewhat disorderly retreat, but in the fighting received fatal wounds. One of his men-at-arms was captured by Qualpopoca, who tore out his heart and cut off his head. The severed head was sent as a trophy to Moctezuma in Tenochtitlan, who received it unbeknownst to Cortés but quickly disposed of it outside the city. Nonetheless, two Spaniards had died at the hands of Moctezuma's tribute collector.

Cortés used the incident at Nautla to arrest Moctezuma in his own palace and throne room. An important justification for taking such swift action was fear of losing the support of Totonacs at then-understaffed and more vulnerable Villa Rica. The Conqueror gained an audience with the emperor in mid-November. As usual, he was accompanied by Alvarado, Sandoval, Velázquez de León, and Ordaz, plus translators Doña Marina and Aguilar. Moctezuma, not expecting anything untoward, was pleased to see Cortés and offered him one of his daughters as a "delicious fruit" as well as items of little value.

The mood changed when the Conqueror accused Moctezuma of attempting to ambush him and his men at Cholula. Despite that terrible offense, don Hernando said he had forgiven the emperor and done everything in his power to please him and be a true friend—yet, as the Conqueror charged, Moctezuma had been responsible for the death of his captain at Nautla as well as one of his conquistadors who had been sacrificed and beheaded. The Conqueror then told the emperor that if he were willing to accompany him to his palace quarters without complaint or crying out, he would forgive all. However, if Moctezuma summoned his bodyguards, Alvarado would kill him then and there.

Moctezuma quite reasonably replied: "My person is not such as can be made a prisoner. Even if I would like it, [because] my people would not suffer it." Back and forth arguments on that point between Cortés's insistence and

Moctezuma's resistance went on for almost four hours. Eventually, Velázquez de León lost his temper and told Moctezuma to either come at once with the Spaniards or he would kill him where he stood. The emperor did not understand the threat and asked Doña Marina what had been said. After translating the words, Marina advised Moctezuma to go peaceably with the Spaniards because they would not dare harm him. But the emperor still refused to leave his throne room. Cortés offered one last compromise that ended the standoff. Through his interpreters, he told Moctezuma he would only have to live among the Spaniards until the truth of what happened at Nautla could be learned. In the meantime, the emperor would have full authority to rule as always but from the palace of his father. That said, Moctezuma agreed to go with Cortés and enter the Axayacatl Palace.

Once the emperor was settled in his new quarters, Cortés demanded that he order Qualpopoca and those in his party who had made war on Spaniards to come to Tenochtitlan and face charges. Within a week or so, Qualpopoca, his two sons, and fifteen Mexica arrived in the Aztec capital. The Conqueror had them brought to the Axayacatl Palace and placed in irons. There followed interrogation with Doña Marina and Aguilar serving as translators. At first, Qualpopoca stated he had acted on his own and that he and his soldiers were responsible. Cortés did not believe him since all orders in the Mexica Empire came directly from Moctezuma. Under intense interrogation, the Conqueror asked the Aztec chieftain: "Did Moctezuma order you to collect tribute from the Totonacs at Nautla?" He replied: "Who else could have?"

Cortés ordered the public immolation of Qualpopoca, his two sons, and the fifteen Mexica in Tenochtitlan's great square at the base of the Templo Mayor. All were burned alive. The victims were apparently fettered to a chain taken from one of the beached vessels and used on the march to Tenochtitlan to tow the Lombard cannons. Fuel for the executions came from the Mexica's armory and it consisted of piles of wooden arrows, sword holders, and other combustibles. Moctezuma was marched to the great square in manacles to witness the executions and help "prevent an uproar." Cortés knew how to humiliate Indian chieftains when it suited his purposes, and Moctezuma saw items in his armory depleted while one of his governors and a tribute collector died along with his sons.

Burning to death as a mode of execution was practiced in Europe at that time, especially heretics condemned by the Spanish and Papal Inquisitions. It will also be remembered that Diego Velázquez in Cuba, with Cortés and probably Bartolomé de las Casas being present among other observers, had burned the Taíno chief Hatuey in 1511. The Mexica themselves burned transgressors for commission of such unpardonable offenses as committing adultery while attending the *Calmecac* school for privileged youths.

Following the executions, Cortés removed Moctezuma's leg irons and the two returned to the Axayacatl Palace. As the Conqueror insisted, Moctezuma continued to rule his empire from there, but Cortés ruled Moctezuma. Over the next four months, the Aztec emperor settled into life among Spaniards but gone were the splendor and power of his own surroundings and privilege. Moctezuma, in fact, soon became liked and befriended by several conquistadors, because he was affable, eager to learn the ways of Spaniards, and even demonstrated a sense of humor.

That was an interval when life became routine for some 330 conquistadors. They were well fed, had nice surroundings, and time on their hands. As mentioned, Gonzalo de Sandoval loved playing chess, and in his personal kit he carried a set of pieces and board. He spent hours playing chess with the Alvarado brothers. Moctezuma became interested and asked Doña Marina to explain the game, which of course she did not understand. Along with the assistance of Aguilar and Marina, Sandoval agreed to teach the basics of chess to Moctezuma, and he loved it.

The emperor then approached Cortés and asked if he could teach the Conqueror to play a popular Aztec game called Totoloque. It involved gambling, long enjoyed by don Hernando. The objective of play was to see which of two players, each having small gold tokens, could come closest to a wall in a series of tosses with bets at stake. Results were kept after each pitch by an agreed upon score keeper, suggested as Pedro de Alvarado by Cortés. Moctezuma was better at the game than Cortés but somehow lost more often than he won. The emperor complained and asked to see the scorecard, while pointing out that Tonatiuh—as the Mexica always called don Pedro because of his unusual reddish blond hair—had cheated him. This had led to a lot of laughter and good-natured joking.

With the emperor in a good mood, Cortés mentioned that among his men were sailors who had expressed interest in boating on the lakes that surrounded Tenochtitlan. Don Hernando suggested a contest in which his boat-builder Martín López could construct bigger and better craft than any Mexica carpenter. Moctezuma took up the challenge, claiming his people knew the lakes better than anyone, and pointed to their fine canoes capable of carrying one-hundred passengers. In fact, the emperor was so confident of winning that he promised to supply hardwoods for the Spanish carpenter. Cortés and Moctezuma ended their discussion by wagering a small amount of gold dust on the impending competition.

More immediately, it was imperative that the Conqueror send a replacement for his deceased captain at Villa Rica. He chose a conquistador named Alonso de Grado to take charge of the Spanish settlement and strengthen the fort. Bernal Díaz and many of Cortés's captains disliked Grado. To them, he not a "man's man," since he was a musician and a skilled writer. Díaz penned a scathing assessment of don Alonso: "Had he been as good a man of war as he was a man of good manners, it would have been to his advantage." But he was not. Grado demanded gold, jewels, and pretty women from the Totonacs and paid no attention to improving the fort. Instead, he spent his time gambling, eating well, drinking excessively, and seducing Indian women. Worse, Grado let it be known that should Diego Velázquez or any of his captains arrive in Mexico, he would gladly join them and give up the land Cortés sought to settle with his preference being to serve the governor of Cuba.

When Cortés learned of Grado's conduct, he ordered him sent to Tenochtitlan. As don Alonso approached the Aztec capital on horseback, he was intercepted by an angry Pedro de Alvarado who unhorsed Grado, tied a rope around his neck, and marched him the final league. Don Pedro put the chastened conquistador in stocks and left him for public ridicule, but not without telling Grado that he would have preferred to hang him—with, of course, the permission of Cortés. The Conqueror somehow liked Grado and set him free, and that would not be the end of don Hernando's favors to Grado—more on this somewhat later.

Grado's removal as captain at Villa Rica forced Cortés to name another successor. Although he disliked losing the services of Gonzalo de Sandoval in

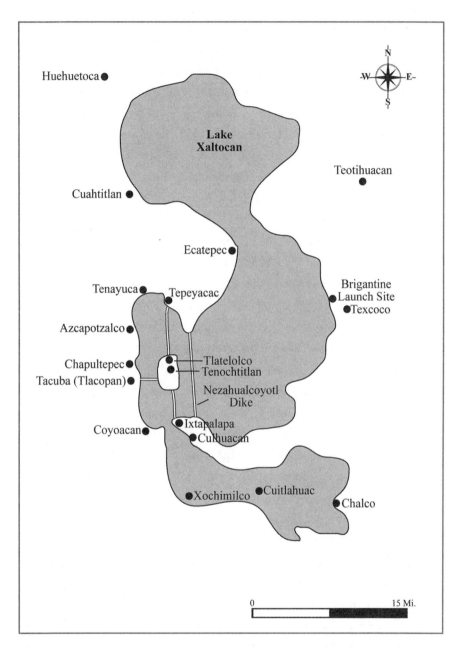

Figure 11. Tenochtitlan and the Lake System.

Tenochtitlan, don Hernando sent his youngest captain to the coast—but likely without his prized chess set, since it had become so popular with Spaniards and Moctezuma in the palace. More relevant to the outcome of the conquest, don Gonzalo upon reaching Villa Rica relayed orders to send back chains, anchors, rigging, and canvas from the beached ships for use by the exceptionally skilled ship and boatwright Martín López. [**Figure 11**]

When the materials arrived in Tenochtitlan, López began outfitting four shallow-draft brigantines made of oak from trees just beyond Texcoco and cedars from more nearby Tacuba to the west of the Aztec capital. Each brig could carry eighty men and two horses. When the first was finished, Cortés invited Moctezuma to sail around part of the lake system. The emperor was much impressed and admitted that don Hernando had won their wager. At the same time, the Conqueror assured Moctezuma that the other craft still under construction were intended only for sailing exercises.

At this time, Cortés's conversations with the Aztec emperor became more casual without the aid of Aguilar. Doña Marina had obvious facility in learning languages, and by early 1520 she could understand don Hernando's Castilian well enough to not require an interlocutor in Aguilar. That gave her exceptional importance among Cortés's inner circle of advisors, because only she could understand Nahuatl. Furthermore, as Bernal Díaz stated, many Spaniards liked Marina and regarded her with respect; and, as the garrulous chronicler added, she was pretty—"for an Indian."

Something resembling cordiality developed between Moctezuma and Cortés as their ease of communication improved without Aguilar and delayed double translations. The emperor asked don Hernando if he would permit four of his daughters and a son to join him in the Axayacatl Palace. Of the five children claimed by Moctezuma, two were legitimate by Aztecs standards, because their mother was the emperor's principal wife as determined by a special marriage ceremony and consummation rites. Son Chimalpopoca was first in order of succession on the death of his father; second was daughter Tecuichpotzin. Cortés said he would allow the children to join their father on the condition that the daughters accept baptism as Christians and accept common Spanish first names for women. After some opposition, Moctezuma agreed.

The five children were admitted to the palace and there joined their father, which resulted in a happy reunion. Fray Bartolomé de Olmedo probably performed the baptismal rites. Tecuichpotzin was christened Isabel; her half-sisters as Ana, María, and Mariana (later known exclusively as Leonor). Moctezuma's children had their own retinue of maids, servants, and guards, and those aides came and went daily. As consequence, they carried news to the emperor of events transpiring in and around Tenochtitlan. Again, only Doña Marina in Cortés's inner circle understood Nahuatl, and her ears could not be everywhere.

The aides informed Moctezuma that provinces subject to Aztec tribute collections, sensing his powers had been lessened as a captive of Cortés, had begun shorting their previous quarterly payments. That had alerted Cacama, the high cacique at Texcoco, and caused him to enforce the original payment schedules but redirect them to himself. The Texcocan chieftain also increased his powers by recruiting half a dozen high Mexica officials to help enforce his scheme, which meant all were at least guilty of undercutting Moctezuma's authority while enriching themselves.

When the emperor learned of Cacama and his associates' plotting, he shared that information with Cortés. The two jointly ordered the arrest of those altering tribute schedules and shackled them to an anchor chain linked to a pillar in the palace. The role of Moctezuma in this is interesting, because even under house confinement he was determined to keep his awesome powers intact while believing his gods would eventually free him. Cortés, however, had different motives. He had managed to acquire a rare Aztec manuscript, the *Matrícula de Tributos* (Register of Tributes), which contained detailed payments made by some sixteen provinces that were subjects of the Mexica. In the future, the Conqueror would take steps to make sure the *Matrícula* was never out of his possession. In the post-conquest era, he knew with certainty which towns were most valuable. Those he awarded in encomienda to himself and his favorites, both Spaniards and Indians. Few people in Mexico could plan better than captain general Hernando Cortés.

As sometimes happens when matters are going well, however, Cortés soon found himself facing his most serious challenge in Mexico. As mentioned, Governor Diego Velázquez in Cuba was often quick to anger and equally quick to forgive, but what Cortés had done in defying him was unforgiveable. In early

March 1520, don Diego decided to force the issue in Mexico with his former friend and partner. He recruited about nine-hundred men-at-arms and sailors and placed them on eleven naos and seven brigantines. Velázquez had initially planned to lead this expedition; however, age and corpulence caused him to reconsider and then appoint a much younger and ambitious captain named Pánfilo de Narváez. Red-bearded don Pánfilo received orders to arrest Cortés at a minimum but hanging him was the preferred option.

The Narváez expedition followed the then-familiar sailing route to San Juan de Ulúa—Cozumel, Yucatan, and Tabasco—before duplicating Cortés's prior landing on the narrow sandy beach at San Juan de Ulúa around April 20. Moctezuma's caciques occupied towns near the landing and farther inland. A Mexica artist drew on cloth a representation of eighteen ships, and a runner set off with it to Tenochtitlan. Once there, the depiction reached Moctezuma in the palace before Cortés knew of Narváez's arrival. The emperor, hopeful of returning to full power and authority, saw an opportunity to ally himself with men he believed inimical to the Conqueror. He replied by runner with a proposal for an alliance between him and the captain in charge of the ships and the hundreds of men he commanded.

Cortés learned of the Spaniards having arrived at San Juan a few days later. His response was immediate. He met the challenge head-on, as was his nature, by force-marching to the coast with a contingent of captains and men-at-arms. It is difficult to estimate the total number of conquistadors in and near Tenochtitlan at that time. Numbers had increased with those accompanying Alonso de Grado's less-than-ceremonial arrival with a rope around his neck but decreased as Gonzalo de Sandoval chose a cadre of trusted men to join him in restoring order at Villa Rica. Also, during protracted calm at the palace, Cortés had sent out several scouting expeditions, and Velázquez de León was on one of those outings from a base in Cholula.

At the beginning of May 1520, Cortés led around 180 conquistadors toward the coast, while leaving Alvarado with about 80 men to guard Moctezuma and keep order at the Palace. The Conqueror held hope of recruiting some four-thousand Tlaxcalan allies as he passed through their homelands but failed to enlist any. Xicotencatl the Elder, a Lord of Tlaxcala, informed don Hernando that he would not allow his warriors to participate in any battle between Spaniards, because he was only interested in killing Aztecs. That meant Cortés had only one other source of allies, it being the 150 men under the command of Sandoval at Villa Rica, but many of them were sailors or men too old to be of use. Thus, in confronting Narváez, the Conqueror would be outnumbered by a ratio of approximately three to one.

When Cortés arrived near Cempoala, he realized that the entirety of don Pánfilo's nine-hundred men had relocated from San Juan to the Totonac town. He bypassed the settlement and continued to Villa Rica where he met with his captains, including Sandoval, to plan strategy. Initially, Cortés tried diplomacy by sending a letter to Narváez in which he stated that he would not surrender because the cabildo of Villa Rica de Veracruz had granted him powers to act in the name of the king. Instead, he suggested that the two men meet and avoid the loss of lives by don Pánfilo's withdrawal to Cuba. Fray Bartolomé de Olmedo carried the letter to Cempoala. On reading it, Narváez and his captains roared with laughter, thinking they held the upper hand due to superior numbers. When the friar returned with his report, Cortés began immediate preparations for battle.

Four units, each containing eighty to ninety men, would attack Cempoala at night. They were fortunate that it started to rain once plans were in place, which served to muffle their movements. Unbeknownst to Cortés, some 150 men under Narváez's command had known don Hernando in Cuba and liked him. They were more than willing to defect from don Pánfilo's command, believing Mexico provided better opportunity for riches than where they had come from in Cuba, but first there would be fighting.

Cortés led the attack around midnight of Whitsunday, May 28-29. His men-at-arms having fought one major battle with the Chontal Mayas and three with the Tlaxcalans were more experienced than those who had arrived with Narváez. The resulting clash of arm was brief. Adding to the fog of combat was a night sky, which at the hour of battle contained thousands of fireflies, and their brief incandescence closely resembled sparks made when steel struck flint prior to the firing of what seemed like many dozens of muskets. The resulting panic prompted hundreds of Narváez's men to surrender. To his credit, don Pánfilo was braver than those he commanded. He retreated several steps up the main pyramid in

Cempoala armed with a two-handed broadsword that he swung in a deadly arc. One of Cortés's footmen began probing at Narváez with a pike, and by chance in darkness it struck the red-bearded commander in the right eye and plucked it out. Bernal Díaz recorded the injured man's outcry: "Holy Mary protect me, for they have killed me and destroyed my eye." The battle, which ended soon after, had not been costly in lives. Fifteen of Narváez's followers were dead, while Cortés's fatalities numbered only two.

Following victory, Cortés employed his talent for using "honeyed words" to good advantage. In a cheerful manner, he spoke to hundreds of men who had come to Mexico with Narváez and asked them to leave behind resentment of defeat. If they would accept his command, he promised to make them rich and give them office for their livelihood. In doing so, they would also serve God and His Majesty King Charles I. Some six-hundred men agreed to serve under his banner, but half that number would not. To the latter, Cortés promised four ships to carry them back to Cuba, which they accepted. After their departure, which came several days later, he ordered the remaining fourteen vessels beached for salvage. On board, were much-needed kegs of gunpowder and more than forty horses. Pleased with hissuccess, the Conqueror next turned his attention to fray Bartolomé de Olmedo and asked him what he had learned in talking to Narváez as his emissary of peace. It was not good news. Don Pánfilo had suborned the Fat Cacique. He and Moctezuma had secretly exchanged gifts and become allies. This information angered the Conqueror, and it henceforth had a decisive effect on his subsequent attitude toward Moctezuma.

Just then came news of events in Tenochtitlan, carried by a Tlaxcalan runner, who reached Cempoala most likely on May 31, 1520. Earlier that month, Toxcatl—the most important festival on the ritual calendar of the Mexica—had been held in Tenochtitlan's great plaza. The occasion, lasting four days, honored the gods Tezcatlipoca and Huitzilopochtli with an extraordinary offering, a special role reserved for a Mexica youth chosen for his exceptional handsomeness and perfection of body. He had been treated like a deity on earth throughout the prior year while plied with rich food and virgins for his pleasure. At the end of Toxcatl festivities, this chosen young man climbed the steps of the Templo Mayor carrying a flute. He broke the clay instrument prior to being flopped on his back and sacrificed in the usual manner. His death perhaps recognized the briefness of youth, but more important it honored the two important gods with the blood offering of a nearly perfect young man—at least by Aztec standards.

The Mexica had asked Alvarado's permissions to hold the festival, and he agreed on condition that the celebrants bear no weapons. With Cortés absent on the coast, there developed in Tenochtitlan an air of uncertainty, including a rumor that don Hernando had been killed. At that same time, the Mexica had stopped delivery of food from the great market to the palace, perhaps in observance of Toxcatl. In any event, Alvarado, then in command, had become increasingly uncertain, fed in part by his Tlaxcalan allies, who had sowed suspicion of Aztec intentions by noting how many of their high nobility had gathered in one place.

Alvarado decided to follow the example set by Cortés at Cholula: He would block three exits to the great plaza and, at the agreed-upon signal, send some sixty Spaniards with swords supported by eager Tlaxcalan auxiliaries to attack the unarmed celebrants. Spaniards in armor with swords and shields began to mingle with the Mexica celebrants. On Alvarado's command of "let them die," the slaughter began. The brilliant fray Bernardino de Sahagún penned a description of the murderous scene that followed: "Some climbed the wall [of the plaza]; they were able to escape. . . . And some escaped among the dead; they got in among those actually dead, only by feigning to be dead. They were able to escape. But if one took a breath, if they saw him, they killed him. And the blood of the chieftains ran like water." The conquistadors then turned on the spectators and killed them, too. The flower of Mexica nobility, all products of the exclusive *Calmecac* school, perished.

When the Spaniards and their Indian allies finally returned to their quarters in the palace, an aroused populace stormed the residence wherein resided Moctezuma, his children, and his brother Cuitlahuac. The attackers tried to set fire to the building; others attempted access to the roof, while still others stormed the main door. Armed conquistadors and their Tlaxcalan allies were barely able to repel the throng, their effectiveness possibly hampered by the fact that no one was clearly in command. Alvarado forced the captive governor of Tlatelolco to appear on a balcony and order the attackers to desist. It had a somewhat calming effect, but thereafter no food or water entered the palace and a siege began.

Cortés, made aware of the crisis in Tenochtitlan, began a two-hundred-mile forced march from Cempoala. With him were around eight-hundred men-at-arms, which included six-hundred who had accompanied Narváez and don Hernando's original contingent of fewer than two-hundred. The Conqueror and his men had added strength by traveling with more than forty horses. But among their Totonac burden bearers, perhaps two or three had been infected with smallpox while at Cempoala.

By early 1519, smallpox germs transmitted by enslaved Africans had reached Cuba and from there spread to Cozumel and Yucatan with terrible consequences as Narváez's forces passed through those regions. Europeans, because of their long association with domesticated cattle, swine, and chickens, had developed some immunity to cowpox and swine and avian influenza. At the same time, the New World, because of its isolation from Europe, was free of influenza, smallpox, measles, malaria, bubonic plague, and perhaps even the common cold. Epidemiologists consider the Americas of that time as "virgin soil." When those diseases struck the native population, they had devastating consequences. It appears smallpox was introduced into Mexico by Narváez's black porter, Francisco de Eguía, who spread the disease to the host Indian family with whom he was lodged, and from there it moved from one family to another in Cempoala.

Meanwhile, Cortés's forced march reached Iztapalapa around mid-June, and there the Conqueror recruited about one-thousand Tlaxcalans from those encamped nearby. He chose not to approach the Aztec capital by the long southern causeway, perhaps fearing an ambush along its nearly seven-mile length. Instead, he chose to reconnoiter Lake Texcoco's eastern and northern shorelines before arriving to the west of Tenochtitlan at Tacuba. From there he and his followers marched into the city while reminding themselves that the elevated walkway had three gaps covered by removable wooden bridges.

Don Hernando with his hundreds of Spanish and Indian followers in tow had no difficulty arriving at the Axayacatl palace. They joined Alvarado and his command as well as Moctezuma and his five children. At that time, little food and water remained for humans or horses. Nevertheless, Alvarado and his men were delighted to see so many familiar men-at-arms, the new arrivals from Narváez's command, and the one-thousand additional Tlaxcalan allies. Not so happy were Cortés, fray Olmedo, and Moctezuma.

Initially, Cortés was not angry at Alvarado, but that changed when the always level-headed Mercedarian friar asked don Pedro why he had attacked unarmed celebrants at a festival in the plaza when he had granted them permission to gather. Alvarado offered the lame excuse that his men had found weapons belonging to Aztecs placed in a room near the great square, but those had probably been stored to comply with his orders that celebrants at Toxcatl not be armed. The Conqueror asked Alvarado if he had indeed granted permission to the Mexica to congregate for the festival, and he acknowledged that he had but decided at the end to follow Cortés's example at Cholula. His explanation was received with much irritation by don Hernando.

The Conqueror next directed his anger at Moctezuma and cursed him thoroughly for his duplicity in sending agents to deal with Narváez. The emperor apologized and said he would do everything he could to regain Cortés's good graces. The Conqueror replied that the emperor could best demonstrate that good faith by reopening the great market in Tlatelolco and restoring food and water to the palace. Moctezuma replied he would be happy to honor the request, but someone other than he would have to reopen the market because he had lost too much authority while captive of the Spaniards. That someone appointed by Cortés turned out to be the emperor's brother, Cuitlahuac. This was a bad mistake because unbeknownst to don Hernando, Moctezuma's brother was a firebrand who had advised driving the Spaniards from Mexico as soon as he learned of their arrival at San Juan de Ulúa.

Once free of the palace, Cuitlahuac not only failed to reopen the great market but also burned the four brigantines built by Martín López, thereby ensuring Spaniards could not escape by water. Cuitlahuac then removed all the wooden bridges spanning gaps in the Tacuba and other causeways. Next, he assumed the leadership necessary to besiege the Axayacatl Palace each day from first light to last. Should the Spaniards and their Indian allies decide to retreat from Tenochtitlan, they would have to do so on one of the elevated causeways—all of which were then interrupted by yawning gaps over Lake Texcoco's waters.

CHAPTER 10

Noche Triste, *Otumba, and Tlaxcala*

The Axayacatl Palace, under siege for about a month, ultimately housed more than eight-hundred Spaniards, Tlaxcalan allies, the governor of Tlatelolco, emperor Moctezuma, and his five children. Matters reached a critical juncture by the last day of June 1520. During the previous weeks, the Mexica had killed or captured several Tlaxcalans and fatally wounded several of Cortés's men in the ranks. Meanwhile, within the palace, Moctezuma remained in irons to prevent any possibility of his escape. The Conqueror, desperate to alleviate the situation, seized the governor and marched him onto the palace terrace, much as Alvarado had done earlier. After a time, the well-respected official of Tenochtitlan's sister city managed to quiet the angry crowd long enough to hear him. Through Aguilar and Marina as translators, Cortés ordered the governor to speak the following words: "We, fellow Mexica, are not the equal of the Spaniards. Let the battle be abandoned; let there be a cessation of war. The Spaniards have put Moctezuma in irons, [and] they have placed irons on his feet."

Angry besiegers would not allow the governor to continue. Many in the throng began jeering and shouting that Moctezuma was a cowardly rogue, followed by pelting the terrace with so many stones the Spaniards had to protect the governor with their shields. Cortés then unshackled Moctezuma and marched him onto the palace battlement. That quieted the crowd for several seconds. However, when the emperor tried to speak, his words were likewise drowned by jeers and whistles. Someone in the crowd armed with a sling launched a rock, perhaps about the size of a pullet egg, that struck the emperor in the head and rendered him unconscious. Spaniards rushed the terrace and carried Moctezuma from it, but he died later that same morning. The emperor's passing, according to Bernal Díaz, caused sadness among some Spaniards who had come to like him.

Some five-hundred years later, scholars still lack agreement on the cause of Moctezuma's death. They concur on little other than it happened while he was in the custody of Spaniards. It seems the emperor bled from one of his ears, which suggests he had suffered a severe concussion. Cortés would later deny all allegations that he had murdered Moctezuma, or that he had ordered it. What seems evident is that Moctezuma had become morose and withdrawn while in confinement. For a man as all-powerful as he had been to have been mocked, humiliated, and stoned must have been dispiriting, but the emperor's emotional state seems an unlikely cause of his death.

Starting in mid-June, Cortés met regularly with his captains to decide what to do about their increasingly desperate situation. They could not repel attacks much longer without food and water for themselves and the horses. The latter, so essential to the Spaniards' advantage in warfare on land, were of little use in street-to-street fighting in an urban environment. Furthermore, while numbering more than forty, by June 30 only a dozen horses were believed strong enough to ride. The inevitable conclusion reached by the Conqueror and his captains was that retreat from Tenochtitlan by one of the causeways was their only option. Since the western causeway was closest to the palace and had only three gaps, it became the preferred means of egress.

To cross gaps in the Tacuba corridor with greater safety, Cortés ordered carpenters, using lumber left over from Martín López's construction of brigantines, to construct a bridge light enough to be carried overhead and placed across the first of the breaks. After everyone and their baggage as well as the horses had crossed, the bridge could be lifted and moved forward to cover the second gap, and then on to the third gap to facilitate reaching Tacuba with safety.

The death of Moctezuma at around noon was the deciding factor in making June 30, 1520, the day of attempted escape from Tenochtitlan. Preparations got underway for a departure near midnight. Of importance to the Spaniards' plans was a doorway in an interior wall near the back of the palace which, prior to their being quartered there, had led to an adjoining anteroom. This room held the gems and treasure that belonged to the sixth Mexica emperor, Axayacatl. Aztec masons had sealed the doorway and plastered around it to hide the existence of an exterior room from the soon-to-arrive Spaniards. When the Spaniards occupied the palace, they noticed the difference in color of fresh plaster on the false exterior wall, and Cortés ordered his carpenters to investigate what had been hidden from their view. Workers discovered the anteroom and revealed its contents. Spaniards had never seen such riches in the Indies: Most likely heavy gold and silver plates, gem-encrusted crowns, gold tableware, beautiful turquoise, gold wristlets and bracelets. The full inventory of these treasures, however, will never be known, because much of it would end up at the bottom of Lake Texcoco during a planned retreat gone wrong. In the short run, however, Cortés had his masons restored the non-weight-bearing wall to disguise the Spaniards' knowledge of the riches that lay beyond it.

Because the Spanish retreat from Tenochtitlan had to be undertaken with as much quiet as possible and in the middle of the night, workers muted the bells on the horses' bridles. They also placed jackets over the chargers' heads to temporarily blind them. Next, the marching order of nearly eighteen-hundred combined men-at-arms and Indian allies had to be worked out. Cortés would lead the Spaniards who carried the bridge, others led the horses and walked, next came Indian allies and Moctezuma's children—but perhaps not all five of them—and finally, Pedro de Alvarado on horseback would man the rear guard. On Cortés's orders, someone probably wrapped the *Matrícula de Tributos* in water-proof canvas and entrusted it to fray Bartolomé de Olmos.

It seems that king Cacama of Texcoco and his associates, who had been chained to a pillar in the palace, had died of undocumented causes, since they are not mentioned in preparations for the retreat. However, before leaving the palace, Cortés ordered his carpenters to destroy part of the wall that separated the main expanse of their living quarters from the anteroom, thereby exposing the hidden treasure. Each conquistador could take whatever he wished to carry on the retreat and claim it for himself, at least temporarily. The temptation for gold-hungry conquistadors to load themselves with heavy objects of great value must have been almost irresistible. However, wise Bernal Díaz took only two small turquoise and placed them in his pocket.

Around 11:30, all those within the palace, with the possible exception of three of Moctezuma's daughters, left in light rain and entered the western causeway. At first all went well, but an elderly Mexica woman who had left her bed to relieve herself spotted the column and shouted: "Mexicans! Come all of you! Already they go forth! Your foes already go forth secretly!" Her cries echoed through the city, and armed Mexica by the hundreds took to their canoes.

In the words of Bernal Díaz: "The bridge was quickly put in place, and Cortés and the others who [*sic*] he took with him in the first detachment and many of the horsemen, crossed over it. While this happened, the cries and whistles of the Mexicans began to sound, and they called out in the language of the people of Tlatelolco, 'come out at once with your canoes for the *Teules* are leaving, cut them off so that not one of them may be left alive.' When I least expected it, we saw so many squadrons of warriors bearing down on us, and the lake so crowded with canoes that we could not defend ourselves. Many of . . . [us] had already crossed the bridge, and while we were in this position, a great multitude of Mexicans charged down on us with the intention of removing the bridge and wounding and killing our men who were unable to assist each other; and as fortune is perverse at times, one mischance followed another, and as it was raining, two of the horses slipped and fell into the lake. When I and the others of Cortés's company saw that we got safely to the other side of the bridge, and so many warriors charged on us, that despite all our good fighting, no further use could be made of the bridge, so that the [next] passage or water opening was soon filled up with dead horses, Indian men and women, servants, baggage and boxes."

The same approach by necessity occurred at the second and final gap in the causeway. Crowding and pushing by panicked Spaniards and Indians in the rear forced those ahead into the water until the break was filled with dead and dying people and wounded horses. Furthermore, Aztecs in canoes on both sides of the walkway fired arrows into those who managed to cross over the remains of humans and horses. Some Spaniards and Indians jumped off the causeway into shallow water and tried to wade ashore. Many of them were overpowered by the Mexica, taken prisoner, and carried off for later sacrifice atop the Templo Mayor. In the mass confusion, Moctezuma's daughter Ana and his son and heir, Chimalpopoca, died from arrows mistakenly fired by Mexica who were trying to rescue them. The emperor's daughters with baptized names Isabel, María, and Mariana were spared that fate. Perhaps they were permitted to stay in the Palace because all were pre-adolescent girls from different mothers and about ten- or eleven-years old. Isabel, born Tecuichpotzin, was legitimate by Aztec standards and despite her youth would later serve briefly as the second interim woman Emperor—the first had been Atotoztli, daughter of the fifth Mexica emperor, Moctezuma Ilhuicamina.

Cortés and others on horses cleared the last break in the causeway, spurred their mounts, and arrived in Tacuba to secure a place for those who survived what the Spanish would call their *"noche triste,"* and for them it truly was a sad night. Had they waited longer on the walkway, Bernal Díaz wrote, "we should all have been put an end to, and not one of us would have been left alive." Those on foot had no weapons other than a few swords, which they used on "those who tried to lay a hand on us." Moreover, the Spaniards had no muskets or crossbows because the weapons had been lost at the first bridge along with many swords. The chronicler also commented that had it been daytime, "it would have been far worse."

All who reached Tacuba congregated in the town's plaza, where Cortés took assessment of his captains only to discover that Alvarado was not among them. As mentioned, don Pedro was rearguard of the column. The Conqueror and a few men who had escaped injury fought their way back onto the causeway to assist Alvarado. They had not gone far when they came upon him badly wounded and on foot because his sorrel mare had been killed. The man called Tonatiuh by the Aztec carried only a spear, which he used to ward off attackers and maintain his balance as he crossed the second and third breaks in the causeway.

As noted, Alvarado was a superb athlete and would become second in fame only to Cortés in the conquest of Mexico, and an apocryphal story gained currency that he had used his spear much like a pole vaulter to accomplish "Alvarado's Leap" over gaps in the western causeway. This has often been repeated and is still to be found in some corners of the internet. The incident is unsupported by the later testimony of many conquistadors in their "merits and services"—accounts submitted to the king in the hope of gaining a stipend for having survived the conquest's perils. Those witnesses had never heard of "Alvarado's Leap." The chronicler Bernal Díaz who late in life wrote his account of the conquest remarked that he, too, had never heard of the "Leap" until several decades had passed.

The death toll for Spaniards during *la Noche Triste* is estimated at about five-hundred, which includes those killed outright and others captured and later sacrificed. Some historians have placed the number of fatalities at six-hundred, but that seems unlikely given the number of conquistadors later needed to fight an enormous battle while trying to exit the Central Valley. Whatever the actual number, it was probably the Spaniards' greatest loss of life in Mexico in a single engagement until the wars for independence from Spain in the early 1800s. The loss of Tlaxcalan lives during the Sad Night and later sacrifices is often placed at eight-hundred. Ironically, many Spaniards who died on that night met their fate by drowning, sinking to the bottom of Lake Texcoco under the weight of the heavy gold objects that they had carried from the palace to satiate their greed.

From the relative safety of Tacuba, surviving Spaniards on the morning following their retreat could hear beating of the great snake-skin drum atop the Templo Mayor that accompanied the sacrifice of their fellow conquistadors. They had been stripped naked, marched up the steps of the Great Pyramid, and there surrendered their hearts to the gods Huitzilopochtli and Tlaloc. There are reliable accounts that Hernando Cortés sat under a cottonwood tree near Tacuba and wept bitter tears as the drumbeat went on. Alamo trees can live for centuries, and it has been a commonplace tour guides to point out the tree under which the Conqueror sat. Don Hernando was further saddened to learn from Alvarado that Juan Velázquez de León lay dead at the bridge, but he was immensely relieved to learn that Martín López, the talented boat and ship builder, was among those who had escaped.

Tacuba had been part of the Triple Alliance with Tenochtitlan and Texcoco since 1428 and was far from a friendly host city. Determined to kill every Spaniard, the Aztecs ordered attacks on them in Tacuba from subject towns to the west of the capital. After repelling those assaults for a day while experiencing the loss of three more conquistadors, Cortés ordered his men to "get out of that town as quickly as [they] could."

The Spaniards' overall goal was to retreat to Tlaxcala, and they faced two options on how best to do that. To the east of Tacuba was the shorter route but more dangerous since it would require traversing a narrow strip of land between Chapultepec heights and Texcoco, during which the column would be more vulnerable to Mexica attacks. Cortés chose the second and longer route, which was to circle the lakes to the north. It was safer and more familiar to him since he had taken that route on returning from the coast prior to entering the western causeway. That choice also guaranteed water for all and grass for some twenty-five horses that needed rest and treatment of their wounds. Unfortunately for the Spaniards, that option also meant finding little food for the men while fending off sporadic attacks by Aztecs.

Once Cuitlahuac, who had assumed command of the Mexica, learned the direction taken by Cortés and his followers, he ordered towns along their way evacuated and food destroyed in nearby fields. As a result, the exhausted and hungry conquistadors experienced the Aztecs' version of scorched-earth strategy. The Conqueror, directing men on foot while repelling a Mexica attack, suffered a glancing blow from a rock that hit him in the head and knocked him to his knees. In the same engagement, the Aztecs killed the horse ridden by one of the Conqueror's captains; the horse's meat, as a result, provided the only rations the conquistadors had received since being forced out of Tenochtitlan.

The men were so weak and tired that covering just ten miles a day was the best they could accomplish. At a campsite muster, Cortés counted only 325 men-at-arms and even fewer Tlaxcalan allies. After circling the northern limits of the lake system, the Conqueror's followers began a sharp ascent to the east toward the town of Otumba. Waiting there on orders of Cuitlahuac, who had been crowned emperor and soon thereafter married by proxy to eleven-year-old Tecuichpotzin (Isabel), were the deputy emperor, three or four sub-commanders, and an estimated twenty-thousand armed Mexica warriors with orders to kill every conquistador and their Indian allies. Looming before them was one of the most fiercely contested battles in the conquest of Mexico, a battle that was fought at Otumba on July 7, 1520.

The small town of Otumba was fewer than thirty miles from Tenochtitlan, but Cortés and his command had traveled almost ninety miles in their circuitous march around the lakes. That brought them near what is now the most famous archeological site in Mexico, San Juan Teotihuacan, with its Pyramids of the Sun and Moon. Fortunately for the Spaniards, on the seventh day since *la Noche Triste* they had camped for two consecutive nights just short of ramparts beyond which stretched the Otumba plain. That provided much-needed rest for half-starved men and exhausted horses. Throughout those nights, however, they were shadowed by Mexica who taunted them with words heard by Doña Marina: "Hasten on! You will find yourselves where you cannot escape." [**Figure 12**]

Early on the morning of July 7, Cortés's command topped the plain's highest point (del sierra) and saw below it a valley filled with Aztec warriors protected by white cotton-quilt armor. As far as their eyes could see, the throng waved banners and displayed a forest of spears that beckoned the conquistadors onward. Historian William H. Prescott centuries later speculated that even Cortés, enfeebled by hunger and fatigue, surely must have entertained the thought that "his last hour had arrived."

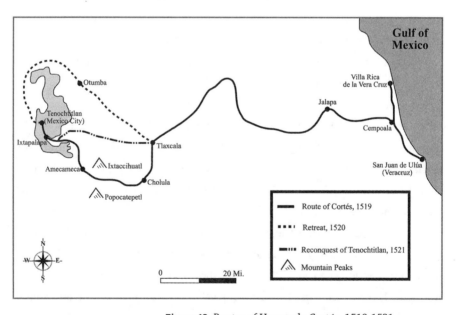

Figure 12. Routes of Hernando Cortés, 1519-1521.

But what choice did the Conqueror have except to continue? He and his conquistadors could not return to the Aztec capital from which they were fortunate to have escaped. Their only course of action was to cut through a mass of armed Mexica or die. Once again, Cortés arranged his more than three-hundred swordsmen in almost arm-to-arm formation and told them they must remain disciplined and depend on the man to their left or right. The Mexica would come at them with wave after wave of attackers, but they would not have to protect their rear. In front they would have perhaps eight mastiffs that had survived *la Noche Triste*, and on their flanks would be twenty cavaliers armed with lances. Led by Alvarado and Cortés, they had orders to aim their steel-tipped lances at the faces of the Aztecs, thereby avoiding their protective armor.

As the fighting began, Cortés's horse was so badly wounded that he had to dismount and saddle one of the baggage animals. Nevertheless, he and the other horsemen created havoc among the attacking Mexica that helped disrupt their ranks. At the same time, conquistador swordsmen became more and more fatigued until they could barely raise their arms to repel wave after wave of Aztecs coming at them. Indeed, those mounted with the best view of Indian combatants described their forward surges as like ocean beakers approaching shoreline. Cortés knew he must do something to turn the tide of battle or his fatigued swordsmen would falter.

The Conqueror stood high in his stirrups to assess the field and spotted a banner waving to the right of a seemingly endless mass of Aztec attackers. It flew over a tent-like covering under which were seated the deputy emperor and three or four high caciques all dressed in feathered finery. While pointing at the banner, the Conqueror shouted above the din of battle and got the attention of Sandoval, Olid, Alvarado, Alonso de Ávila, and Juan de Salamanca with these words: "Follow me and support me! There is our mark!" The six horsemen spurred their chargers and dashed through Mexica footmen toward the banner and pavilion.

Under rules of "decent warfare" practiced by the Aztecs when fighting Indian opponents, kings and their retinue who directed their men in battle were not in danger, as their lives were sacrosanct. Accordingly, the deputy emperor (*Cihuacoatl*) and his entourage must have appeared wide-eyed in astonishment as six riders with lances sped toward them. Cortés rode down the deputy emperor and sent him sprawling on the ground—whereupon Salamanca dismounted and killed him with his lance. The lesser military commanders could scarcely move due to their feathered war garments, and they died as well. Salamanca grabbed the banner and waved it as he circled his horse in view of the astonished Aztec footmen. "It was the work of a moment" because the Aztec attackers, deprived of their commanders, threw down their weapons and ran. Those fleeing were cut down by suddenly invigorated swordsmen, lanced by cavaliers, and set upon by half a dozen mastiffs.

Hernando Cortés regarded the battle of Otumba as one of his greatest triumphs in the conquest of Mexico. Afterward, he allowed his men-at-arms to loot the bodies of the fallen Aztec warriors. The hundreds of suits of cotton-quilted armor that were more successful in stopping or turning an arrow than Spanish mail and metal armor would prove to be of great value in the fighting that lay ahead. These protective suits resembled present-day flak jackets, and of course they were cooler to wear in sunlight and hot weather than traditional European armor. Otumba has long been regarded as a crucial battle in the conquest of Mexico. If one visits Cortés's birthplace in Medellín, the small town has an impressive statue of the town's hero in its square. Around its base are plaques commemorating battles he won in Mexico, with Tlaxcala, México (Tenochtitlan), and Otumba among them.

Cortés permitted his tired captains and footmen to spend the night at the battle site. On July 8, 1520, the victorious conquistadors and their Indian allies resumed their upward march. On the following day, the mountains of Tlaxcala hove into view. They were welcomed at the first Tlaxcalan town they entered, and even better news followed. Xicotencatl the Elder and kings of the other two political entities in the confederation were on their way to likewise welcome the Spaniards and offer succor. Cortés, himself, admitted that had the Tlaxcalan Kings and their warriors turned on them, they were doomed. The exhausted musketeers had no gunpowder, and the crossbowmen were without arrows or bolts. In short, the Tlaxcalans could have ended the Spanish conquest of Mexico in the early days of July 1520. But they chose instead to honor an alliance with Spaniards that continued into the seventeenth century and beyond on the northern frontier of Mexico.

For probably the first time in his life, Cortés had to trust Indians because his situation was so desperate. He was forced to acknowledge that the Tlaxcalans held the upper hand, and they would soon take advantage of it. However, at first there was joy demonstrated by Xicotencatl the Elder and other powerful caciques. They expressed sadness over the condition of the Spaniards and assured them they would have time to rest, heal their wounds, and enjoy food. Cortés thanked the high Tlaxcalan caciques for their generosity, and there followed three weeks of rest and recovery for the Spaniards. Accounts of the battle of Otumba vary, with some contending Cortés may have lost two fingers on his left hand in the fighting. What seems certain is that he sustained injury to that hand to the extent that he could not control the reins of a charger, and his skills as a caballero thereafter were diminished.

During the rest time, Cortés and Alvarado sat down to discuss their best course of action. Both agreed on what was certain to be a forthcoming unpopular order from the Conqueror. Everyone must surrender any gold, silver, or gems they had managed to carry out of Tenochtitlan on the *Noche Triste* or suffer severe punishment for failure to comply. When the assembled men were told what they had to do, there was so much grousing and profanity that fray Olmedo had to cover his ears and walk away. Cortés addressed the protests by using his most persuasive and "honeyed" words, according to Bernal Díaz. He told his men that he knew it was difficult for them to surrender their treasure, especially given the danger and privation they had just experienced. However, there was a greater objective ahead: to avenge the death of their fellow conquistadors and in doing so defeat the Aztecs, reoccupy Tenochtitlan, and distribute its riches.

The collected treasure would remain in Tlaxcala until Gonzalo de Sandoval had once again taken command at Villa Rica and established order. Following that and under heavy guard, the treasure would be transported to Sandoval to pay any captain of a ship arriving at Villa Rica who was willing to return to an island in the Caribbean for needed supplies and reinforcements. There would be opportunity to buy gunpowder, weaponry, and attract men needed to complete the conquest of Mexico, and in doing so it would please God and King Charles I. Cortés reminded his command of the treasure sent to Spain in July 1519 with

Puertocarrero and Montejo. A second shipment containing the gold and silver disks had also been sent to Spain on the better of the two remaining caravels. Sandoval had dispatched the vessel carrying them before returning to Tenochtitlan after the defeat of Narváez and his men. Surely, argued Cortés, ships from their homeland would soon arrive expressing the gratitude of the king and providing them with much-needed supplies. What Cortés did not know was that the beautiful disks aboard the caravel had been seized near the Azores by an armed French vessel, transported to Paris, and there melted into bars to enrich the coffers of Spain's then most deadly enemy, King Francis I.

There was still another matter Cortés did not know about until later. During the early days in which the Spaniards would enjoy rest and respite, the recently crowned Aztec emperor, Cuitlahuac, sent six Aztec ambassadors to the Tlaxcalans, and they had accepted them in secrecy and listened to their proposal. The Mexica diplomats pointed out that they and the Tlaxcalans had many interests in common: They shared the same ancestry, spoke the same language, and revered the same gods. Yes, there had been unpleasantness and even warfare in recent years when the two Mexican people had been divided. However, it was time to return to older and more pleasant times. The Spaniards were a menace to both Mexica and Tlaxcalans because they had mocked their gods, violated their temples, stolen their riches, and worst of all reduced the status of Moctezuma to that of a cowardly puppet monarch.

The Aztec ambassadors suggested that the Mexica and Tlaxcalans join forces to kill the strangers in their weakened condition. There would then be an opportunity to eliminate the horses and dogs of war. Those animals had helped the Teules win battles fought with both Mexican nations. The diplomats finally offered what they hoped was the clinching proposal. If the Tlaxcalans would join the Mexica in putting an end to the strangers and their animals, then Tlaxcala would be welcomed in a permanent alliance and given a status comparable to that which had long been enjoyed by Texcoco and Tacuba.

Xicotencatl the Younger urged acceptance because "he had never abandoned his unrelenting hatred of Cortés." The young firebrand urged the killing of all Spaniards as soon as possible, which could easily be done in view of "their beaten condition." He, however, did not speak for his father or the warrior king

Maxixcatzin of the confederation. Both said it would be unworthy of them to inflict death on men in such need and with whom they had so recently pledged friendship. Maxixcatzin also pointed out that the Mexica had been guilty of habitual treachery in breaking every agreement when it suited "their customary cruelty and arrogance." When the younger Xicotencatl protested, his father, despite his "great age," pushed him down a staircase, and that ended the matter.

Without admitting to Cortés what had taken place in secret conversations with the Mexica diplomats, Maxixcatzin told don Hernando: "now you are in your own house, you have come where you can rest and recover from your labors." At that same time, and again unknown to Cortés, the "Mexica ambassadors had left in haste and secrecy." Maxixcatzin next assured the Conqueror that the alliance with his people would continue, but there would be a quid pro quo explained to him by Xicotencatl the Elder.

When Cortés met with the Tlaxcalan king, he would learn the bitter reality of having to deal with Indians who negotiated from a position of strength. Xicotencatl drove a hard bargain with don Hernando in return for helping him so substantially. First, the Spaniards must grant Cholula to the Tlaxcalans, thereby dissolving the recent alliance of Cholulans and Aztecs. Second, when Tenochtitlan fell to the combined forces of Tlaxcalans and Spaniards, the latter must allow the former to build a fortress within the city, man it, and thereby never again have to face Aztec arms and perfidy. Third, the Tlaxcalans demanded half of all booty gained in the fall of Tenochtitlan. Fourth, the Tlaxcalans required perpetual freedom from paying tribute to whoever ruled the former Mexica capital. Cortés agreed to all those terms because he had no other choice. However, that did not mean the Conqueror intended to honor those commitments when he again held the upper hand.

The next demands of Xicotencatl angered Cortés, but again he had to accept them. The Conqueror was informed he could no longer urge the Tlaxcalans to give up their gods and stop human sacrifice. Furthermore, the Spaniards could not erect a cross in the plaza of the city in which the high Tlaxcalan king lived, nor could the Spaniards hold religious services there. Those conditions convinced don Hernando that he must found a second town in Mexico. It had to be located close to Tlaxcala but also serve as a partial base of operations for the defeat of the Aztecs and the reoccupation of Tenochtitlan. Not least in importance to Cortés, Catholic Mass could be held in the new villa.

After three weeks of rest at Tlaxcala, Cortés asked the high caciques for five-thousand warriors to punish a town where Spaniards had died on their march to Tenochtitlan. His object was Tepeaca, located six or seven leagues southeast of Tlaxcala on the road to Villa Rica. The caciques gave him four-thousand fighters because they also hated the Tepeacans.

The Tepeacans unwisely met the Spaniards and their Indian allies on a plain, and the ensuing battle was fought almost entirely with swords because the Spaniards had no gunpowder. Twenty cavaliers on healthy horses and armed with lances helped men-at-arms and native allies carry the day. The loss of lives for the Tlaxcalans amounted to three. Two horses were wounded, one so seriously that it died. Only two Spaniards were wounded, but neither "in a manner to cause them any danger," as Bernal Díaz wrote.

After the battle, Spaniards entered Tepeaca and renamed it Segura de la Frontera (secure frontier town.) As was typical, magistrates and councilmen were chosen. Once in control of the villa, Cortés ordered its men and women branded on the face as slaves, and their children were likewise enslaved. The victorious Castilians erected a chapel for religious services, and they felt safe, knowing that Tlaxcalans guarded the entire frontier.

Shortly after founding Segura de la Frontera, the Spaniards learned from an Otomi informer that smallpox had spread with horrific results to Tenochtitlan, wherein a terrible odor rose throughout the city from the dead. The disease killed both high- and low-ranking Mexica, including emperor Cuitlahuac only sixty days into his reign. His young wife Tecuichpotzin (Isabel) survived. She nonetheless had been widowed a second time. Her first marriage by proxy when she was ten was to Atlixcatzin, a presumed successor to Moctezuma. That high cacique, the son of Emperor Ahuitzotl, had died of unrecorded causes. As mentioned, Tecuichpotzin served briefly as interim empress after the death of Cuitlahuac before marrying a third time by proxy at age eleven to Cuauhtemoc, nephew of Moctezuma, who is honored to present-day times as the great Aztec defender of Tenochtitlan and other cities during the Spanish conquest.

When Cuauhtemoc learned Tepeaca had fallen, he took immediate steps to protect his empire. He feared the Spaniards would overrun Oaxaca in the south and other outlying areas, so he sent ambassadors to alert those living there and warned them to be vigilant. He gave jewels to some of the high caciques and to others remitted tribute payments, and most important the new emperor sent garrisons of warriors to aid in their defense. In every regard, Cuauhtemoc would lead his fellow Mexica in defense of the hated Spanish. His defiant message as often repeated to Cortés was: "I am no Moctezuma."

After Cortés organized the new town of Segura de la Frontera, he received letters from Villa Rica informing him that another ship had arrived there. Its captain, Pedro Barba, after whom the aforementioned Maya interpreter had been named, was a close friend of the Conqueror. Barba brought with him only thirteen footmen and two horses because his ship was small, and he carried letters from Diego Velázquez to Pánfilo de Narváez in the belief his captain would then be in command of Mexico. Don Pedro, however, soon defected to Cortés after hearing the wonders of Tenochtitlan. He, his men, and two horses set out for Tepeaca where he was welcomed by the Conqueror. Then additional letters from Villa Rica reached Cortés with news that yet another ship had dropped anchor off the town. It bore one horse, six footmen, and more importantly, six crossbows and many balls of twine for making crossbow strings.

By this time, the treasure that Cortés had collected from his captains and men-at-arms, an estimated 45,000 gold pesos, had reached Gonzalo de Sandoval on the coast. He was able to send ships and their captains to ports in the Caribbean to recruit additional men and pay for supplies, weapons, and gunpowder. That commerce continued for several months while Cortés in Tepeaca rebuilt his depleted command and armed more conquistadors.

In late summer 1520, Cortés conceived the idea of building shallow-draft brigantines in the mountains of Tlaxcala that would give him naval power when later launched on Lake Texcoco. He believed it essential to have watercraft to counter the hundreds of canoes armed with archers possessed by the Aztecs. The Conqueror sat down with Martín López who was no ordinary carpenter, boat builder, or shipwright. Born in Seville and related to a family of carpenters, his brothers Pedro and Miguel were likewise skilled wood workers. As mentioned, he had previously built four brigantines in Tenochtitlan, each capable of carrying around eighty men and two horses. Those craft, intended as means of evacuating Spaniards across the waters of Lake Texcoco should that become necessary, had been burned by Cuitlahuac. Confronting the twenty-four-year-old master craftsman from Seville was a feat that would rarely be duplicated in history.

Cortés asked the boatwright if he could build thirteen brigantines, twelve approximately fifty feet in length and a larger flagship at sixty-five feet. He had to test them on a dammed river in the mountains of Tlaxcala, knock them apart, transport the pieces some seventy miles to a shore on Lake Texcoco, and then reassemble them. The twelve smaller vessels had to be equipped with paddles and sails, carry twenty-five to thirty men, and be armed with brass cannons. The flag ship, however, would carry a heavier medium-sized Lombard cannon. Both men knew that trying to assemble these vessels at a lake shoreline, which would take an extended amount of time, and leave the operation open to attack by superior numbers of Mexica warriors.

López replied that he could do as don Hernando requested but would need the help of hundreds of Tlaxcalan workers to do the heavy lifting. The project would have to be finished in four months before the rainy season began in late December. Then rain would swell the river contained by an earthen dam long enough for him to test the craft and then remove them from the stream for disassembly. Cortés agreed to speak to Xicotencatl the Elder about acquiring the Indian laborers. He believed the Tlaxcalan leader would willingly supply the workers if it would help defeat the hated Aztecs. López followed by requesting that master blacksmith Hernán Martín and his forge at Villa Rica be brought to the construction site to sharpen the tools he would need, and the Conqueror agreed to arrange that as well.

Work began almost immediately on the thirteen brigantines with the approval and support of the Tlaxcalan cacique. Perhaps only woodsmen who have cut down a tree without power equipment can appreciate the incredible hard work that lay ahead. Even more difficult was cutting a tree trunk into boards used to build boats with hand tools. When López had been a shipwright in Seville, he could eye a tree with branches that spread from the trunk and cut part of a vessel's hull that formed its V-shape. Brigantines were simpler to build in that they required a flat bottom to traverse the shallow lakes that surrounded the Aztec capital. Even so, the work was extremely demanding.

Anyone familiar with hand tools used by carpenters can relate to those employed by López and his helpers in sixteenth-century Mexico: axes, adzes, crosscut saws, mauls, chisels, drawknives, and wood rasps—the last two for detailed work. Boatwrights preferred to use wooden pegs rather than nails to join pieces of lumber because they would expand in water and form a better bond. Under the direction of Martín López, these tools shaped the thirteen brigantines requested by Cortés. At the same time, Tlaxcalan workers with shovels formed an earthen dam and lake on the Río Zahuapan. All work was completed before heavy rains began. As the river rose toward the top of the dam, the thirteen brigantines performed well in buoyancy and maneuverability, whereupon they were removed from the river, disassembled, and the pieces stored separately for each craft.

While work progressed, men in ranks with little to do and in need of recreation asked Cortés and two of the Alvarado brothers to play cards with them. Details are lacking on what games were played, but one may have resembled draw poker. Tens, face cards, and aces were probably given values of one to five. Players sat on the ground and played on a blanket. However, the Conqueror and either Pedro or Jorge de Alvarado always sat opposite each other amidst three or four other players so they could read the backs of each other's marked cards, as well as those on their left or right. The men-at-arms wagered a bit of gold they had acquired in exchange for trifles, and they invariably lost. (As a side note, Professor Scholes at the University New Mexico urged me to write a research article on gambling with cards in the conquest of Mexico and agreed to help, but other matters intervened.)

The Conqueror, anticipating fighting that lay ahead, again summoned Gonzalo de Sandoval to Segura de la Frontera along with Lombard cannons and heavier field ordnance salvaged from beached vessels. Cortés followed by organizing military operations designed to secure a portion of lakeshore as launch site near Texcoco and east of the Nezahualcoyotl dike. Thanks to several ships arriving at the Spanish settlement on the coast, by late 1520 Cortés had acquired eighty crossbowmen and musketeers and eight or nine field cannons. Numbers of men in the ranks had increased to 550, and they were organized into nine companies of about sixty men each. To this force he probably added about ten-thousand Tlaxcalans. In planning his return to Tenochtitlan, the Conqueror's motives were different from when he first entered the city some fourteen months prior. At that time, he had planned to use Moctezuma as his puppet and rule through him, which had worked well for a time. But his second entry into the Aztec capital would have to follow the defeat of Cuauhtemoc.

The first night away from Tlaxcala was December 28, 1520, and the nine companies spent it on a pass at more than twelve-thousand feet in uncomfortable cold. The following day, don Hernando began a descent toward the lake country and, perhaps, the dim image of Tenochtitlan in the distance. The preferred launch site for the thirteen brigantines was just north of Texcoco, the second most important city in the Central Valley. It was the Conqueror's good fortune that the Texcocan prince Ixtlilxochitl had decided to become a Christian in fall 1520, and he had traveled to Tlaxcala to receive baptism from fray Olmedo. While there the prince and Cortés became friends, a relationship that lasted throughout the conquest. To honor the Conqueror, Ixtlilxochitl chose Hernando as his baptismal name. Their close friendship made it safer to reassemble the brigantines in that locale, and even more so when the King of Texcoco was summoned to Tenochtitlan by Cuauhtemoc to help prepare the defense of the city. Accordingly, when Cortés and his entourage reached Texcoco, they were welcomed by Ixtlilxochitl who provided food and apartments for their comfort.

Using Texcoco as Cortés's base of operations was much better than having to camp in the open along the eastern shore of Lake Texcoco. It was also important to secure the region around the city to provide safety in reassembling parts for thirteen brigantines when they arrived from Tlaxcala. To that end, Sandoval carried out a successful campaign that captured the town of Chalco and won the allegiance of its caciques. Don Hernando himself led a sortie that marched on Ixtapalapa at the entry to the southern causeway and captured that city with little loss of Indian lives and no conquistador fatalities.

Cortés decided to try diplomacy as a last option to avoid having to attack and destroy the great city of Tenochtitlan. He chose eight prisoners taken by Sandoval at Chalco and sent them down the southern causeway with a peace offer to Cuauhtemoc. He begged the Emperor to surrender and thereby spare many lives. Don Hernando reminded Cuauhtemoc that it was easy to remedy a war in the beginning but difficult toward its middle and end. Should the Mexica capitulate, the Conqueror promised to treat him and his people with great honor. The eight Indians gained an audience with the emperor, but he refused to send a reply to Cortés.

With defiance, the emperor went forward with plans to strengthen the defenses of his capital. He increased food stores, and he rebuilt defenses along the three causeways by deepening the gaps in them in several places and making sure the portable bridges could easily be removed or destroyed. Cuauhtemoc also sent reassuring messages to the caciques of subject towns offering remission of tribute in exchange for their assistance in defending Tenochtitlan. And, finally, if they could capture any of the *Teules*, they should be sent to him, whereupon he would sacrifice them to the gods Huitzilopochtli and Tlaloc.

By early 1521, it was clear war was inevitable. Cortés took all measures he thought necessary to protect the disassembled brigantines that had not arrived from Tlaxcala. He selected two-hundred men-at-arms, twenty musketeers and crossbowmen, fifteen horsemen, and a large company of Tlaxcalan allies and sent them under the command of Sandoval on the road to Tlaxcala. In the meantime, the Conqueror prepared a launch site for the brigantines on the eastern shore of Lake Texcoco. For weeks, hundreds of Tlaxcalans had been digging a channel wide enough, deep enough, and long enough to assemble within it the thirteen brigantines. Excavation started a few yards east of the shoreline and once everything was placed within it, the short distance from the western end of the flume to the lakeshore could be dug away. In-rushing water would then supply flotation for the vessels and give them access into the entire lake system.

With good reason, Cortés worried that the Mexica would attack the column bearing brigantine parts and food supplies that would stretch for two leagues, or about six miles. The entire "parade" of men and lumber was vulnerable—front, middle, and end. Sandoval was more than halfway to Tlaxcala with intent of providing additional security when he met Martín López, who supervised the transport of disassembled brigantine parts. The procession reached Texcoco on February 15, 1521. It was a sight to behold, with drums beating and conch shells sounding. Shouts of conquistadors and Indians alike were joyous. The former cried out *"Viva, viva el emperador, nuestro señor;"* the latter, *"Castilla, Castilla, y Tlaxcala, Tlaxcala!"*

CHAPTER 11

The Siege and Fall of Tenochtitlan

The feat of transporting thirteen disassembled brigantines seventy miles overland, putting the craft together, and launching them on a lake as naval units in the conquest of Mexico was remarkable. But the resolve of Tlaxcalans in aiding the Spaniards so importantly in defeating their Mexica cousins, who spoke the same language, worshipped many of the same gods, and shared similar pasts, was also little short of astonishing. In conversations between Moctezuma and Cortés when both were residents of the Axayacatl Palace, the emperor asked don Hernando why he placed so much value on Tlaxcalans as allies when at any time during his reign he could have crushed them just as easily as stepping on a bug. When Cortés later told Xicotencatl the Elder about Moctezuma's boast, the aged cacique was dismissive and said the Mexica emperor had never accepted his inability to conquer Tlaxcala.

The chant of the Castilians as they arrived at Texcoco, which honored their "*emperador*," meant that news had reached Mexico by late 1520 that King Charles I of Spain had added a second title, that of Charles V of the Holy Roman Empire. Furthermore, Cortés, writing from the new town of Segura de la Frontera, addressed his second letter, dated October 30, 1520, to his "Most High Mighty and Catholic Prince, Invincible Emperor and our Sovereign Liege." The Conqueror understood that his status with the Crown, and most likely his life, depended on events that would unfold over the next six months as he attempted to reenter Tenochtitlan by dint of arms.

Prior to the two-mile-long column's arrival with the brigantine parts at Texcoco, Spaniards there had supervised Tlaxcalans who had dug and enlarged the channel that would permit the ships' entry into Lake Texcoco. In the last two weeks of February 1521, Martín López and other carpenters began reassembling the improvised watercraft. Parts of the thirteen brigantines had been kept separate in transit because they were peculiar to each handcrafted vessel. After reconstruction of the vessels had begun in the channel, the site was guarded day and night, because Cuauhtemoc on three occasions sent armed men in canoes with orders to burn the ships. Each time they were driven away by Gonzalo de Sandoval, whom Cortés had entrusted to protect his prized naval unit.

Cuauhtemoc perhaps got a second indication of Cortés's tactics when the Conqueror set off near the end of February on his second reconnaissance around the lakes (the first had been while waiting for brigantine parts to arrive at Texcoco). On this occasion, Cortés took half his command: around three-hundred on foot, three heavy cannons, twenty-five horses under the command of Alvarado, and several hundred Tlaxcalan allies. When the combined force approached the town of Xaltocan to the north, Indian allies pointed out the existence of a half-abandoned causeway that allowed them to cross to the western side of Lake Texcoco without having to circle farther to the north. In gratitude, Cortés gave the Tlaxcalans permission to sack Xaltocan.

The primary purpose of the second reconnaissance was to scout towns and surrounding areas that were located near entries to the northern and western causeways—Tepeyacac and Tacuba, respectively. The Conqueror and his command reached Tacuba on the fifth day after departing Texcoco. At Tacuba, don Hernando viewed the causeway that had cost so many lives of Spaniards and Tlaxcalans on the Sad Night of the previous June 30–July 1. After a minor clash with warriors defending Tacuba, Cortés and his command entered the western causeway that gave access to Tenochtitlan.

Instead of opposing the Spaniards with force, Cuauhtemoc urged them farther toward the city with taunts from his warriors. Once the conquistadors were within range of small stones launched from the flat rooftops of buildings that extended into the water on one side of the causeway, the Mexica used atlatls and slings to unleash a barrage of projectiles that killed a half-dozen conquistadors and wounded many others. Cortés, recognizing his mistake, ordered a somewhat panicky retreat to Tacuba. Again, the message sent from the young Aztec emperor to the would-be Conqueror was: "I am no Moctezuma."

Nonetheless, Cortés used Aguilar and Doña Marina to send a message to Cuauhtemoc that expressed the Conqueror's desire to speak with the emperor and arrange peace, but that approach came to naught. The Conqueror next sent a warning that he would cut off food to the city and starve its inhabitants into submission. In defiance, Cuauhtemoc replied that his people would not suffer from hunger because they would eat the arms and legs of defeated Spaniards. To further emphasize his point, the emperor sent a warrior onto the flat roof of a house near the causeway armed with maize tortillas, which he sailed toward the Spaniards while shouting what Doña Marina heard as "Eat these, because we are in no need of them."

Cortés and his command stayed in Tacuba for six days, during which the Conqueror made several feints up the causeway but stayed well beyond the range of deadly stones. Don Hernando later admitted that his appearance at Tacuba with a sizable force was designed to persuade Cuauhtemoc to negotiate. That failing, he would weigh the advantage of using brigantines for naval support during the siege of Tenochtitlan, which would get underway in about two months. In the immediate future, Cortés and his command returned over the same route they had followed to Tacuba and arrived at Texcoco around mid-March, having fought minor clashes with Aztecs along the way.

While awaiting the final reassembly of the brigantines and their launching into Lake Texcoco, which did not occur until April 28, 1521, Cortés conquered towns east of Texcoco that were tributaries of the Aztecs. The campaigns had a two-fold purpose: to demonstrate the power of Spanish arms while blunting the municipalities' capacity to send supplies and manpower to Tenochtitlan when the city came under siege.

Almost all tributary towns were located to the east, south, or west of Tenochtitlan. Caciques in those settlements faced a dilemma that waxed and waned throughout the conquest. On the one hand, they would welcome not having to pay tribute to the Mexica if the Spanish prevailed. On the other, what if they committed themselves as allies of the Spaniards as the Tlaxcalans had done, but the small number of conquistadors then proved unable to defeat thousands of Aztecs? Should that happen, they would inevitably face terrible retribution from Cuauhtemoc and his legions. Those dilemmas remained undecided even as the siege began. The Tlaxcalans, under the banner of Xicotencatl the Younger, might waver in their allegiance with the conquistadors if the tide of battle turned against them, since the foreigners had no Indian allies other than the Tlaxcalans. Such considerations were life-and-death matters for the towns' chieftains and their people. As in any war, it is best to be aligned with the victors.

Meanwhile, work had progressed on the channel dug by thousands of Tlaxcalan workers under the supervision of Hernando Ixtlilxochitl. When completed off the eastern shore of Lake Texcoco, it was more than a mile in length, twelve-feet deep, and twelve-feet wide. When reassembled within it, the thirteen brigantines were all floated when water from Lake Texcoco entered the flume, thereby giving the vessels access to the extensive lake system that surrounded the Aztec capital. Cortés took command of the flagship, and his naval units began attacking and destroying Mexica water traffic. A combination of musketeers and crossbowmen along with the sheer size of brigantines compared to canoes hollowed from the trunks of trees gave the Spaniards an overwhelming advantage, and they lost no brigantines in the early phases of fighting. It was also psychologically advantageous for Spaniards to sail unopposed around the northern shores of Lake Texcoco and then beyond to Lake Xaltocan farther north. Indians living in the few coastal towns of importance in those regions such as Huehuetoca, Cuauhtitlan, and Ecatepec were ill disposed to favor Cuauhtemoc after being confronted from time to time by the Spaniards' version of gunboat diplomacy.

Meanwhile at Villa Rica, a few ships bearing mostly would-be conquistadors from Santo Domingo continued to arrive. Those vessels carried kegs of gunpowder, iron ingots for ballast, balls of twine for crossbows, and canvas for sails. Cortés's men on the coast welcomed the newcomers and sent them along with their supplies and Totonac burden bearers to Tlaxcala, but not beyond, on orders of the Conqueror. Almost seven-hundred conquistadors were concentrated at Texcoco, but the road beyond Tlaxcala was considered unsafe without armed escort.

At about this time when things seemed to be going well, Cortés learned of a plot to assassinate him. Perhaps it was Sandoval, who spent more time among rank and file men than did his fellow captains, who learned of a plan that involved perhaps more than two-hundred conquistadors. They planned to kill Cortés and replace him with Francisco Verdugo, Diego Velázquez's brother-in-law. The leader of the conspiracy was Antonio de Villafaña, a malcontent and close friend of Pánfilo de Narváez who had been allowed to return to Cuba. Don Antonio's strategy was to get near Cortés while he dined with his captains by bearing what he purported was a letter from Cortés's father that had just arrived from the coast. While the conqueror's hands were occupied in reading the forgery, Villafaña would stab him in the neck with a dagger.

Cortés responded to news of the plot by ordering Sandoval to arrest Villafaña. The Conqueror then demonstrated his characteristic deviousness by announcing that at the time of the malefactor's arrest the would-be assassin had a list containing the names of everyone in the conspiracy, thereby sending a chilling message to men in the ranks who were complicit. In truth, only fourteen prominent enemies of the Conqueror were mentioned, and none was a surprise to him. Villafaña was tried by a court presided over by Cortés as chief magistrate and sentenced to death by hanging. Prior to his execution, Villafaña confessed to fray Juan Díaz. Cortés, having escaped a plot to murder him, never revealed that he had the names of fourteen enemies. To better protect himself, the Conqueror selected a bodyguard and kept his sword close at hand.

Soon after the Villafaña matter was resolved, Cortés began final preparations for the siege of Tenochtitlan. He was pleased to learn that along with additional ships at Villa Rica a second blacksmith and his forge had reached the coastal town. When combined, the smithies forged quarrels for crossbows, iron tips for lances, and metal points for arrows. At this juncture, Cortés also selected his captains who would lead advances on the three causeways that linked Tenochtitlan with surrounding shorelines: Gonzalo de Sandoval from the south with headquarters at Ixtapalapa; Cristóbal de Olid from the north with base of operations at Tenayuca; and Pedro de Alvarado with command center in Tacuba. Each captain received about one-fourth of some ninety horses and a large, hard-to-determine number of Indian allies who would serve as auxiliaries in the conquest (the total for each subcommander was likely close to five-thousand Tlaxcalans). An additional fourth division was held in reserve for assignment where needed.

It was still necessary for don Hernando to find a way to get his brigantines through the Nezahualcoyotl dike, which had been built in the second half of the fifteenth century. The dike ran continuously for just fewer than six miles and sealed off the more saline waters of Lake Texcoco to the east of Tenochtitlan and Tlatelolco. The problem proved less difficult than it might otherwise have been due to sluice gates that could be opened to reduce the threat of flooding in the two cities during the longer rainy season that began in late June or early July. The Conqueror chose to breach the great dike near its northern end by using the flagship's Lombard cannon to open a gap wider than the width of the sluice gate, which permitted the thirteen craft to cross the barrier to the west side of the lake. Thereafter, Cortés left three brigantines to support Olid on the eastern side of the northern causeway, and he assigned the same number of armed ships to the eastern limits of the southern *calzada*. [**Figure 13**]

As noted earlier, the Aztecs had dug deeper breaks in places on the walkways to make it more difficult for the Spaniards and their Indian allies to fill those gaps with dirt and rocks. Near Ixtapalapa the remaining six brigantines and flagship used such a deepened causeway span to cross to the western side of the more than six-mile southern arterial approach to Tenochtitlan. Thus, Cortés had seven armed ships to assist the advances of both Sandoval and Alvarado on the Aztec capital. The deployment of all naval vessels remained the same during the eighty-day siege that lay ahead—with one exception. Fighting on the western causeway became so intense the Conqueror had to breach the western walkway near Tacuba to ensure brigantine support on both sides of that approach to the Aztec capital. This final deployment of ships also permitted the Conqueror to intercept canoe-borne supplies to the Mexica capital on waters between Tacuba and Tenayuca.

The besieged Aztec capital had been weakened when smallpox took the life of Emperor Cuitlahuac after his reign of only two months. His successor, Cuauhtemoc, survived the contagion, and he became an even more formidable opponent than his uncle had been. Nonetheless, the outbreak of smallpox among people with no immunity to many European and African diseases had taken its toll. As historian David J. Weber wrote, smallpox had "devastated and dispirited Indians," and it served to weaken the entire population of Tenochtitlan. Then, on the eve of siege in 1521, there was a shortage of food that the Mexica were accustomed to eating.

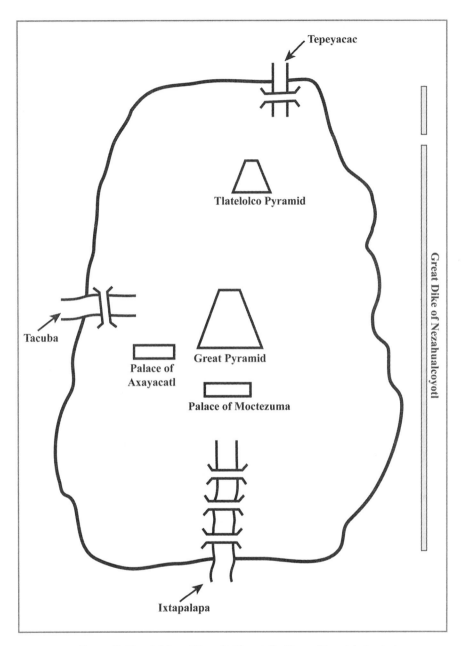

Figure 13. Sketch Map of Tenochtitlan at the Time of Spanish Contact.

It is also noteworthy that Cuauhtemoc and the Mexica had no concept of Spanish strategy because amphibious warfare was unknown to the Mexican experience. Finally, Cuauhtemoc had probably erred in summoning the kings of Texcoco and Tacuba to the capital to bolster its defense, thereby making those important cities more easily overrun by Spaniards. Both cities would serve as bases for assaults on the southern and western walkways, and Spanish-occupied Texcoco had helped guard Tlaxcalan workers who dug the access channel to Lake Texcoco.

The naval advantage that Cortés used in occupying Tenochtitlan was briefly offset by the defection of the Tlaxcalan commander Xicotencatl the Younger, who had never disguised his hatred of the Conqueror. As fighting began to intensify on the causeway approaches to the Aztec capital, the Tlaxcalan prince abandoned his command and returned to Tlaxcala along with dozens of warriors. At first, Cortés sent Texcocan and Tlaxcalan caciques to Tlaxcala who tried to persuade Xicotencatl to return, but he refused. The Conqueror followed by sending Alonso de Ojeda and Juan Márquez to Tlaxcala with orders to place the firebrand in irons and return him to Texcoco "in all haste," which they did.

In Tacuba, Cortés gave Xicotencatl the choice of returning to command or hanging. The defiant prince chose the latter, whereupon the Conqueror ordered his public execution as an example to anyone who challenged his absolute authority. At that point, however, Alvarado tried to save the condemned man. Don Pedro is often portrayed as pitiless toward Indians, and he frequently was, but he also would speak in support of what he considered a just cause. The Conqueror nonetheless rejected his friend's appeal and carried out the execution. Fortunately for him, there were no overt protests from his Tlaxcalan allies.

In the second half of the nineteenth century, historian William H. Prescott addressed Cortés's hanging of the Tlaxcalan prince: "Thus perished Xicotencatl, in the flower of his age—as dauntless a warrior as ever led an Indian army to battle. He was the first chief who successfully resisted the arms of the invaders; and, had the natives . . . been animated with a spirit like his, Cortés would never have set foot in the [Aztec] capital." Along with Cuauhtemoc, revered to this day in Mexico for his bravery in opposing Spanish conquistadors, the younger Xicotencatl likewise deserves remembrance as another example of indigenous pride. When he died at the end of a rope in 1521, Tlaxcalan patriots demanded his garments, which they cut into small pieces and distributed as sacred relics to those with similar regard for the Spaniards. Nevertheless, Cortés had made his point, and his attempts to conqueror and occupy Tenochtitlan continued unabated and without further opposition in ranks.

Thanks to reinforcements in personnel and supplies arriving from Villa Rica, the Conqueror had about seven-hundred men-at-arms, around one-hundred and twenty each of crossbowmen and musketeers, three large field guns, and at least a dozen brass cannons all mounted on the smaller brigantines. With his usual attention to detail, the Conqueror issued orders on how every conquistador was to be equipped and comport himself throughout the battles ahead, and sentence of death hung over anyone who dared to disobey his orders. This was harsh discipline for men who had had to equip themselves with quilted body armor, neck guard, leggings, steel helmet, sword, and shield. The Conqueror also gave orders that no one was to sleep without armor on body and feet in sandals. No one was permitted to go into any village for food, and gambling was not allowed. Finally, mistreating an Indian ally carried lashes as punishment, and execution was the price for sleeping on guard duty or attempted desertion.

As Cortés and his main captains continued attacks on the three causeways, they encountered stiff resistance by Mexica warriors armed with lances the likes of which the Spaniards had never encountered. During the disastrous retreat from the Aztec capital on the Sad Night, some five-hundred Spaniards had either drowned, died fighting, or were sacrificed following capture. Whatever the cause of death, they had left behind weapons. Among them were probably two-to-three-hundred swords. The Mexica carved long wooden lances and lashed the appropriated sword blades to the end of them. Those weapons were dangerous for any Spaniards engaged in hand-to-hand fighting on the narrow causeways, and the irony of conquistadors being impaled by their own Toledo blades will not be lost on the reader.

Another problem among the many the attacking Spaniards faced was their inability to use horses on the narrow walkways, and it took time and hard work on the part of their Indian allies to fill in gaps in causeways each morning. At the end of a day spent fighting Aztecs, the conquistadors and Indian allies retired to their camps to eat and sleep. However, Tenochtitlan was so populous that Cuauhtemoc could wage defensive warfare around the clock. At night, Mexica workers removed the fill dirt and rocks from breaks in the *calzadas*, or roadways, and work of the previous day had to be repeated by the Spaniards' Indian allies.

From available sources, the most detailed accounts of events that took place on the three causeways center on the western one from Tacuba. Perhaps this was because Alvarado, second in command to the Conqueror, was initially in charge there. However, early in the fighting don Pedro suffered a wound to his sword arm that temporarily disabled him, whereupon Cortés left the flagship under the command of a subordinate captain and led the campaign from the west for the remainder of the siege—even after Alvarado recovered and joined him. Accordingly, the Conqueror had the advantage of leaving written accounts of his experiences while other captains did not.

Prior to his injury, don Pedro had led a shoreline campaign from Tacuba that would figure importantly in the outcome of the reconquest. At the head of a small group of horsemen, Alvarado attacked Chapultepec, or "Grasshopper Hill," a landform that rose high above Tenochtitlan. There he destroyed a portion of the parallel aqueducts that had carried fresh water into Tenochtitlan since the reign of Moctezuma Iluicamina in the fifteenth century. Thereafter and throughout the siege, residents of the Aztec capital had to rely in part on water from a few wells in the capital. Less dependable was water transported in earthen jars by canoes that had to run a naval blockade enforced by half a dozen brigantines.

Progress toward Tenochtitlan, whether led by Alvarado or Cortés, was measured by advancing beyond the first gap in the Tacuba causeway, securing it, moving on to the second, and then, to the third and final gap. All progress meant fighting and dying for Mexica and Spaniards alike. The Conqueror estimated the ratio of fatalities at one conquistador to twenty-five Aztec warriors. But even that disparity was unacceptable, because Cuauhtemoc's warriors numbered in the tens of thousands.

During the siege of Tenochtitlan, Tlaxcalan allies served primarily as auxiliaries. In that capacity, they brought supplies and ammunition from camps to conquistadors who did most of the fighting. Communication, however, became a problem between conquistadors and Indians. Under combat conditions and din of battle, it would have been unwise to risk the lives of translators Aguilar and Doña Marina. After securing passage beyond the first gap in the causeway, the captains and their men-at-arms advanced on the second that was bridged for the convenience of Mexica defenders. However, there were occasions when Spaniards had to retreat when overwhelmed by vastly superior numbers. They found it dangerous when crowded from behind by throngs of Indian allies. It seems Doña Marina offered a non-verbal solution to the problem. She suggested that rear guard conquistadors circle their swords overhead as the signal to advance but place shields on their backs to indicate the need for withdrawal. Indeed, some Mexica picture manuscripts, or codices, depict scenes of defeat with shields covering the backs of fleeing warriors.

When Spaniards and Tlaxcalans progressed beyond the second gap in the Tacuba causeway, the following weeks became "slow, painful, and difficult for them." From the roofs of houses that extended into the water on the south side of the western walkway, the Mexica again unleashed small stones with great velocity when propelled by slings and atlatls. Cortés countered by ordering the flagship brigantine with its Lombard cannon to sail within range, and over the course of two or three days the medium-sized cannon leveled the houses.

The resourceful Aztecs countered by working at night to embed sharpened wooden stakes just below the surface of lake waters on both sides of the causeway between the third gap and the western approach to Tenochtitlan. These impediments prevented both the flagship and smaller brigantines from providing supporting fire to the Spaniards and Indian allies who were trying to enter the city. Mexica carpenters, working at night, built wooden ramparts to replace the houses that had been destroyed, and from atop them warriors again hurled stones at the advancing Spaniards.

Along the two north-south causeways, one of which extended from Tenochtitlan to Tenayuca in the north and the other that ran from Tenochtitlan to Ixtapalapa in the south, things were likewise not going well for Olid and Sandoval, respectively. Each day Tlaxcalans and a few other Indians allies had to fill gaps in the walkways that had been cleared in the night. Morale was low as day-after-day fighting took place over the same sections of the two causeways. Weary captains and footmen also complained of having to wear armor and sandals even in sleep as demanded by Cortés.

Those who served on the brigantines fared better than conquistadors assigned to the causeways. It was safer destroying canoe traffic than engaging in hand-to-hand fighting, and at times mariners could approach an unguarded portion of Tenochtitlan, carry out successful raids in the city, and enrich themselves by looting. Afterward, they could return at night to their camps. Since each of the twelve smaller brigantines had a crew of twenty-five to thirty—and the flagship thirty-five to forty—about half of the seven-hundred men-at-arms under the Conqueror's overall command fought in the reconquest from brigantines.

By late June 1521, Cortés and Alvarado had fought their way past the third break in the Tacuba walkway and arrived at houses and buildings on the western outskirts of Tenochtitlan. However, this meant their supply lines from camp became longer and more vulnerable to attacks. That danger was at least partially offset by brigantines operating on both sides of the walkway, but the submerged sharpened stakes near Tenochtitlan inhibited close supporting fire from musketeers and crossbowmen. Nonetheless, both main captains and their support group were able to retreat in safety, but having set foot inside the city from which they had been driven on the Noche Triste sent a message to Cuauhtemoc. He was quick to respond, and in the nights ahead the Mexica dug and made use of deeper pits armed with sharpened stakes near the capital on both sides of the western approach.

At approximately this time, Cortés learned that Olid, whom he regarded as the least dependable of his causeway commanders, had been lax and allowed food and supplies to reach the hilled city of Tenayuca near entry to the northern causeway. The Conqueror was unhappy but did not think he could spare Alvarado to address the problem. Instead, don Hernando turned to ever-dependable Gonzalo de Sandoval at Ixtapalapa. In a complicated maneuver, the youthful conquistador captain supported by twenty-three horse guard, eighteen crossbowmen, and about a hundred men-at-arms circled to the north and reached the northern end of the Coyoacac *calzada* and arrived at Tenayuca. And at that juncture, "Tenochtitlan was quite surrounded" and in the control of the Spaniards.

With the Aztecs denied food carried by canoes, and the twin aqueducts having been severed at Chapultepec by Alvarado, Tenochtitlan was an isolated city dependent on its own reserves of food and supplies, which were far from adequate.

Cortés worsened matters for the city's defenses by ordering captains and crews on the brigantines to land anywhere on the unprotected outskirts of the Aztec capital, enter streets, and burn houses. Siege strategy by then had lapsed into total war, and it seemed that on the night of June 30, the anniversary of the Noche Triste, the fall of Tenochtitlan was imminent. But that did not happen.

Trouble started when Cortés as first captain made a serious mistake. He and Alvarado, supported by men-at-arms and a dozen horses, again fought their way into Tenochtitlan. With satisfaction, they burned the Axayacatl Palace, which had housed Spaniards and later Moctezuma Xocoyotzin as a captive and his five children from late 1519 to June 30, 1520. They then razed other buildings in the city.

Cuauhtemoc responded by asking the high caciques of Tlatelolco for their assistance. It will perhaps be remembered that Tlatelolco was located to the north of Tenochtitlan and had lost its independent status after a brief and bloody civil war, but matters had changed by 1521. The Tlatelolcan chieftains agreed to aid the emperor, but their price for cooperation was a promise that their independent status would be restored for helping defeat the Spaniards. Cuauhtemoc accepted those terms, which brought many hundreds of Tlatelolcan warriors into the defense of Tenochtitlan.

Cortés worsened his error by launching a second incursion into the Aztec capital that reached the great square in Tenochtitlan and the Templo Mayor. He set up one of his field cannons and fired several shots at the great pyramid, "doing much damage," as he later wrote. The audacity of the hated Spaniards defiling the most important religious structure in Tenochtitlan infuriated the Aztecs and their new-found Tlatelolcan allies. They launched a counterattack so fierce that it forced Cortés to abandon the cannon and retreat toward the safety of the causeway. However, the two brigantines intended to protect them as they withdrew toward Tacuba became ensnared in underwater obstructions and had to be abandoned. Both captains were killed, including Cortés's friend, Pedro Barba.

Worse, the aroused Mexica attacked the break in the walkway that was nearest the city and removed part of the rocks and dirt that filled it. In the crowding and panic that followed, reminders of the Noche Triste no doubt surfaced, and more than sixty conquistadors were overwhelmed and marched off as captives. Three Aztecs warriors overpowered Cortés in the melee, and had they chosen to kill him instantly rather than later offer his heart as the ultimate prize to their gods, his rescue would not have been a possibility. But Cristóbal de Olea, one of his men-at-arms, freed the Conqueror by cutting off the hands of his captors. Thanks to him, Cortés barely survived, but shortly thereafter the heroic Olea became a fatal casualty.

Overall victory went to Cuauhtemoc, and it gave him a psychological weapon he used to great advantage. The emperor took his time in sacrificing and dismembering the Spanish captives, who numbered sixty-four according to Bernal Díaz. Initially, five were sacrificed and their bodies decapitated. The Mexica threw the severed heads onto a portion of the Tacuba causeway they had recaptured to mock and horrify the conquistadors. The next ten heads were mounted on the great skull rack near the base of the Templo Mayor to appease the Mexica's gods. Four horses had died in the fighting, and their heads were likewise mounted on the Tzompantli.

Bernal Díaz wrote a graphic description of what happened to the remaining conquistador captives. Their death rituals began with blasts of conch horns, followed by beating the great snake-skin drum that could be heard for more than five miles. The intended victims were stripped naked and forced up the steps of the great pyramid by throngs of Mexica. Once atop the cue, feathered headpieces were placed on them, and they were forced to dance before images of Huitzilopochtli and Tlaloc. Immediately afterward, the Aztecs flopped the victims on their backs over a convex stone, "and with stone knives they sawed open their chests and drew out their palpitating hearts and offered them to idols that were there, and they kicked the bodies down the steps, and Indian butchers who were waiting below cut off the arms and feet. . . . [Their] entrails and feet they threw to . . . carnivores [in the zoo.]" Perhaps of interest, flesh from arms and legs of sacrificed Spaniards was later consumed with *chilmole* (perhaps chocolate sauce).

Cuauhtemoc sent heads and other body parts of Spaniards as well as scraps of horsehide to the city states of Cholula, Texcoco, Huexotzinco, and Huehuetoca that had allied themselves with the conquistadors when they appeared to be winning. Their caciques likely foresaw a different outcome in the future. At least twenty conquistadors had been killed in the fighting, and dozens more had lost their lives on the sacrificial stone atop the Templo Mayor. The dead foreigners were assuredly not *Teules* with extraordinary powers, and it was questionable if not foolish for Indians to be affiliated with them. Consequently, Indians from several communities were ordered home by their caciques. Even more troublesome, thousands of Tlaxcalan warriors likewise left, perhaps remembering the warning spoken by Xicotencatl the Younger about consorting with vile Spaniards. Probably more injurious to the Spaniards' cause, the Tlaxcalans sent their women home. They had made maize cakes and cooked food every day in the white strangers' camps.

The Spanish retaking of the Aztec capital ground to a halt, and it remained that way for at least two weeks in July 1521. Slowly, the magnitude of defeat on the western entrance to Tenochtilan began to sink in. Olid and Sandoval traveled by boats to Tacuba and Cortés's camp to find out what had happened and receive their orders. While there, the captains heard the terrifying horns and drumbeats as Cuauhtemoc made it a point to sacrifice five or more Spaniards every day. Captives with delayed executions were forced atop the Templo Mayor to watch their fellow conquistadors die and be butchered. Added to the horror were the groans of the wounded men in the Tacuba camp, making it "one of the worst moments of the expedition."

At least there was unified command when the two division captains met with Cortés and Alvarado. Almost all Indian allies by then had returned to their homes. One moment they had been filling in gaps in causeways, hauling guns, and providing food; the next, they were gone. For four days in July, the conquistador captains met in Tacuba, guarded by brigantines on both sides of the western walkway. During this bleak time, several Castilian women took up residence in Cortés's camp and served as caregivers to the wounded. Among them, Isabel Rodríguez's ministrations had a "healing touch," and the mulatta Beatriz de Paredes likewise provided sympathy and care.

In the short run, Cuauhtemoc benefited most from the Spaniards' sense of defeat. The caciques of Chalco, Xochimilco, Cuernavaca, and elsewhere received severed heads, as well as the hands of conquistadors. The message from the emperor sent to those towns was that half the invaders were dead, and the other half wounded. Best of all, enthused Cuauhtemoc, the Spaniards had lost their Indian allies. But the emperor soon overplayed his hand. Cortés learned that

Mexica had raided Cuernavaca and punished its people for their alliance with the invaders. A small number of Cuernavacan chieftains traveled to Tacuba and asked for help. The Conqueror seized the opportunity to regain an important ally by sending Andrés de Tapia with eighty footmen and ten horsemen over a mountain range to the town with orders to do what was necessary to punish the offending Aztecs, which they did.

Cuernavaca was an important turning point for Cortés because events there demonstrated what would likely happen once the Spaniards were defeated. Cuauhtemoc would not only exact revenge on those who had betrayed him but also become just as arrogant and demanding of tribute as Moctezuma and Cuitlahuac had been. At that same time, the Texcocan prince Hernando Ixlilxochitl, who had been so helpful to the Spaniards in supervising the thousands of Tlaxcalans who dug the trench that allowed the brigantines to enter Lake Texcoco, devised a plan of importance. He visited towns along the northern edge of the lakes whose people had fleets of canoes. Indians there received permission to attack Mexica watercraft and keep the spoils for themselves.

The Spaniards still had seven or eight of the original thirteen brigantines and used them to deny Tenochtitlan's access to food and water from outside the lakes. They also had enough manpower to block the entrances of the three causeways. That strategy worked, and Indian allies along with their women began returning to the camps, but for a time it was Spaniards who had to fill in causeway breaches every day. In doing such hard work, they noticed something had changed. The Mexica no longer responded by sending squadrons in the night to undo their labor. At first, Spaniards attributed this to their superior work in making causeway repairs, but in fact the explanation lay with the Aztecs' fatigue and shortage of food and water.

That energized Cortés, and once again he used his "honeyed words" to inspire tired and wounded conquistadors. Bernal Díaz, then serving under Alvarado's command, wrote that the Conqueror "was always writing to tell us all what we were to do and how we were to fight." Then in July the longer rainy season began, and it seemed to buoy the spirits of Europeans while discouraging tired and hungry Mexica warriors who nonetheless had not lost the will to defend their city. At night, the Aztecs gamely regained some part of what they had lost the previous day by reopening causeway gaps. Then, around the middle of July that stopped, meaning the Spaniards and their Indian allies did not have to expend time and energy each morning to advance on approaches to Tenochtitlan.

Next, something so dramatically unlikely occurred that it stunned the Spaniards and spoke volumes about Cuauhtemoc's beleaguered defense of Tenochtitlan. The emperor began using women warriors and dressing them accordingly. Such a thing had never happened in the Spaniards' experience in the Indies, although many of them were familiar with the legend of Amazon women that held sway into the 1530s and beyond. The women warriors on the causeways were not Amazons, but they demonstrated bravery and resolve in helping defend their people and way of life.

With Tlaxcalans and other Indian allies again serving as auxiliaries and fighters, Alvarado and his command advanced almost daily into the western outskirts of Tenochtitlan. On one occasion, they came upon a freshwater spring that provided a small amount of potable water and destroyed it. Increasingly, Mexica in Tenochtitlan had to drink foul lake water, and as a result "many died of a bloody flux."

Another source of renewed confidence for the Spaniards came with the arrival of gunpowder, crossbows, and even a few more men-at-arms. All came from Villa Rica following the landing there of a ship that had been part of Ponce de León's search for the Fountain of Youth in Florida. Without doubt, the most welcome item was gunpowder. It had become in such short supply that Cortés had ordered Francisco de Montano to again descend into to the crater of Popocatepetl and collect sulfur. The element could be used to supplement gunpowder's explosiveness, but again there was no local source of potassium nitrate.

On one foray into Tenochtitlan, Spaniards came close to again reaching the somewhat battered great square, but Cortés ordered his men to halt when he received word Cuauhtemoc wished to negotiate terms for surrender. That, however, was a ruse designed to halt advancing conquistadors and allow the Aztecs time to rally defenses and attack with arrows and javelins. Cortés and his command were able to counter that thrust and in doing so captured three prominent Mexica caciques, while Ixlilxochitl took prisoner his brother Coanacochtzin, the king of Texcoco. The Aztec chieftains were released and sent to Cuauhtemoc as a peace gesture. Once again, this amounted to little more than a momentary pause in fighting. More important, the caciques of Tlatelolco began to question the wisdom of their alliance with Tenochtitlan and accuse the Mexica of cowardice—hardly a fair charge. Indians in the twin city had never been able to achieve full common cause with Tenochtitlan after their defeat in a civil war.

Soon after, Cortés and Alvarado fought their way toward the great square in Tlatelolco but had to retreat when faced with massive opposition. However, they rallied and attacked again on the following day. In this second engagement, Spaniards used horses to good advantage and seized the city's pyramid, allowing Cortés to climb its steps. This cue had been more securely held by Tlatelolcan defenders because of its remoteness from the western approach to Tenochtitlan. Atop the pyramid, the Conqueror found the heads of Spaniards captured while fighting on the northern causeway and later sacrificed. Still, from the advantage of having perhaps seventy-feet of height, Cortés estimated that about seven-eighths of Tenochtitlan and Tlatelolco was in the hands of Spaniards.

Starting on July 22, Cortés, joined by Sandoval who had advanced the full length of the Ixtapalapa causeway, carried out an ambush by using horses hidden in a palace outside the main square. The Spaniards attacked with their men-at-arms and then feigned retreat while pursued by excited Mexica who anticipated victory but were cut down by the horse guard. In a second engagement, the two captains killed dozens of Mexica, including a few women and their children who had entered Tlatelolco in search of food. The occasion underscores an important interpretive point. If the Aztecs were "cannibals pure and simple," there were plenty of dead bodies to eat. In truth, commoners were not permitted to eat human flesh, and the nobility who could eat it often did so symbolically, or ritualistically, to honor their gods rather than for sustenance.

On July 27, Alvarado, following a battle with men and women combatants, won control of the great marketplace in Tlatelolco, which had long been without food. Don Pedro celebrated by leading the horse guard in galloping around empty stalls. He paid tribute to Francisco de Montano by appointing him standard-bearer. That celebration, however, ended when Aztecs launched a massive attack that forced Alvarado to retreat, but he gained a measure of revenge by burning Moctezuma's huge palace.

The last bastion of Aztec defense centered in Tlatelolco proper with its narrow streets and many flat-roofed houses topped with stones of varying sizes. Aztec defenders were able to block entry to streets with barricades of stones and rubble that prevented Spaniards from using horses in final engagements that would last just more than two weeks. During that interval, the Conqueror brought Indians accustomed to doing hard manual labor into the city and gave them forged tools—pickaxes, sledgehammers, and prybars. Their job, while protected as much as possible by Spanish arms, was to dismantle houses one-by-one and clear the barricades that blocked streets. It was slow going and dangerous work, resulting in many laborers dying from arrows or heavy stones dropped on them from rooftops.

At this juncture, Cristóbal de Olid fought his way into the Aztec capital from the north, and all approaches to Tenochtitlan were controlled by Spaniards. By then, Cuauhtemoc was more disposed to surrender, but his military commanders still urged resistance to the last heartbeat of a Mexica defender. The emperor ultimately agreed with them, while calling on the gods to save him. In these final throes of the great Aztec empire, the Spaniards were unnerved by the apparent relish Tlaxcalans had in killing Mexica women and children who were trying to surrender. Cortés set up his command center in a tent, emblazoned with a crimson canopy, on the roof of a house near the last zone of Mexica resistance in Tlatelolco, and even his harshest critics agree he was appalled by what he saw. The Conqueror hoped to avoid further bloodshed, but the Aztecs still occupied dozens of houses with stones atop their roofs. While deciding what to do, the Spaniards had captured several Mexica prisoners, and one of them when interrogated seemed to think the Conqueror was the sun. He asked Cortés why he, with the power to travel across the sky each day, did not end the fighting by killing him and other Mexica so they could go to heaven and be with Huitzilopoctli.

In late July, Cuauhtemoc sent five prominent caciques to discuss terms for surrender with Cortés. The ambassadors said that their emperor was afraid to approach the Spanish commander because he feared for his life. There followed back and forth communications until Cuautemoc finally agreed to meet with Cortés in Tlatelolco's Great Market while protected by his guards. Don Hernando went there with his own guard and waited four hours, but Cuauhtemoc did not appear.

So, the siege continued into the second week of August 1521, and during that time Cuauhtemoc apparently concluded defeat was inevitable; but he could not bring himself to offer the gesture of submission. The emperor told his closest advisors to surrender, but he would leave the city and seek shelter, perhaps in Azcapotzalco where the effigy of Huitzilopochtli had been moved out of concern for its safety. As it turned out, Cuauhtemoc's hope of escape had no chance of success.

On the morning of August 13, Cortés met with Alvarado and Sandoval to plan the end of the eighty-day siege. By then, the Spaniards had moved heavy cannons into Tlatelolco and trained them on the last remaining flat-roofed houses, still defended by die-hard Mexica warriors. Those residences were then leveled by field pieces. Following that phase of warfare, Alvarado was to lead the final attack, supported by Tlaxcalan allies and a division of men captained by Olid with orders to drive the surviving Aztecs into lake waters. Sandoval had meanwhile been stationed offshore in command of about seven brigantines, all armed with small cannons, crossbows, and muskets. On a different shoreline, Cuauhtemoc had assembled about fifty pirogues to use in his attempt to escape the city.

The deputy emperor sought and gained a last-minute meeting with Cortés in which he delivered a message from Cuauhtemoc to the effect that he preferred to die rather than surrender, which was not true. The Conqueror, unimpressed, replied if that were indeed the case, then all those resisting in Tlatelolco would die. On the afternoon of August 13, 1521, the last battle of the reconquest began, and it went exactly as the Spanish first captain had warned. The few remaining houses were demolished by heavy cannon fire. Some survivors rushed to the edge of the lake seeking safety, while others tried to surrender. The latter included many dozens of women and children. Cortés had given his Indian allies strict orders through Aguilar and Doña Marina to spare the lives of anyone who chose to surrender, but it mattered little. The Tlaxcalans clubbed small children to death and sacrificed a few adults by cutting out their hearts where they lay. Unable to prevent such senseless murder, the Conqueror later wrote: "There was not one man among us [Spaniards] whose heart did not bleed at the sound of these killings." The Mexica who had made it to the shoreline of Lake Texcoco did not fare well either.

Driven by panic, they waded farther and farther from shore until many drowned or were killed by crossbowmen and musketeers firing from the brigantines.

In the meantime, Cuauhtemoc, the king of Tacuba, and many high Mexica caciques launched their fleet of canoes and paddled for safety. The emperor lay prone and out of sight in a fast-moving pirogue. Those pursuing on the brigantines were aware of Cortés's orders to look for Cuauhtemoc and heed the Conqueror's admonition, "we need him alive." García Holguín, a brigantine captain, identified what he regarded as a canoe "carrying distinguished passengers on board" and decided to approach it alongside with his faster vessel. Holguín signaled the canoe's rowers to stop, but they paddled onward—whereupon he trained his brass cannon on the vessel and threatened to destroy it. At that point, Cuauhtemoc stood up and identified himself. The emperor surrendered, as did the king of Tacuba. One of Holguin's men-at-arms boarded the canoe and put fetters on Cuauhtemoc and the Tacuban monarch with the formidable name of Tetlepanquetzatzin.

The triumphal Spaniards on Holguín's brigantine set off to take their prized captives to Cortés. However, Sandoval demanded possession of the men as the overall naval commander. Holguín refused Sandoval's orders, and they quarreled all the way to Cortés's headquarters, situated in one of the few buildings that remained standing in Tlatelolco. As the Conqueror took possession of Cuauhtemoc, the emperor speaking through Doña Marina and Aguilar said: "I beg you to end my life." Cortés passed off the suggestion by assuring the Aztec's heroic defender of Tenochtitlan that he had nothing to fear. But like all of Hernando Cortés's promises to Indians—especially when he held the upper hand—his words would prove deceitful.

But what of the Mexica caciques in the other canoes who remained on Lake Texcoco with no place to go? When Cuauhtemoc was pressured by Cortés and Sandoval to order their surrender, the deposed emperor scoffed at the idea—explaining that without his command they were of no danger to anyone. Of more importance, where was Cuauhtemoc's young wife Tecuichpotzin, known to the Spanish by her baptismal name of Isabel? In his account, Bernal Díaz placed her in the pirogue with her husband, as did William H. Prescott centuries later. But Cortés near the end of his third letter to the Emperor Charles V made no mention of her. The distinguished British historian Sir Hugh Thomas is probably correct in placing her, along with two half-sisters, elsewhere in Tenochtitlan. That safe house was made known to the Spaniards, and they had likely placed a protective cordon around it. In any event, the previously mentioned Isabel, Mariana (Leonor), and the short-lived María (identified by their baptismal names) survived the eighty-day siege. The first two, but especially Isabel and her descendants, would become important in Mexico and even in Spain well beyond the sixteenth century, matters that will be dealt with in the following chapter.

CHAPTER 12

Hernando Cortés and Post-Conquest Mexico, 1521-1529

The night of June 30 to July 1 of 1520 became known as the Sad Night for Spaniards in the conquest of Mexico; August 13, 1521, was the Sad Day for Aztecs. Their great capital, which one of Cortés's sailors compared favorably to Constantinople, lay in ruins. Gone were thousands of houses and dozens of buildings, including palaces. The Great Market in Tlatelolco contained not a morsel of food, the *Calmecac* school for Mexica *gente decente* was gone, and an estimated population of 180,000 people in 1519 had been reduced to a beggarly few thousand.

From the perspective of present-day times, we can only imagine the suffering of the defeated during the final days of siege, but fortunately there is poignant eyewitness commentary, recorded in some instances years after Tenochtitlan fell to the Spaniards. Those sources are contained in *The Broken Spears: The Aztec Account of the Conquest of Mexico*, an edited work by the late Miguel León Portilla, one of Mexico's most brilliant and gifted historians and anthropologists.

The testimony of Aztecs was in Nahuatl, a sophisticated language that in the pre-Columbian era lacked a true alphabetic writing system. In the post-conquest era, the three mendicant orders of the Catholic faith responsible for imparting the Christian doctrine to the Indians of New Spain arrived in the mid-1520s and early 1530s. The Franciscans came in 1524; the Dominicans, in 1526; and the Augustinians, in 1533. Starting with the Franciscans, members of the order began to learn Nahuatl. The pioneer in that endeavor was fray Bernardino de Sahagún, credited by some scholars as the New World's first ethnographer.

Learning Nahuatl vocabulary often started with Franciscan friars sitting down in the dirt with children or adolescents, pointing at an object, and asking, "What do you call this?" In short, they learned a new language the way children do, by remembering and repeating words. Joining Sahagún were fellow Franciscans Alonso de Molina and Andrés de Olmos. But their genius went well beyond learning the language of the Aztecs by ear alone. They used the Castilian alphabet to approximate and record the Nahuatl language. This technique, by which a language previously transmitted exclusively by oral means is rendered into written format is called transliteration.

This process permitted Sahagún and others to record what the Aztecs themselves had to say about the Spanish conquest of Mexico and the fall of their capital—again, from the perspective of the defeated. The Indian informants used beautiful but anguished words that read like poetry, and it was they who provided the title of the book edited by Miguel León-Portilla in which this poem appears:

> Broken spears lie in the roads;
> We have torn our hair in grief.
> The houses are roofless, and their walls
> Are red with blood.
> Worms are swarming in the streets and plazas,
> And the walls are splattered with gore.
> The water has turned red, as if it were dyed,
> And when we drink it,
> It has the taste of brine.
> We have pounded our hands in despair
> Against the adobe walls,
> For our inheritance, our city, is lost and dead.
> The shields of our warriors were its defense,
> But they could not save it.
> We have chewed dry twigs and salt grasses;

We have filled our mouths with dust and bits of adobe;

We have eaten lizards, rats and worms . . . .

There followed this comment made by an anguished Mexica informant: "When we had meat, we ate it almost raw. It was scarcely on the fire before we snatched it and gobbled it down. They [the Spaniards] set a price on all of us: on the young men, the priests, the boys and girls. The price of a poor man was only two handfuls of corn, or ten cakes made from mosses or twenty cakes of salty couch-grass. Gold, jade, rich cloths, quetzal feathers—everything that once was precious was now considered worthless."

Such sophisticated words were spoken by Aztec intelligentsia, some of whom had begun to question human sacrifice as well as espouse the notion that life in the world they lived in had value. But the old gods still reigned supreme in 1519 because what was there to suggest they had failed the Mexica? As recorded in the Matrícula de Tributos, Indians in sixteen provinces from Totonac lands in the north to those in the Valley of Oaxaca to the south, plus northern regions of Central America, paid tribute to the Aztec Empire. And there was little to indicate the Aztec Empire had reached its fullest extent of expansion. Nevertheless, there existed outlying indicators that more humanitarian impulses among Aztec elites had begun to take root. For example, fray Bernardino de Sahagún in the *Florentine Codex* translated into Spanish the prayer of an Aztec chieftain at the time of the conquest; an excerpt from this poem is translated into English:

Grant me, Lord, a little light,

Be it no more than a glowworm giveth

Which goeth about by night,

To guide me through this life,

This dream which lasteth but a day,

Wherein are many things on which to stumble,

And many things at which to laugh,

And others like unto a stony path,

Along which one goeth leaping.

Poetic words were one thing, but what was Hernando Cortés to do with Cuauhtemoc and the kings of Tacuba and Texcoco, and what were his plans for the ruined city of Tenochtitlan? The Aztec monarchs were imprisoned in Texcoco because there was no appropriate place to confine them in the capital. The Conqueror, however, never permitted Tecuichpotzin to live again with her husband—no doubt because he did not want the royal couple to bear a child who someday might compromise Spanish control of post-conquest New Spain. In addressing other matters in the devastated capital, Cortés readily honored the Aztecs' request to bury their dead, which went on for several days.

At the conclusion of burials, Cortés ordered all Mexica to leave Tenochtitlan and relocate to Tacuba, Texcoco, or elsewhere. He assigned his captains to oversee the clearing of rubble in various districts of the city, using most of it to fill in canals that became streets. There was nonetheless one exception to Spaniards' supervision of this labor. Perhaps the reader will recall that in prior centuries the Aztecs had established fictitious ties to Tula to legitimate their descent from the ancient Toltecs, and to strengthen their assertion Emperors Acamapichtli and Axayacatl had married princesses from the ruling house of Tula.

Before Moctezuma's coronation as Aztec emperor in 1503, he had married princess Miahuaxochitl in Tula and fathered a son by her named Tlacahuepan. When Miahuaxochitl's father was accidentally killed in a flower war, Moctezuma claimed hegemony over Tula because of his wife's prominence. Their son remained in Tula until the siege of the Aztec capital had ended. Cortés then brought Tlacahuepan to the ruined city where he was baptized and given the Christian name of Pedro. The youth, likely in his early twenties, received appointment by the Conqueror as supervisor over a district in Tenochtitlan alongside his captains. Pedro maintained close ties with Cortés for many years and even traveled to Spain with him in the late 1520s.

In the earlier years of that decade, Moctezuma's daughter, María, died of undocumented causes, and at that time Cortés recognized only three heirs of Moctezuma: Isabel, Mariana, and Pedro. The last was older than his half-sisters, who then were about fourteen- or fifteen- years of age. All would later receive rich encomiendas that were unique, not because they as Indians held others in liege, but rather because as Indian royalty they had their vassals bestowed upon them in perpetuity, a most unusual occurrence with long-range consequences.

Meanwhile, Cortés, still without royal sanction of his conquest of New Spain, occupied himself for the better part of 1521–1522 with the rebuilding of Tenochtitlan as a Spanish city. There was little doubt that the former Aztec capital would serve in the same capacity for Spanish-controlled Mexico. Its central location and status as the nexus of authority in pre-conquest Central Mexico made it without peer. And the psychological importance of ruling Mexico from the great metropolis of the lake country, just as the Aztecs had presided over the Triple Alliance from the city between 1428 and 1521, again made it not just an obvious choice, "but the only one." For many years in the sixteenth century the capital of New Spain would bear the hyphenated name: "México-Tenochtitlan," and finally just "México."

In building México-Tenochtitlan, Cortés again demonstrated careful planning. He no longer acquired warhorses beyond those already in Mexico. Instead, the Conqueror needed draft animals and two-wheeled carts for transporting materials. He began acquiring dependable mules, probably from Santo Domingo where European animal husbandry had existed longest. Meanwhile, carpenters fashioned carts, and wheelwrights gave them mobility for hauling. Both were essential in constructing the new Spanish capital.

As work progressed, Spaniards found little treasure beyond what Cuauhtemoc and the Mexica caciques had placed in their canoes prior to fleeing Tenochtitlan. Cortés faced mounting pressure to interrogate the captive emperor and the king of Tacuba regarding the location of gold and gems that seemed so apparent in the Axayacatl Palace prior to Noche Triste. The monarchs repeatedly denied knowledge of any hidden treasure. At that point, Julián de Alderete, treasurer for Charles V, demanded that don Hernando permit him to torture the two men— the king of Texcoco, perhaps as a favor to his brother Ixtlilxochitl, was spared the procedure. Cortés would later testify that he had objected to what was about to take place, but had he chosen to prevent it, he could have.

Spaniards tied Cuauhtemoc to a pole with a rope around his neck. His feet were dipped in oil and set alight. The pain was so severe the emperor tried to hang himself. Spaniards did the same to the king of Tacuba. Tetlepanquetzatzin in his agony begged Cuauhtemoc to help him. The latter looked at him and replied: "Am I enjoying some kind of delight or bath?" Both Indian rulers were so crippled they thereafter walked with a limp, but in the end Cuauhtemoc admitted having given orders to throw some treasure into the lake. However, Indian divers found only a few ornaments of little value when the emperor pointed to where items had been discarded.

There followed a final division of the gold and gemstones that did exist. Cortés and his captains as well as Martín López claimed the lion's share. Bernal Díaz, speaking for himself and probably for fellow men in the ranks, claimed he received less in value than two-hundred gold pesos—about two-thirds the price of a good horse. And when one remembers that "most conquistadors were in New Spain in the first place because they wanted wealth," it is not surprising that strong sentiment arose to expand the conquest into regions outlying Tenochtitlan.

The first new conquest was the Tarascan Kingdom, situated northwest of the capital in the present-day Mexican state of Michoacán. Tarascans were independent of the Aztec Empire, and a failed attempt to conquer them in the fifteenth century had ended in defeat for the Mexica "with great loss of life." In early 1522, there were a few forays into Tarascan lands in search of food that amounted to little. But later in summer of that year, Cortés commissioned Cristóbal de Olid to lead an invasion of Michoacán, and it departed México-Tenochtitlan in July. The Tarascan king, known as the Cazonci, has been described by historian Benjamin Warren as "an absolute monarch aided by a group of appointed individuals who were always subject to his will."

Olid arrived at the Tarascan capital Tzintzuntzan with twenty cavaliers, another twenty crossbowmen, and one-hundred and twenty footmen. The size of the Spanish forces and the Tarascans' almost paralyzing realization that the foreigners had defeated the Aztecs and destroyed their city may have lent the impression that opposition was pointless. Olid, however, apparently saw complacency as cowardice and proceeded to sack the Cazonci's palace while looking for gold. The Spanish captain also threw down idols from the main temple. The Tarascan king then offered formal acceptance of Spanish presence in his kingdom, but his pledge fell well short of accepting servile status. Later, the Cazonci's intransigence would prompt a major conquest of Michoacán in the early 1530s that lies beyond the scope of this study.

With the situation in Michoacán in hand, Cortés turned his attention to the province of Pánuco, an ill-defined region in Mexico that lay inland from the present-day city of Tampico, which seemed most likely to fall under control of rival conquistador Francisco de Garay. As mentioned, the governor of Jamaica had profited from an enormous gold nugget found on his mining property in Santo Domingo. When monetized, it placed at his disposal the equivalent of 60,000 one-ounce silver pesos, which he used to good advantage in petitioning the Crown for the right to colonize the Gulf region explored in 1519 by Alonso Álvarez de Pineda.

On June 4, 1521, Garay received a royal license to settle the province of Amichel, which included all lands from peninsular Florida to the town of Nauhtla, situated on the border between Totonac-claimed lands to the south and those within the boundaries of Pánuco. It is not precisely known when Cortés, then engaged in building México-Tenochtitlan, learned of this concession to Garay, but it was likely in early 1522. The Conqueror responded by instructing his agents at Court, which included his father Martín Cortés, to seek revocation or at least greater limitation of Garay's grant.

However, a sudden, unexpected, and most unwelcome event soon took precedence in the affairs of Hernando Cortés. Arriving unannounced by ship, his wife Catalina Suárez reached Villa Rica in June or July of 1522. With doña Catalina came her sister and her brother Juan Suárez, at one time Cortés's best friend and co-encomendero in Cuba. For many reasons, this was a most unfortunate happening for don Hernando. He had not seen in wife in three years, and only twice in that time had he mentioned in his accounts that he was married—once when he declined to wed the Fat Cacique's daughter, or niece, at Cempoala, because he had a wife; and second, when he refused to accept one of Moctezuma's daughters as "a special fruit."

But in summer 1522, Doña Marina had carried Cortés's child nearly to term, and the Conqueror had brought her, as well as a collection of Castilian and Indian mistresses, to his residence in Coyoacan near Tenochtitlan. Soon after the arrival of his wife in Mexico, Doña Marina gave birth to Cortés's child, a mestizo son named Martín after don Hernando's father. This will not surprise Spanish legal scholars and historians familiar with Castilian family law, but Cortés would become fond of Martín and reward him well in his will. At the same time, he disinherited another son named Luis whom he viewed as unworthy and the product of Cortés's affair with another Indian woman.

Nonetheless, in late summer and autumn 1522, Catalina Suárez replaced all other women competitors and lived with Cortés as his wife for months. On All Saints Day, November 1, there was a banquet at Coyoacan, followed by dancing. Catalina at one point began banter with one of the Conqueror's friends on the proper employment of Indians. Don Hernando overheard his wife say, "I promise you that, before many days, I will do something with my Indians [,] which no one will understand." Cortés, probably jokingly, said: "With *your* Indians? I do not want to hear anything about *your* things." Catalina felt abashed, left the dance, and retired to her room. Shortly thereafter, Cortés joined his wife.

In the middle of the night, don Hernando summoned his majordomo and told him his wife was dead. The aide, with Cortés's approval, sent a cryptic message to Juan Suárez notifying him that his sister had died, but he was not to come and see her body. In the inquest held to determine the cause of doña Catalina's death, a maid who did see the body testified there were bruises on the neck and that the head had turned blue. Still another maid claimed that doña Catalina had complained to her that Cortés often threw her out of bed and she had said: "One day you will find me dead from the way I live with don Hernando." Two of Cortés's closest associates asserted Cortés had murdered his wife, one of whom was the priest and translator Gerónimo de Aguilar.

Perhaps most suspicious, early the following morning Cortés buried his wife with a scarf wrapped around her neck. Don Hernando's testimony in his own defense contended that he was awakened in the night by his wife's gasping for breath, and then her heart stopped. He began shaking her by the neck and shoulders to resuscitate her, and that had caused bruising. Perhaps in fairness to Cortés, doña Catalina's brother testified that heart failure was common among women in the Suárez family, and that his mother and another sister had both died of what were probably heart attacks. Be that as it may, Cortés's wife was only the first of several suspicious deaths linked to the Conqueror.

After his wife's burial and the inquest into the cause of her death, Cortés—having heard nothing from his agents in Spain for months—made plans extending into late November and early December 1522 to occupy Pánuco. His basis for doing so was contrived by claiming the Huastecs who attacked and killed most of Álvarez de Pineda's colony were seeking exoneration for having killed Spaniards. These Indians allegedly informed Cortés they had killed the foreigners who had provoked them, because they were not followers of the great captain who had defeated their Aztec enemies. The Indians had then invited don Hernando to enter their lands and protect them from possible reprisals should other Spaniards approach their lands.

Initially, Cortés delayed entering Pánuco because Cristóbal de Olid had taken many of his best men-at-arms into Michoacán, and Pedro de Alvarado had led most of the remaining ones on a campaign into the Valley of Oaxaca in the south. But the Conqueror later received disturbing information of events in Cuba via a ship arriving at Villa Rica. It brought news that the Second Admiral Diego Columbus had entered an alliance with the *adelantado* Diego Velázquez and Francisco de Garay. The three men planned to enter New Spain along with other enemies of Cortés and "do him as much damage as possible."

By then, Olid and Alvarado had returned from campaigns with their forces intact, and that permitted Cortés to organize a coordinated advance into Pánuco. He would lead an incursion by way of the Moctezuma River Valley with a force consisting of four-hundred men-at-arms, among whom was Bernal Díaz; and, if we may believe the chronicler, about ten-thousand Tlaxcalan allies. Later, an armed caravel with cannons, musketeers, and crossbowmen would sail north from Villa Rica and anchor near the mouth of the Río Pánuco.

Preparation of the two-pronged contingent suggests Cortés had not received an invitation from Huastecs to enter their lands. The Indians' assertion seems unlikely given the Huastecs' response to every Spanish contact from Juan de Grijalva in 1518 to what was about to occur in December 1522. As mentioned, the Huastecs in Pánuco had copper-clad weapons, which has prompted some historians to speculate that they had contacts with Tarascan technology in prior years. In any event, their reputation as fighters plus the questionable point of occupying a land lacking readily exploitable wealth had dissuaded the Aztecs from invading their lands and conquering them.

Cortés, who had fought the Chontal Mayas, the Tlaxcalans, and of course the Aztecs, later commented that he had never faced such fierce opposition as the Huastecs mounted in defense of their lands. Their warriors refused to surrender under any circumstances, and battles ended when the last man standing was killed. Fighting began along upper reaches of the Río Pánuco along its right bank, as Cortés and his forces moved eastward toward the Gulf where they anticipated support from the armed caravel—although that never came about due to poor planning and lack of execution. But flat terrain along the streambed gave significant advantage to Spaniards and their horse guard. Cortés, however, was never an accomplished caballero after the Battle of Otumba. Some sources contend he lost two fingers on his left hand, while others assert that the Conqueror suffered so much injury that he could no longer control reins on his charger. In any event, after Otumba the best caballeros in Mexico were Alvarado without doubt and probably Sandoval.

There is also an important factual matter worth emphasizing, and one I have had a role in establishing. Some historians in Texas, and above all lay persons in the state, continue to assert that the short-lived colony founded by Álvarez de Pineda on a river to the north of Villa Rica de Veracruz was on the lower Río Grande. Those who support this contention cite Paul Horgan's Pulitzer Prize winning two-volume book, *Great River: The Rio Grande in North American History*. But first-hand evidence from the Cortés expedition established beyond a reasonable doubt that the Álvarez de Pineda colony was located on the Río Pánuco in Mexico. And here even more credit goes to Bernal Díaz. Without his unexpurgated writing, we likely would not know the name Alonso Álvarez de Pineda.

As Cortés continued eastward along the right bank of the Río Pánuco and about nine miles from a town named Chila, he and his expedition found grisly remains of the former Spanish colonists. The Huastecs had flayed skins of the dead and preserved them like the leather used in fine gloves. Identities of some of the deceased were recognizable from their hair and beards as old acquaintances from the Caribbean islands. Other unmistakable evidence of the location of the Álvarez de Pineda colony was soon discovered. Since the Huastecs controlled the river with war canoes and brought in defenders from the left bank, Cortés needed watercraft. He and his native allies came upon two or three ships the Indians had been unable to burn because they were partially sunk in the river. Salvaged planking from the vessels provided the material carpenters needed to construct half a dozen barges and equip them with paddles. The improvised craft, to quote Bernal Díaz, "were made from the wood of old vessels that belonged to the captain sent by Garay, who had been killed." The chronicler with his usual detail identified the captain as Álvarez de Pineda. (Bernal Díaz remains the sole reference to the identity of this man; and even the Naval Archive in Madrid has no record of him.)

We need not dwell on the remainder of the conquest of Pánuco. Cortés and his command, then reinforced by barges on the river, encountered heavy resistance beyond Chila. And in two weeks, marked by bitter Huastec resistance, the Conqueror had reached the Indians' last holdout on an island in Tamiahua lagoon. For several days, don Hernando tried to negotiate a peaceful surrender of the Huastecs, but again his efforts failed.

Before the last battle in the conquest of Pánuco, Cortés spent the night transporting horses by barges to the island. At dawn, the horse guard held off Huastec attacks while the entire force of Spaniards and their Indian allies were ferried into position by barges and captured Indian canoes. The battle ended when the last Indian defender was killed. At that time, Cortés commented on Huastec warriors being the most fearsome he had faced in the Indies.

On December 22, 1522, Cortés founded the third villa in New Spain and named it Santiesteban del Puerto. The town was a short distance from Chila and was located on the right bank of the Río Pánuco. The municipality was later renamed Pánuco, Veracruz. Just as the Conqueror had appointed mayors and councilmen at Villa Rica de Veracruz and Segura de la Frontera, he did the same at Port Saint Stephen. Pedro de Vallejo was Cortés's choice as alcalde of the new villa, and before returning to his residence at Coyoacan, the Conqueror awarded encomiendas to several of his conquistadors. The date on one of these grants is

March 1, 1523, but there is no evidence it was the first of such concessions. What is certain is that Cortés had no legal authority to allocate Indians in encomienda to anyone at this time. That, however, would change in several months because of events taking place in Spain.

As noted, King Charles I left Spain in May 1520 to confront Martin Luther in Germany and receive a second more important title of Charles V of the Holy Roman Empire. Also as mentioned, the young king had left a country in the throes of a strange internal conflict known as the Revolt of the Comuneros (April 1520– October 1521). When Charles began his return to Spain in 1522, he was aware the country was at peace thanks to Crown loyalists. The emperor also knew of a conquistador captain named Hernando Cortés, because of letters he had received from him from a land called New Spain some five-thousand miles across a great ocean. The young monarch likely remembered riches he had received as gifts from that distant land before leaving Spain. And last, Charles knew that Bishop Juan de Fonseca, left in charge of Spain during his absence, had an intense dislike of that conquistador captain.

The emperor arrived at Valladolid, Spain, which he regarded as Spain's capital, on August 25, 1522. In the four years since Charles had first set foot in Spain as an awkward sixteen-year-old youth who did not know a single word of Castilian, he had transformed himself into a great monarch. The king had faced Martin Luther at Worms and witnessed the beginning of the Protestant Reformation, grown a magnificent beard to hide his projected Hapsburg jaw, and learned much. Although a devout Catholic, Charles was at least mildly opposed to the political power of the Roman Catholic Church in Spain and was therefore not over awed by Fonseca, who had been the most powerful cleric in Spain for more than thirty years.

Charles V had developed wide-ranging interests, including an appreciation of art and learning. In late summer at Valladolid, the emperor began organizing councils by dismissing some people and appointing others. Included was a special committee charged with advising him on what to do about the man who had been labeled a renegade conquistador by Diego Velázquez, the royal governor and *adelantado* of Cuba. Significantly, Bishop Fonseca was not a member of that advisory group, because Charles was suspicious that the high cleric had withheld information regarding Cortés from him that would have cast the Conqueror in a more favorable light. The emperor's distrust of Fonseca intensified during fall 1522 as committee members read the Conqueror's extensive correspondence sent to Charles V. Throughout those deliberations, Fonseca continued to lose even more favor and was ultimately sent to live out the remainder of his life in Burgos, the see of his bishopric. The high churchman died on November 4, 1524. Prior to his death, most of his staff was incorporated into the Royal Council of Indies. The Council would evolve from its creation in 1524 into the highest administrative agency of matters relating to Spain in the Indies, although it always acted in the name of the King, and it served as the court of last resort in all legal matters arising in the Indies.

Without doubt Cortés had made enemies, including some who had joined plots to assassinate him, but there was never serious doubt raised about the man's loyalty to the Crown or his commitment to militant Catholicism. Furthermore, given the emperor's intellectual interests, he no doubt admired don Hernando's ability to write literate Castilian spiced with occasional phrases in Latin. Still, some committee members expressed doubts about Cortés's character. In one letter from an enemy of the Conqueror, the writer insisted the first captain had the conscience of a dog—a bad analogy since canines can display guilt. The committee members nonetheless reprimanded Diego Velázquez for sending Pánfilo de Narváez to Mexico against the express orders of the Audiencia of Santo Domingo. Perhaps most important, the committee ordered don Diego "not to meddle in Cortés's affairs anymore."

Emperor Charles V, on hearing the committee's overall favorable comments on the Conqueror, agreed to the following concessions on October 11, 1522: He appointed Cortés *adelantado* and commander-in-chief with political responsibilities; *repartidor* (distributor of Indians in encomienda); and governor and captain-general (supreme military commander) of New Spain. This was total victory for Cortés in that he received royal confirmation of privileges that he had enjoyed since the fall of Tenochtitlan. As a final triumph, the emperor sent a personal letter to Cortés in which he "spoke warmly and enthusiastically of his achievements."

However, along with glad tidings for the Conqueror, Charles V and his advisors appointed four bureaucrats to assist and oversee all decisions made by

Cortés; an especially important step given the extraordinary powers that had been conferred on him. Two of those appointees would bedevil don Hernando beyond anything Diego Velázquez had likely ever considered. Alonso de Estrada would travel to New Spain as treasurer; Gonzalo de Salazar, as *factor*; Rodrigo de Albornoz, as accountant; and Pedro Almíndez de Chirino, as inspector general. An examination of the quartet's instructions reveals a key element of Crown control over the administration of New Spain. Each appointee was praised for his service to the Crown but enjoined to monitor all actions taken by the other three who were regarded as less trustworthy. The principle of "divide and rule," combined with mutual suspicion, were vital components of royal absolutism that lasted throughout the centuries of Spain in America.

It was one thing for the emperor to empower and congratulate Cortés by decree in Spain but quite another for that news to reach New Spain—in fact, in the words of Sir Hugh Thomas, it took the "unconscionably long time" of one year. Spanish bureaucracy moved with glacial slowness and there was the odd decision that two cousins of Cortés, Rodrigo de Paz and Francisco de Las Casas, "should be the bearers of the good tidings." This unfortunate delay would ultimately result in chaos and death for Spaniards and Huastecs alike in Pánuco.

Trouble began when Francisco de Garay, governor of Jamaica, led a huge expedition to settle lands along the Gulf of Mexico previously explored by his captain Álvarez de Pineda. In sailing to New Spain, Garay stopped in Cuba to take on supplies and there learned Cortés had conquered Pánuco, founded Villa Santiestaban del Puerto, awarded encomiendas to his followers, and appointed Pedro de Vallejo as captain in charge of one-hundred colonists. This information prompted Garay to land farther north on the Gulf Coast from Pánuco on the Río de Las Palmas, the present-day Río Soto la Marina, where he arrived on June 25, 1523.

The Garay-led expedition consisted of six-hundred men, about half of whom were armed, and eleven ships. The armada anchored near the mouth of the Palmas, an exception being a shallow-draft brigantine and its crew sent upriver to explore. There, Garay's men found nothing but a barren land devoid of any exploitable wealth, and on returning they described what they had seen with one contemptuous word: "*despoblado*" (uninhabited place). By that time, disappointment along with supplies running low prompted about three-hundred men to go ashore and forage their way to the Río Pánuco, approximately a ninety-mile trek. The remaining three-hundred on the eleven ships lifted anchor and sailed down the coast to the river.

The presence of nearly seven-hundred Spaniards in a land that could barely sustain one-hundred was certain to cause trouble, especially when the newcomers began making demands for food and women. Mounting abuses led to an Indian uprising that cost the lives of three-hundred Castilians and left a recently pacified province in revolt. To address the crisis, Pedro de Vallejo appealed to Cortés at Coyoacan for reinforcements. Don Hernando had recently fought a minor battle with Indians near México-Tenochtitlan and in the fighting sustained a left arm wound that even further prevented his controlling a charger. In his stead, the Conqueror sent Gonzalo de Sandoval with several-hundred men-at-arms and thousands of Indian allies on a forced march to Pánuco. On arrival there, the expedition crushed the revolt, and Sandoval followed by sending an indelible message to rebellious Indians. He tied three-hundred Huastec caciques to trees or metal stakes anchored in the ground and burned them alive—one for each Spaniard who had died in the revolt.

On recovering from his wound, Cortés traveled to Pánuco and began issuing slaving licenses to settlers there who rounded up Huastecs, whether troublesome or not, branded them on their faces as slaves, and shipped the unfortunates off to labor-desperate islands in the Caribbean in exchange for livestock—the exchange rate being one slave for fifteen cattle. But far too many Spaniards occupying poor lands gave rise to vagrants (*vagabundos*) who wandered the countryside and preyed on defenseless Indians.

When news of Cortés's multiple appointments finally reached New Spain in mid-fall 1523, included was a Crown decree that compelled Francisco de Garay to relinquish all claims to Pánuco. He could, however, settle inland along the Río de las Palmas—a concession he rejected, knowing full well there was nothing worth having. Cortés, having won all, invited Garay, who had relocated to the capital, to spend Christmas 1523 with him at Coyoacan. The two men attended midnight Mass, followed by breakfast at the home of don Hernando. After dining, Garay fell violently ill and died two days later. It was the second suspicious death linked to the Conqueror. In defense of don Hernando, there was little reason for him to have poisoned Garay, having won everything he might have desired in concessions granted by Charles V. In fact, when Cortés had first learned of his multiple titles, it had touched off a three-day celebration at Coyoacan, and the Conqueror was so elated he remarked that he would gladly kiss the emperor's feet a hundred times. Nonetheless, the following year 1524 would be a bad one for don Hernando, and it would begin his decline in fortune until reversal came in 1529.

In summer 1524, Cortés equipped Cristóbal de Olid with ships, musketeers, and crossbowmen for an expedition to the coast of Honduras, which was rumored to be so rich that Indians there used gold for fishhooks. Dreams of El Dorado where streets were paved with gold would persist for decades. Honduras, known to Spaniards as Higueras, held promise as such rich land. On Olid's departure from Villa Rica, Cortés gave him strict orders to avoid Cuba or have any contact with Diego Velázquez—a command don Cristóbal chose to ignore. He stopped in Santiago and defected to the Conqueror's old nemesis Diego Velázquez before continuing to Higueras, where he founded a colony on its north coast.

When the Conqueror learned of Olid's betrayal, he responded by organizing a sea expedition that consisted of five ships, fifteen cavaliers, and about three-hundred footmen with half that number armed with muskets and crossbows. Under don Hernando's command, and on three occasions during the hurricane season in 1524, the assembled ships left Villa Rica only to be driven back to port by contrary winds.

After the third failed attempt, the Conqueror altered his plans, perhaps acknowledging that God's will had prevailed against him. He decided on an overland expedition to Higueras, but at the same time sent his cousin Francisco de las Casas on a fourth attempt to reach there by sea. The latter finally succeeded, but Cortés—out of contact with the vessel—had gone forward with plans to trek through difficult and uncharted lands. The undertaking included Doña Marina, Cuauhtemoc of Tenochtitlan, Coanacochtzin of Texcoco, and Tetlepanquetzatzin of Tacuba. Before leaving México-Tenochtitlan, Cortés had to decide what to do with the four treasury officials who had joined him on orders of Charles V. The bureaucrats had arrived believing exaggerated accounts of the treasure Cortés had sent to Spain, and all expected to get rich quickly after their arrival. They, however, soon saw the difficulty of attaining instant wealth in New Spain. Rumors spread that multi-titled don Hernando Cortés at his residence in Coyoacan had stored vast amounts of gold, silver, and gems—and that he had cheated the Crown by failing to pay the royal *quinto*. Two of the four treasury officials, Salazar and Chirino, repeated those rumors to excite their partisans, but Estrada and Albornoz did not believe such tales and supported Cortés in comments made to his followers. Recognizing this factionalism, the Conqueror did not wish to leave behind the two officials who had conspired against him, so he insisted that Salazar and Chirino join his march to Honduras, while leaving Estrada and Albornoz in charge during his absence.

When the overland expedition reached Coatzacoalcos, a supply ship arrived there with word that New Spain had fallen into near-complete chaos. *Vagabundos* without encomiendas to support them wandered New Spain and abused Indians, while Estrada and Albornoz were powerless to stop them. Cortés then made a strategic error by allowing Salazar and Chirino to leave the expedition and return to New Spain on the supply ship. When the men arrived in the capital, they claimed Cortés had empowered them with complete authority to restore order, although he had not done so. The new arrivals nonetheless incarcerated Estrada and Albornoz, revoked encomiendas held by Cortés's partisans, and arrested Cortés's young cousin Rodrigo de Paz who had been left in charge of don Hernando's household at Coyoacan.

Seeking information on where Cortés had allegedly hidden vast amounts of treasure, Salazar and Chirino interrogated Paz. When he replied truthfully that there was no cache of valuables, the two officials had him tortured in the same manner used on Cuauhtemoc: They set ablaze oil on his feet until he could no longer walk. Still convinced Paz was lying, Salazar and Chirino ordered him carried to the gallows and hanged. They then began revoking Cortés's encomienda grants to conquistadors who had defeated the Aztecs and followed by reassigning them to their partisans who had done little or no fighting. Such unfairness prompted a counter revolt, during which adherents of Cortés freed Estrada and Albornoz. They, in turn, arrested Salazar and Chirino and confined them to a cage set up in the great plaza of México-Tenochtitlan where they were taunted and ridiculed. The pro-Cortés officials also restored the original encomienda grants to

Conqueror's partisans. This unseemly chorus of events took place during the nearly two years Cortés was absent from the Spanish capital.

Meanwhile, and before the Honduran expedition left Coatzacoalcos, Doña Marina found her aged mother who had sold her into slavery among the Chontal Mayas to please her second husband. As a Christian convert, Doña Marina forgave her mother; but she had also been comfortable with the old Mexica gods Huitzilopochtli, Tezcatlipoca, and Quetzalcoatl—and why not, since they likewise had given her solace.

Shortly afterward, as the Honduran expedition continued toward coastal Higueras, Cortés decided to end his long and intimate relationship with Doña Marina, although she would continue to serve him as translator. Marriage to an Indian woman for a man of don Hernando's stature and titles was of course out of the question. Nonetheless, there is ample evidence that Cortés was fond of Marina and treated her well, especially as the mother of his mestizo son Martín. That said, he forced her to marry a reluctant conquistador named Juan Jaramillo whose opposition to matrimony was tempered by Cortés's forcing him to drink large amount of pulque, a cheap alcoholic drink made from fermented corn. When the drunken ceremony was complete, Doña Marina was separated from the Conqueror, whom she knew well having rarely spent a day apart from his company in five years.

Well before reaching Honduras, Cortés thought it necessary to bring charges that related to a plot to kill him and his fellow conquistadors, which implicated the kings of Tacuba, Tenochtitlan, and Texcoco. In a column of Spaniards and their Indian allies that numbered in the hundreds, it was impossible to prevent the native monarchs from having contact with local Indians at various places along the way. And since the three chieftains were famous, plans to free them were made in secret. Cortés likewise had his informants, and they convinced him an ambush was imminent.

After torturing one or more of the kings, Cortés learned more incriminating details. The former Indian monarchs were tried in the field by a commission appointed by the Conqueror, found guilty of conspiracy, and sentenced to hang. According to historian France V. Scholes, who read details of the trial and its aftermath, Cortés spent a sleepless night pondering whether to allow the hangings, but he nonetheless permitted them to proceed. The executions of the three Kings, especially Cuauhtemoc, has enraged Mexicans to the present-day. Many of them regard Cuauhtemoc as a martyr—perhaps with justice—but at least he was tried for conspiracy with corroborating testimony, not summarily lynched.

During the months that Cortés spent reaching Honduras, in 1524 Pedro de Alvarado advanced from México-Tenochtitlan toward present-day Guatemala and El Salvador. After the fall of Tenochtitlan, followed by the disappointment of there being so little treasure to distribute—even Cortés's main captains received only two-thousand gold pesos—Alvarado became a conqueror in his own right. His first conquest began in the southeast corner of the present-day state of Chiapas where it borders Guatemala. Don Pedro encountered heavy fighting in taking the town of Utatlan, the capital of the Cakshiquel Maya. Throughout the subsequent conquest of Guatemala, Alvarado's force of more than four-hundred Spaniards and thousands of Indian allies were aided by smallpox that swept before them and weakened native opposition. In the end, Alvarado established his headquarters at present-day Guatemala City and from there expanded control over El Salvador and part of Honduras. For the next seventeen years, Alvarado served as royal governor of portions of Central America, and in the early 1530s he even ventured into South America where he had a minor role in the conquest of Ecuador. To repeat, Alvarado may well be regarded as the "ubiquitous conquistador" in the Spanish Indies.

Meanwhile, Cortés was in the field for just fewer than two years and finally arrived in Honduras with the intent of punishing Cristóbal de Olid. To his surprise, there had been no need for him to have made the trek, for don Cristóbal was dead. The Conqueror had sent his cousin Francisco de las Casas by sea to persuade Olid to surrender and face consequences for his alliance with Diego Velázquez. When Las Casas arrived as intended, he hoped to join forces with an earlier settler in Honduras named Gil González de Ávila, a friend of Cortés.

Both Las Casas and Gil González were apprehended as enemies by Olid and incarcerated for a few weeks. During that time, the captives began to cajole don Cristóbal and remind him of when he was a favorite of Cortés and one of his principal captains in the conquest of Mexico. Olid apparently loved flattery and began to lower his guard to the point of taking meals with his erstwhile enemies. In a playful manner, either Las Casas or Gil González rose from the table on day and first yanked on don Cristóbal's beard and then stabbed him in the neck with a table knife, it being the only available weapon. A scuffle ensued in which Olid was soon overpowered. Following that, "the captain of the guard, the ensign and the lieutenant were taken prisoner in a moment, no man being killed, and Cristóbal de Olid in the uproar escaped into hiding"—thus wrote Cortés in his fifth letter to the Emperor Charles V.

Within a day or two, Olid was apprehended and brought to trial by a commission consisting of judge and jurors selected by Las Casas and Gil González. Not surprisingly, the defendant was found guilty of treason, marched to the central plaza of the town he had founded, and beheaded him. Having learned this on his arrival in Honduras, Cortés left the colony in hands of partisans and sailed at the first opportunity to Villa Rica, along with Doña Marina as the bride of Juan Jaramillo.

By then, the pro-Cortés faction in charge of México-Tenochtitlan was about to fall again under the rule of Salazar and Chirino who spread a rumor that Cortés had died of a fever on the march to Honduras. To their chagrin, an emaciated and exhausted don Hernando Cortés stepped off a vessel at Villa Rica de Veracruz in May 1526. Some who had known the Conqueror for years did not recognize him. But the enfeebled governor and captain general soon regained his strength and resolve.

Cortés rode horseback to México-Tenochtitlan and on entering the city received a tumultuous welcome from his partisans. The Conqueror was saddened to learn that his young cousin Rodrigo de Paz was dead, but he ordered the transfer of Salazar and Chirino from a cage in the plaza to confinement in the municipal jail where they awaited trial. Cortés then moved promptly to bestow encomiendas on three children of Moctezuma.

Doña Isabel (Tecuichpotzin) had been widowed a third time with the hanging of Cuauhtemoc, and Cortés thought she should have a Castilian husband. But why don Hernando chose Alonso de Grado as groom remains a mystery, especially when one remembers that Pedro de Alvarado had previously wanted to hang Grado as a worthless and cowardly drunk who liked music. In any event, Isabel was only seventeen when widowed a fourth time, because it seems that Grado died of debauchery in early 1527. By then, doña Isabel had received one of the richest encomiendas in Mexico on June 27, 1526. Every eighty days she received revenue from more than eleven-hundred tributary units in Tacuba and its subject towns, and possession was in perpetuity (*para siempre jamás*).

At the same time, Isabel's half-sister Mariana (thereafter known exclusively as Leonor) received the large lakeside city of Ecatepec and all its houses as her encomienda. The encomienda was likewise awarded to her and her heirs "forever." Next came Moctezuma's son don Pedro, and he along with his heirs also received a permanent grant of revenue from Tula and nearby Tultengo. Pedro's legacy would have the greatest importance and longevity. However, by the middle of the seventeenth century there were no male descendants named Moctezuma. The imperial surname would nevertheless continue through the third countess, Gerónima María de Moctezuma, whose husband José Sarmiento de Valladares added the title, Count of Moctezuma. Don José served as the last Viceroy of Mexico (1696–1701) in the Spanish Hapsburg era. Astonishingly, heirs of don Pedro Moctezuma would continue receiving revenue from Tula and Tultengo throughout the colonial era in Mexico that ended in September 1821. The independent Mexican government then continued to pay a stipend to twentieth-century heirs of Pedro Moctezuma until the interim presidency of Abelardo L. Rodríguez (1932–1934).

Unknown to Cortés in 1526 when he bestowed encomiendas on the three surviving Aztec nobility, he had reached the apogee of power and influence in Mexico. As part of establishing the Crown's long arm of absolute monarchy into the Indies, every literate Spaniard—and even those illiterate if they could pay someone able to write a letter—could send a complaint about a superior and address it to the Council of the Indies or to the king himself. It is only slight exaggeration to state that during the almost two years Cortés had marched through uncharted Mexico and Central America, a "blizzard" of mail airing complaints about him reached authorities in Spain. There, king and Council of the Indies began to listen. How could the Conqueror with so many powers recently conferred on him have allowed New Spain to fall into near-complete anarchy—encomiendas awarded, then revoked, only to be reallocated—while he was away on an unnecessary trek to Honduras? By November 1525, Spain's highest governmental officials were determined to bring an end to Cortés's authority in New Spain. Charged with that responsibility, Luis Ponce de León was sent to New Spain with orders to remove Cortés from power and bring him to trial by *residencia* for possible malfeasance in office. At the same time, Nuño de Guzmán received appointment as governor of Pánuco, which was to become a separate jurisdiction from New Spain but was then under the control of Cortés and settled by his adherents.

There is no doubt that Ponce and Guzmán received dual appointments with the goal of "trimming the sails" of Hernando Cortés. Ponce's instructions made specific reference to Guzmán by name, stating: "If by his reception [in Pánuco] or in matters of his government he should need your assistance, give it to him . . . as between you there is no difference or competency whatever by reason of limits of your governments." Guzmán, in turn, was ordered to assist Ponce in the capital should he have need of his help.

The appointees sailed together and arrived in Santo Domingo a few weeks after Cortés had returned to New Spain. Soon afterward, Guzmán fell ill with a fever, probably malaria, and was bedfast for eight months. Ponce, unable to wait for don Nuño's recovery, continued alone and arrived in México-Tenochtitlan in July or August 1526. He presented his commission to the Conqueror, which removed the many titles and powers conferred on him by Charles V, and don Hernando immediately bowed to the royal decree. To demonstrate his willingness to undergo *residencia*, an exhaustive inquiry into a Crown-appointed officeholder's tenure, Cortés invited Ponce to dine with him. Shortly after eating, Ponce complained of a severe stomach disorder, apparently from eating contaminated bacon. He died within a day or two but not before transferring his commission to an aged conquistador, Marcos de Aguilar.

Aguilar was hardly the man to take charge. His mental faculties were hampered by senility, and he became so incapacitated that he had to take nourishment from a wet nurse. The old man soon died, and although he had not recently dined at the table of Cortés, there was nonetheless suspicion cast on the Conqueror. From his death bed, Aguilar had roused himself long enough to place Alonso de Estrada, aided by Gonzalo de Sandoval, in command but without the right to conduct Cortés's *residencia*. Nothing at that point had changed in curbing the power of the Conqueror because of don Hernando's close friendship with the co-governors.

Matters remained unsettled until Nuño de Guzmán regained his health in Santo Domingo and assumed the governorship of Pánuco. Don Nuño was yet another example of how family mattered in gaining royal appointments in the Indies. His relatives had supported King Charles during the Revolt of the Comuneros. Don Nuño's father was a familiar (informer) of the Spanish Inquisition; a brother held one of the highest positions in the Franciscan Order; another sibling was an ambassador to the Republic of Genoa; and Guzmán himself had been an honored youth of a prominent family at the King's court and sailed with Charles I to Flanders in 1520.

Guzmán finally arrived at Villa Santiesteban del Puerto in May 1527 along with a retinue of servants and men-at-arms. Trouble began immediately when don Nuño revoked encomienda grants made by Cortés and reassigned them to his stalwarts. Those dispossessed of income left Pánuco and carried their grievances to Cortés and his associates at Coyoacan. From early summer 1527 into December, border clashes occurred between Pánuco and México-Tenochtitlan proper, and near-civil war ensued—followed by another barrage of complaints sent in letters addressed to king and council in Spain. In the meantime, Guzmán followed Cortés's example by expanding the slave trade in exchange for livestock badly needed in Pánuco.

Things changed when Nuño de Guzmán learned that the king and the Council of the Indies had created the Audiencia of New Spain and appointed him as president of this supreme agency of government. News of the appointment reached Guzmán in late 1527, and within were directives: don Nuño was to leave Pánuco while retaining his governorship there, travel to México-Tenochtitlan, remove Alonso de Estrada and Gonzalo de Sandoval as co-governors, and then set in motion plans to conduct the *residencia* of Cortés. To assist Guzmán, four judges had been sent across the Atlantic to serve with him on the Audiencia. Of interest, two of the magistrates, called *oidores* (judges who heard cases), died within days after reaching New Spain without repast at the table of Cortés. In a rare personal letter penned by Guzmán to a friend in Pánuco and sent from the capital in January 1528, don Nuño commented on the frequency of newcomers dying in New Spain after eating contaminated food: "Those who came with me are afflicted with severe diarrhea, and some are already dead, while others are sick . . . I am not certain why I have been spared death for in the . . . months I have been in these parts more than six-hundred Spaniards have died." Such comments might bring a sympathetic smile from travelers in the past who have visited Mexico and thereafter suffered digestive disorders. But Guzmán's comments also serve to lift the veil of suspicion that surrounded Cortés on the deaths of those who dined with him. More important, Nuño de Guzmán and the two surviving judges of Audiencia of New Spain were ordered to begin the massive *residencia* of Cortés. The Conqueror in 1528, recognizing that political winds had shifted against him, began preparations to return to Spain, the birth country he had not seen since leaving it around 1506. Traveling with him in March were many Castilian friends that included Gonzalo de Sandoval and Andrés de Tapia, as well as a few prominent Indians—the most important of whom being Pedro Moctezuma who had been appointed encomendero of Tula and Tultengo.

Cortés was well received at Court by Charles V, although the Emperor was reserved in his comments while awaiting the results of *residencia* proceedings underway in New Spain. Cortés's father Martín had died in 1527, after being at Court many years as an effective advocate for his famous son. The Conqueror then left Court and visited Medellín for a happy reunion with his mother.

While in Spain, don Hernando began a search for a Castilian bride who was appropriate to his station. His choice was Juana de Zúñiga. Doña Juana was the daughter of the Count of Aguilar and niece of the Duke of Béjar—a surname familiar to San Antonians and other Texans when spelled with an "x." The Duke was the most powerful and rich nobleman in western Spain, and doña Juana brought a substantial dowry of 10,000 ducats into her marriage to Cortés. Even Charles V was complimentary of Cortés's choice for nuptials, and when don Hernando fell ill at Burgos, the Emperor visited his bedside—an almost unheard-of honor.

Still, Cortés's future rested on the outcome of his *residencia* conducted by a magistrate chosen by Nuño de Guzmán and the two surviving judges of the Audiencia of New Spain. Testimony and documentation related to that proceeding created more than three-thousand pages. The formal inquest ended in 1529, and the judge's conclusions were forwarded to Spain. When Charles V was informed that Cortés had received almost total vindication for his actions and conduct in

New Spain, he asked don Hernando to sit beside him on the throne. The Emperor then made don Hernando a nobleman with the impressive title of Marqués of the Valley of Oaxaca in southern New Spain, and the marquisate was conferred in perpetuity.

With the title came an encomienda that initially comprised 21,000 vassals. Cortés without Crown consent would increase the number of tributaries to 50,000. Don Hernando, while wealthy for the rest of his life, would no longer serve as governor of New Spain, a matter that hurt him deeply. He did keep his military designation as Captain General, but it amounted to little more than an honorary title. Henceforth, political power in New Spain was vested with audiencias headed by Viceroys of New Spain. Significantly, Antonio de Mendoza was also appointed as New Spain's first Viceroy in 1529 but was delayed from taking office for six years because of various commitments in Spain. Mendoza was worth waiting for, because no individual would be as important as he from 1535 to 1550 in bringing stability to New Spain from the foundations that Hernando Cortés had established there.

AFTERWORD

This study concludes in 1529 with the establishment of stable government in Mexico, but a caveat is needed. The Audiencia of New Spain, 1528–1532, headed by Nuño de Guzmán as president, failed dismally, and it became noted for especially bad governance when judges Juan Ortiz de Matienzo and Diego Delgadillo joined. The trio accelerated the number of Indian slaves sent to the Caribbean islands in exchange for livestock, using Pánuco as their main conduit. The president and *oidores* were biased in actions taken against partisans of Cortés by revoking their encomienda grants and reassigning Indian tributaries to themselves and their friends. Matienzo and Delgadillo became notorious for keeping harems of Indian women. When removed from office by the Second Audiencia of New Spain and subjected to *residencia* proceedings, the audiencia judges were convicted of gross malfeasance in office and sent to Spain where they died in prison. Guzmán received a lighter sentence, but even with prominent family connections, he was placed under house arrest at Court from 1540 until he died at Valladolid on October 26, 1558. Stable government arrived with the Second Audiencia in 1532, and its judges were further empowered when joined by Viceroy Antonio de Mendoza in 1535.

It is of interest here to comment on the later years of some of the prominent men and women introduced in this study and relate the circumstances of their deaths as reported by existing sources. As mentioned in the opening chapters on Christopher Columbus, the mariner died at Valladolid, Spain, on May 20, 1506.

Unlike many conquistadors in Yucatan and Mexico, he died in bed in the company of his sons. Columbus was never poor late in life, although he felt disappointment in not having reached the Orient by sailing west. As suggested earlier, perhaps it was best that he died without realizing how far he had been from Japan and Asia even at the western extent of his discoveries in the Caribbean.

Two cities, Seville and Santo Domingo, have vied too long in claiming to house the bones of Christopher Columbus. Spaniards as late as 2002 have allowed DNA testing of bone fragments taken from the famous Tomb of Columbus that resides within Seville's huge gothic cathedral, where it is held aloft on the shoulders of four Castilian nobles dressed in finery. Spaniards are confident they have at least some bones of the famous mariner. In Columbus's will, he expressed the desire that his remains be sent to the Indies, but that did not immediately happen. Instead, his bones were moved several times in Spain and became disarticulated. Within the Seville Cathedral are the verifiable remains of Columbus's brother Diego and the Admiral's son, Hernando. There is apparent DNA match of some bone fragments from the three burials. Officials in the Dominican Republic, however, still insist that they have Columbus's remains but refuse to open the so-called "Lighthouse Tomb" in Santo Domingo, arguing that remains of the dead should lie undisturbed.

Gonzalo de Sandoval, Cortes's "Constant Captain," and later short-term co-governor of New Spain along with Alonso de Estrada, accompanied Cortés when he sailed to Spain in March 1528. In the more than forty days at sea, don Gonzalo—probably still in his late twenties—became ill of undetermined causes. After disembarking at Palos in early May, he was taken to a hostelry (*mesón*) where he remained bedfast until May 23. During his stay at the inn, one of his strongboxes was broken into, probably by the hostel owner, and several ingots of gold were taken. Friends tried to save the young conquistador by carrying him to Seville where there were better medical facilities, but his condition rapidly worsened. He died at an inn in Niebla before midnight of May 24, 1528.

Doña Marina and her conquistador husband Juan Jaramillo received an encomienda, located about fourteen leagues to the northwest of México-Tenochtitlan, and lived in its *cabecera* (head town) of Xilotepec. The couple's daughter María married Luis de Quesada, a resident in México-Tenochtitlan.

Little more is known of Doña Marina's life or death that can be documented. Born Malinalli, her command of Nahuatl and Maya and role as translator greatly facilitated the conquest of Mexico by Spaniards. She, in my opinion and in that of others who admire her, has been unfairly vilified by some in Mexico who have labeled her a traitor to her people while serving as Cortés's concubine (*puta*). However, one might well ask, "who were her people?" A Nahuatl mother who sold her into slavery among the Chontal Maya? Doña Marina probably did what she thought was best for herself, just as anyone in her situation might have done.

To my knowledge, there is no recent, archival-based biography of Pedro de Alvarado in any language. Perhaps because such a study would be extremely difficult to research, given the variety of theaters and capacities in which he served: his role as a ship captain in 1518, his emergence as one of the most skilled horsemen in Mexico, his role in the conquest of Mexico as first captain under Cortés, his remarkable escape as the last Spaniard out of Tenochtitlan during the Noche Triste, his seventeen years as governor and captain general of portions of Central America, and even his brief role in the conquest of Ecuador.

In 1540-41 don Pedro, then in his mid-fifties and still eager for adventure, partnered with Viceroy Antonio de Mendoza to explore by sea the northwest coast of Mexico and provide naval support for the Francisco Vázquez de Coronado expedition, which was then in the field. Early on, Alvarado chose to refit his ships at Puerto Navidad on the west coast of Mexico and while there was recruited by the viceroy to help suppress an Indian revolt in the region. Unknown to Alvarado, behind a large natural rock formation known as the Peñol of Nochistlán in the province of New Galicia were Indians unlike any he had ever faced. These semi-sedentary First People were masters of the bow and arrow. In two assaults on the Peñol, thirty of Alvarado's one-hundred men-at-arms lay dead, a result unheard of at that time for Spaniards in wars with Indians. Forced to retreat in rain along a ravine while pursued by Indians, don Pedro took up a rearguard position while leading his horse on foot. Another cavalier decided to assist his captain by joining him, but his horse on muddy and slippery ground became entangled with Alvarado's mount. The struggling animals knocked don Pedro off his feet and into the ravine, and his horse rolled over him on its way down.

Fellow conquistadors carried his broken body to Guadalajara, New Galicia, where he died on July 4, 1541. It was a strange way to die for Alvarado, who was regarded as the ultimate warrior.

When Isabel Moctezuma (Tecuichpotzin) was widowed a fourth time after the death of Alonso de Grado in 1527, Cortés moved the Aztec princess under his roof and soon thereafter into his bed. When doña Isabel was six or seven months' pregnant with his child, don Hernando arranged for her to take a fifth husband, Pedro Gallego de Andrade. There followed a pre-nuptial understanding with Gallego that at birth the infant would be placed in the home of Cortés's cousin by marriage, a prominent lawyer named Juan Gutiérrez de Altmirano, who would became administrator of the Conqueror's vast properties in New Spain. Doña Isabel bore a daughter by don Pedro named Leonor Cortés Moctezuma, who was the granddaughter of both Cortés and Moctezuma. While beyond the range of this study, at maturity doña Leonor married a rich miner twice her age and bore three children on the northern mining frontier of New Spain at Zacatecas. One of her daughters married Juan de Oñate, the future governor and *adelantado* of New Mexico province.

In 1530, doña Isabel and her fifth husband Pedro Gallego birthed a son named Juan de Andrade (Gallego) Moctezuma. Shortly thereafter, Gallego died of undetermined causes, and the Aztec princess was widowed a fifth time. One might reasonably posit, given the fate of five former husbands, that suitors would be wary of nuptials with Isabel Moctezuma, but she was too rich not to attract the attention of many suitors, including a conquistador named Juan Cano. Their marriage would result in five more children, bringing doña Isabel's total offspring to seven. She died at about age forty-one in late 1550, leaving considerable wealth to her son by Pedro Gallego and a bequest to doña Leonor, her daughter fathered by Cortés. Her last will and testament spawned immediate challenges in lawsuits filed by her widowed husband Juan Cano and his three sons. Those legal challenges almost without exception were settled in favor of the Canos. Two daughters of Juan Cano and doña Isabel took the veil and were not involved in lawsuits. Widower Juan Cano moved to Spain and there built an impressive palace that still stands in his birth city, Cáceres, Extremadura. It was financed by continued tribute payment imposed on the Indians of Tacuba. This splendid reconstructed castle may be viewed by Googling "Aldea del Cano Castle Cáceres Province of Cáceres, Extremadura."

Hernando Cortés returned to New Spain with his high-born wife Juana Zúñiga, his mother, and four-hundred others in 1530. They left Seville in summer and arrived at Villa Rica on July 15. His mother died shortly thereafter at Texcoco before she could properly appreciate her son's achievements. Initially denied admission to the capital by Nuño de Guzmán and judges of the Audiencia of New Spain, don Hernando and his wife relocated to Cuernavaca, where Cortés built a palatial home with an adjoining flower garden. The former Conqueror would live another seventeen years—years filled with frustrations, numerous lawsuits launched by him and against him, and a sense of failure due to his overweening ambition to conqueror new lands to the north of New Spain that were believed to be richer than Central Mexico. In that endeavor, he faced competition from his archenemy Nuño de Guzmán for settlement of the northwest coast of Mexico and beyond, as well as by Viceroy Mendoza in attempts to find the rumored rich Seven Cities of Cíbola and a strait to the Orient. His numerous lawsuits with Guzmán occupied him for years, but they did not significantly drain his vast wealth.

Cortés's wife Juana Zúñiga with her ties to the highest tier of Spanish nobility gave birth to two daughters and a son who was also named Martín like the Conqueror's mestizo offspring with Doña Marina. The second son would later inherit the title Second Marqués del Valle de Oaxaca. Disappointments, perhaps well deserved for a man who had destroyed a great Indian nation in Mexico even if he had not intended to do that, gnawed at don Hernando during his later years. He returned to Spain in 1539 to handle affairs at Court while spending most of his time in Seville. He planned on several occasions over the next eight years to return to New Spain and die there, but that did not happen. On December 2, 1547, at the age of sixty-three and on the verge of sailing the Atlantic a third time, Hernando Cortés fell ill and died outside Seville in the small hamlet of Castilleja de la Cuesta. The house where he drew his last breath remains standing, with a placard announcing the passing therein of Hernando Cortés.

A specific provision in Cortés's will in which he bequeathed to his son the Second Marqués the right to collect tribute from 50,000 vassals in the Valley of Oaxaca bears evidence of his great wealth. In an early draft of his testament, Cortés included a bequest to his mestizo son Luis, likewise born to an Indian consort. He changed his mind in a few days and disinherited him. As mentioned earlier, don Hernando was generous to his illegitimate son Martín born to Doña Marina. Like Isabel Moctezuma, he also left a bequest to his daughter Leonor Cortés Moctezuma. Cortés asked that his remains be sent to New Spain where his greatest accomplishments had taken place, and eventually that did happen.

Figure 14. Cortés Monument and Castle of Beatriz Pacheco, Countess of Medellín. Photo by author.

Cortés's first interment was in a small church outside Seville. His bones did not arrive in Texcoco until 1566, and they stayed there until around 1794 when they were transferred to the church of Jesús Nazareno in Mexico City and remained there until 1829. At that time, anti-Spanish fury beset Mexico as the result of a failed invasion from Spanish-held Cuba aimed at restoring colonial rule from Madrid. Crowds coursed through Mexico City intent on destroying reminders of Spain, and some ten-thousand pro-royalist sympathizers were exiled from the country. Lucas Alamán, a staunch conservative politician and noted historian, fearing the desecration of Cortés's remains, carried them into the National Cathedral and placed them in a sealed niche. Astonishingly, Alamán forgot to return them to the church after the crisis had passed. After Alamán died in 1853, the location of Cortés's bones remained unknown until 1946 when workers repairing the National Cathedral opened the niche. The bones of Hernando Cortés were again placed in the church of Jesus of Nazareth in Mexico City, where they now repose.

In the Extremaduran region of Spain lies the small town of Medellín. By far the most famous person to have been born there was Hernando Cortés. Situated in the town's plaza is a fine statue of the local hero. [**Figure 14**] Around the statue's base are plaques commemorating his most famous battles in Mexico, including Mexico (Tenochtitlan), Tlaxcala, and Otumba. The small house where Cortés was born in 1484 remains standing near the statue on one side of the plaza. Above the town are remains of the large castle once owned by doña Beatriz Pacheco, Countess of Medellín. One might in fantasy picture young Cortés playing the game of *matamoros* on the castle's ramparts, but this would never have happened. No common inhabitant of Medellín dared set foot on the fortications surrounding doña Beatriz's domicile, and that included the child named Fernando Cortés by his parents at birth but known to posterity, and referred to throughout this book, as Hernando Cortés.

BIBLIOGRAPHY

CHAPTER 1

Cohen, J. M., Ed., Trans. *The Four Voyages of Christopher Columbus*. By Hernando Colón. New York: Penguin Books, 1969.

Gibson, Carrie. *Empire's Crossroads: A History of the Caribbean from Columbus to the Present Day*. New York: Grove Press, 2014.

Mann, Charles C. *1491: New Revelations of the Americas before Columbus*. New York: Vintage Books, 2006.

Morison, Samuel E. *Admiral of the Ocean Sea: A Life of Christopher Columbus*. Boston: Little, Brown, and Company, 1974.

Phillips, William D. Jr., and Carla Rahn Phillips. *A Concise History of Spain*. Cambridge University Press, 2013.

Phillips, William D. Jr., and Carla Rahn Phillips. *The Worlds of Christopher Columbus*. Cambridge University Press, 1992.

Weddle, Robert S. *Spanish Sea: The Gulf of Mexico in North American Discovery, 1500–1685*. College Station: Texas A&M University Press, 1985.

CHAPTER 2

Cohen, J. M. ed., trans. *The Four Voyages of Christopher Columbus*. By Hernando Colón. New York: Penguin Books, 1969.

Díaz del Castillo, Bernal. *The Discovery and Conquest of Mexico, 1517–1521*. Ed. Genero García, trans. A. P. Maudslay, Intro. Irving A. Leonard. New York: Grove Press, 1956.

Gibson, Carrie. *Empire's Crossroad: A History of the Caribbean from Columbus to the Present Day*. New York: Grove Press, 2014.

Hanke, Lewis. *The Spanish Struggle for Justice in the Conquest of America*. New intro. Susan Scafidi and Peter Bakewell. Dallas: Southern Methodist University Press, 2002.

Morison, Samuel E. *Admiral of the Ocean Sea: A Life of Christopher Columbus*. Boston: Little, Brown and Company, 1970.

Phillips, William D. Jr. and Carla Rahn Phillips. *A Concise History of Spain*. New York: Cambridge University Press, 2013.

Phillips, William D. Jr. and Carla Rahn Phillips. *The Worlds of Christopher Columbus*. New York: Cambridge University Press, 1992,

Weddle, Robert S. *Spanish Sea: The Gulf of Mexico in North American Discovery, 1500-1685*. College Station: Texas A&M University Press, 1985.

CHAPTER 3

Gibson, Carrie. *Empire's Crossroads: A History of the Caribbean from Columbus to the Present Day*. New York: Grove Press, 2014.

Hanke, Lewis. *Aristotle and the American Indians: A Study in Race Prejudice in the New World*. Chicago: Henry Regnery, 1959.

Hanke, Lewis. *The Spanish Struggle for Justice in the Conquest of America*. New intro. by Susan Scafidi and Peter Bakewell. Dallas: Southern Methodist University Press, 2002.

Phillips, William D. and Carla Rahn Phillips. *The Worlds of Christopher Columbus*. New York: Cambridge University Press, 1992.

Simpson, Lesley B. *The Encomienda in New Spain*. Berkeley: University of California Press, 1950.

Thomas, Hugh. *Conquest: Montezuma, Cortés, and the Fall of Old Mexico*. New York: Simon and Schuster, 1993.

Wagner, Henry R. *The Rise of Fernando Cortés*. Berkeley: Cortés Society, 1944.

Weddle, Robert S. *Spanish Sea: The Gulf of Mexico in North American Discovery, 1500-1685*. College Station: Texas A&M University Press, 1985.

CHAPTER 4

Chipman, Donald E. *Nuño de Guzmán and the Province of Pánuco in New Spain, 1518–1533*. Glendale: The Arthur H. Clark Company, 1967.

Díaz del Castillo, Bernal. *The Discovery and Conquest of Mexico, 1517-1521*. New York: Farrar, Straus, and Cudahy, 1956. Trans, A. P. Maudslay.

Gibson, Carrie. *Empires's Crossroads: A History of the Caribbean from Columbus to the Present Day*. New York: Grove Press, 2014.

Hanke, Lewis. *The Spanish Struggle for Justice in the Conquest of the Americas*. New intro. Susan Scafidi and Peter Bakewell. Dallas: Southern Methodist University Press, 2002.

Las Casas, Bartolomé de. *A Short Account of the Destruction of the Indies*. London: Penguin Books, 1992. Trans, Nigel Griffin.

Phillips, William D. Jr., and Carla Rahn Phillips. *A Concise History of Spain*. New York: Cambridge University Press, 2013.

Thomas, Hugh. *Conquest: Montezuma, Cortés and the Fall of Old Mexico*. New York: Simon & Schuster, 1993.

Weddle, Robert S. *Spanish Sea: The Gulf of Mexico in North American Discovery, 1500-1685.* College Station: Texas A&M University Press, 1985.

CHAPTER 5

Davies, Nigel. *The Aztecs: A History.* New York: G. P. Putnam's Sons, 1973.

Díaz del Castillo, Bernal. *The Conquest of New Spain.* Trans. and Intro. by J. M. Cohen. New York: Penguin Books, 1985.

Gardiner, C. Harvey. *Martín López: Conquistador Citizen of Mexico.* Lexington: University of Kentucky Press, 1958.

Gardiner, C. Harvey. *Naval Power in the Conquest of Mexico.* Austin: University of Texas Press, 1956.

Las Casas, Barolomé de. *Historia de las Indias.* 3 vols. Madrid: M. Aguilar, n.d.

Scholes, France V., and Ralph L. Roys. *The Maya Chontal Indians of Acalan-Tixchel: A Contribution to the History and Ethnography of the Yucatán Peninsula.* Washington, DC: Carnegie Institution of Washington, 1948.

Thomas, Hugh. *Conquest: Montezuma, Cortés, and the Fall of Old Mexico.* New York: Simon and Schuster, 1993.

Varner, John G., and Jeanette Johnson Varner. *Dogs of the Conquest.* Norman: University of Oklahoma Press, 1983.

Weber, David J. *The Spanish Frontier in North America.* New Haven: Yale University Press, 1992.

Weddle, Robert S. *Spanish Sea: The Gulf of Mexico in North American Discovery, 1500–1685.* College Station: Texas A&M University Press, 1985.

CHAPTER 6

Brotherson, Gordon. "Tula: Touchstone of the Mesoamerican Era." *New Scholar* 10 (1986): 19–39.

Brundage, Burr C. *A Rain of Darts: The Mexica Aztecs.* Austin: University of Texas Press, 1972.

Carrasco, David. *Quetzalcoatl and the Irony of Empire: Myths and Prophecies in the Aztec Tradition.* Rev. ed. Boulder: University of Colorado Press, 2000.

Chipman, Donald E. *Moctezuma's Children: Aztec Royalty under Spanish Rule.* Austin: University of Texas Press, 2005.

Chipman, Donald E. "Isabel Moctezuma: Pioneer of *Mestizaje.*" In *Struggle and Survival in Colonial America.* Eds. David G. Sweet and Gary B. Nash. Berkeley: University of California Press, 1981.

Davies, Nigel. *The Aztecs: A History.* New York: G.P. Putnam's Sons, 1973.

Davies, Nigel. *Toltec Heritage: From the Fall of Tula to the Rise of Tenochtitlan.* Norman: University of Oklahoma Press, 1980.

Durán, Diego. *Book of the Gods and Rites and the Ancient Calendar.* Trans., eds. Fernando Horcasitas and Doris Heyden. Norman: University of Oklahoma Press, 1971.

Harris, Marvin. *Cannibals and Kings*. New York: Vintage Books, 1978.

León-Portilla, Miguel. *The Aztec Image of Self and Society: An Introduction to Nahua Culture*. Salt Lake City: University of Utah Press, 1992.

Ricard, Robert. *The Spiritual Conquest of Mexico: An Essay on the Apostolate and the Evangelizing Methods of the Mendicant Orders in New Spain, 1523–1572*. Berkeley: University of California Press, 1974.

Peterson, Frederick A. *Ancient Mexico: An Introduction to the Pre-Hispanic Cultures*. New York: G. P. Putnam's Sons, 1959.

Prescott, William H. *History of the Conquest of Mexico*. Intro. James Lockhart. New York: The Modern Library, 2001.

Soustelle, Jacques. *Daily Life of the Aztecs*. Sanford University Press, 1961.

Thomas, Hugh. *Conquest: Montezuma, Cortés, and the Fall of Old Mexico*. New York: Simon and Schuster: 1993.

Townsend, Camilla. "Burying the White Gods: New Perspectives on the Conquest of Mexico." *American Historical Review* 108 (June 2003): 659–687.

CHAPTER 7

Chipman, Donald E. *Nuño de Guzmán and the Province of Pánuco in New Spain: 1518-1533*. Glendale, CA: The Arthur H. Clark Company, 1967.

Chipman, Donald E. and Harriett Denise Joseph. *Spanish Texas, 1519-1821*. Rev ed. Austin: University of Texas Press, 2010. See p.25, for 1519 sketch map of the Gulf Coast. Archivo General de Indias, Seville, Spain: Mapas y Planos, México 5.

Díaz del Castillo, Bernal. *Discovery and Conquest of Mexico, 1517-1521*. New York: Grove Press, 1956.

Díaz del Castillo, Bernal. *Historia verdadera de la conquista de Nueva España*. 2 vols. Mexico City: Editorial Porrúa, 1955.

Morris, J. Bayard, trans. *Hernando Cortés: Five Letters, 1519-1526*. New York: W. W. Norton & Company, 1991.

Prescott, William H. *History of the Conquest of Mexico*. Into. James Lockhart. New York: The Modern Library, 2001.

Thomas, Hugh. *Conquest: Montezuma, Cortés, and the Fall of Old Mexico*. New York: Simon and Schuster, 1993.

Weber, David J. *The Spanish Frontier in North America*. New Haven: Yale University Press, 1992.

Weddle, Robert S. *Spanish Sea: The Gulf of Mexico in North American Discovery, 1500-1685*. College Station: Texas A&M University Press, 1985.

CHAPTER 8

Chipman, Donald E. *Nuño de Guzmán and the Province of Pánuco in New Spain, 1518-1533*. Glendale, CA: The Arthur H. Clark Company, 1967.

Cortés, Hernando. *Five Letters to the Emperor*. Trans. and Intro. J. Bayard Morris. New York: W. W. Norton, 1991.

Díaz del Castillo, Bernal. *The Discovery and Conquest of Mexico, 1517-1521.* New York: Farrar, Straus, and Cudahy, 1956.

Díaz del Castillo, Bernal. *Historia verdadera de la conquista de Nueva España.* 2 vols. Mexico City: Editorial Porrúa, 1955.

Prescott, William H. *History of the Conquest of Mexico.* Into. James Lockhart. New York: The Modern Library, 2001.

Sahagún, Bernardino de. *Florentine Codex: General History of the Things of New Spain.* Trans. Arthur J. O. Anderson and Charles E. Dibble. Book 12. Santa Fe: School of American Research and the University of Utah, 1950-1982.

Thomas, Hugh. *Conquest: Montezuma, Cortés, and the Fall of Old Mexico.* New York: Simon and Schuster, 1993.

Weddle, Robert S. *Spanish Sea: The Gulf of Mexico in North American Discovery, 1500-1685.* College Station: Texas A&M University Press, 1985.

CHAPTER 9

Chipman, Donald E. "Alonso Álvarez de Pineda and the Río de las Palmas: Historians and the Mislocation of a River." *Southwestern Historical Quarterly* 98 (January 1995): 369-385.

Chipman, Donald E. *Moctezuma's Children: Aztec Royalty under Spanish Rule, 1520-1700.* Austin: University of Texas Press, 2005.

Chipman, Donald E. *Nuño de Guzmán and the Province of Pánuco in New Spain.* Glendale, CA: The Arthur H. Clark Company, 1967.

Cortés, Hernando. *Five Letters of Cortés to the Emperor.* Trans. and ed., J. Bayard Morris. New York: W. W. Norton, 1991.

Díaz del Castillo, Bernal. *The Discovery and Conquest of Mexico, 1517–1521.* New York: Farrar, Straus, and Cudahy. 1956.

Díaz del Castillo, Bernal. *Historia verdadera de la conquista de la Nueva España.* 2 vols. Mexico City: Editorial Porrúa, 1955.

Phillips, William D. Jr., and Carla Rahn Phillips. *The Worlds of Christopher Columbus.* New York: Cambridge University Press, 1992

Prescott, William H. *History of the Conquest of Mexico.* Intro. by James Lockhart. New York: The Modern Library, 2001.

Sahagún, Bernardino de. *Florentine Codex: General History of the Things of New Spain.* Trans. Arthur J. O. Anderson and Charles E. Dibble. Book 12. Santa Fe: School of American Research and the University of Utah, 1950-1982.

Thomas, Hugh. *Conquest: Montezuma, Cortés, and the Fall of Old Mexico.* New York: Simon & Schuster, 1993.

Weddle, Robert S. *Spanish Sea: The Gulf of Mexico in North American Discovery, 1500-1685.* College Station: Texas A&M University Press, 1985.

CHAPTER 10

Chipman, Donald E. *Moctezuma's Children: Aztec Royalty under Spanish Rule, 1520–1700.* Austin: University of Texas Press, 2005.

Chipman, Donald E. *Nuño de Guzmán and the Province of Pánuco in New Spain.* Glendale, CA: The Arthur H. Clark Company, 1967.

Cortés, Hernando. *Five Letters of Cortés to the Emperor.* Trans. and ed., J. Bayard Morris. New York: W. W. Norton, 1991.

Díaz del Castillo, Bernal. *The Discovery and Conquest of Mexico, 1517–1521.* New York: Farrar, Straus, and Cudahy, 1956.

Díaz del Castillo, Bernal. *Historia verdadera de la conquista de la Nueva España.* 2 Vols. Mexico City: Editorial Porrúa, 1955.

Gardiner, C. Harvey. *Naval Power in the Conquest of Mexico.* Austin: University of Texas Press, 1956.

Prescott, William H. *History of the Conquest of Mexico.* Intro. by James Lockhart. New York: The Modern Library, 2001.

Sahagún, Bernardino de. *Florentine Codex. General History of the Things of New Spain.* Trans. Arthur J. O. Anderson and Charles E. Dibble. Book 12. Santa Fe: School of American Research and the University of Utah, 1950–1982.

Schroeder, Susan. "Introduction." In *Indian Women of Early Mexico*, eds. Susan Schroeder, Stephanie Wood, and Robert Haskett. Norman: University of Oklahoma Press, 1997.

Thomas, Hugh. *Conquest: Montezuma, Cortés, and the Fall of Old Mexico.* New York: Simon and Schuster, 1993

Weddle, Robert S. *Spanish Sea: The Gulf of Mexico in North American Discovery, 1500–1685.* College Station: Texas A&M University Press, 1985.

CHAPTER 11

Chipman, Donald E. *Moctezuma's Children: Aztec Royalty under Spanish Rule, 1520–1700.* Austin: University of Texas Press, 2005.

Cortés, Hernando. *Five Letters of Cortés to the Emperor.* Trans. and ed., J. Bayard Morris. New York: W. W. Norton, 1991.

Davies, Nigel. *The Aztecs: A History.* New York: G. P. Putnam's Sons, 1973.

Díaz del Castillo, Bernal. *The Discovery and Conquest of Mexico, 1517–1521.* New York: Farrar, Straus, and Cudahy, 1956.

Díaz del Castillo, Bernal. *Historia verdadera de la conquista de la Nueva España.* 2 vols. Mexico City: Editorial Porrúa, 1955.

Prescott, William H. *History of the Conquest of Mexico.* Intro. by James Lockhart. New York: The Modern Library, 2001.

Sahagún, Bernardino de. *Florentine Codex: General History of the Things of New Spain.* Trans. Arthur J. O. Anderson and Charles E. Dibble. Book 12. Santa Fe: School of American Research and the University of Utah, 1950-1982.

Thomas, Hugh. *Conquest: Montezuma, Cortés, and the Fall of Old Mexico.* New York: Simon & Schuster, 1993.

Weber, David J. *The Spanish Frontier in North America*. New Haven: Yale University Press, 1992.
Weddle, Robert S. *Spanish Sea: The Gulf of Mexico in North American Discovery, 1500–1685*. College Station: Texas A&M University Press, 1985.

CHAPTER 12

Altman, Ida. *The War for Mexico's West: Indians and Spaniards in New Galicia, 1524-1550*. Albuquerque: University of New Mexico Press, 2010.
Chipman, Donald E. "Alonso Álvarez de Pineda and the Río de las Palmas: Historians and the Mislocation of a River." *Southwestern Historical Quarterly* 98 (January 1995): 369-385.
Chipman, Donald E. *Moctezuma's Children: Aztec Royalty under Spanish Rule, 1520-1700*. Austin: University of Texas Press, 2005.
Chipman, Donald E. *Nuño de Guzmán and the Province of Pánuco in New Spain, 1518-1533*. Glendale, CA: The Arthur H. Clark Company, 1967.
Cortés, Hernando. *Five Letters of Cortés to the Emperor*. Trans. and ed., J. Bayard Morris. New York: W. W. Norton, 1991.
Díaz del Castillo, Bernal. *Historia verdadera de la conquista de la Nueva España*. 2 vols. Mexico City: Editorial Porrúa, 1955.
Hollingsworth, Ann P. "Pedro de Moctezuma and His Descendants, 1521-1718," Ph.D. dissertation. North Texas State University, 1980.
León-Portilla, Miguel. *The Broken Spears: The Aztec Account of the Conquest of Mexico*. Expanded and updated ed. Boston: Beacon Press, 1992.
Prescott, William H. *History of the Conquest of Mexico*. Intro. by James Lockhart. New York: The Modern Library, 2001.
Stuntz, Jean A. *Hers, His, and Theirs: Community Property Law in Spain and Early Texas*. Lubbock: Texas Tech University Press, 2005.
Thomas, Hugh. *Conquest: Montezuma, Cortés, and the Fall of Old Mexico*. New York: Simon & Schuster, 1993.
Warren, J. Benedict. *The Conquest of Michoacán: The Spanish Domination of the Tarascan Kingdom in Western Mexico, 1521-1530*. Norman: University of Oklahoma Press, 1985.
Weber, David J. *The Spanish Frontier in North America*. New Haven: Yale University Press, 1992.
Weddle, Robert S. *Spanish Sea: The Gulf of Mexico in North American Discovery, 1500-1685*. College Station: Texas A&M University Press, 1985.

AFTERWORD

Altman, Ida. *The War for Mexico's West: Indian and Spaniards in New Galicia, 1524-1550*. Albuquerque: University of New Mexico Press, 2010.
Bakewell, Peter J. *Silver Mining and Society in Colonial Mexico: Zacatecas, 1546-1700*. Cambridge: Cambridge University Press, 1971.

Carrasco, Pedro. "Indian-Spanish Marriages in the First Century of the Colony. In *Indian Women of Early Mexico*, eds. Susan Schroeder, Stephanie Wood, and Robert Hasket. Norman: University of Oklahoma Press, 1997.

Chipman, Donald E. "Isabel Moctezuma: Pioneer of *Mestizaje*." In *Struggle and Survival in Colonial America*, eds. David G. Sweet and Gary B. Nash. Berkeley: University of California Press, 1981.

Chipman, Donald E. *Moctezuma's Children: Aztec Royalty under Spanish Rule, 1520-1700*. Austin: University of Texas Press, 2005.

Chipman, Donald E., trans. The Will of Nuño de Guzmán, President, Governor, and Captain General of New Spain and the Province of Pánuco, 1558. Reprinted from *The Americas* 35 (October 1978); 238-248.

Conway, G. R. C. *The Last Will and Testament of Hernando Cortés, Marqués del Valle*. Mexico City: Privately Published, 1939.

García Iglesias, Sara. *Isabel Moctezuma: La última princesa azteca*. Mexico City: Ediciones Xochitl, 1946.

Gibson, Charles. *The Aztecs under Spanish Rule: A History of the Indians of the Valley of Mexico, 1519-1810*. Stanford: Stanford University Press, 1964.

Google Search. "The Tombs of Christopher Columbus in Seville and Santo Domingo;" see also, "Tomb of Christopher Columbus" @ atlasobscura.com. Accessed 02/16/20.

Himmerich y Valencia, Robert. *The Encomenderos of New Spain, 1521-1555*. Austin: University of Texas Press, 1991.

Ortega y Pérez Gallardo, Ricardo. *Historia genealógica de las familias más antiguas de México*. 3d ed. 3 vols. Mexico City: Imprenta de A. Carranza, 1908-1910. See vol 3: "Testamento de la Princesa Isabel Moctezuma, Hecho en 10 de Diciembre de 1550.

Powell, Philip W. *Soldiers, Indians, and Silver: The Northward Advance of New Spain, 1550-1600*. Berkeley & Los Angeles: University of California Press, 1952.

Scholes, France V. "The Last Days of Gonzalo de Sandoval: Conquistador of New Spain. In *Homenaje a Don José de la Peña y Cámara*. Madrid: Edicioners José Porrúa Turanzas, 1969.

"Testamento de Juan Cano," September 3, 1572. Archivo General de Indias, Seville. Contratación, 209, N. 1, R. 7, fols. 7-14v.

Thomas, Hugh. *Conquest: Montezuma, Cortés and the Fall of Old Mexico*. New York: Simon and Schuster, 1993.

INDEX